D0082725

SHIR HAMA'ALOT L'DAVID
(Song of the Steps)

and

KTAV HITNAẒẒELUT L'DARSHANIM
(In Defense of Preachers)

by DAVID DARSHAN

ALUMNI SERIES OF THE HEBREW UNION COLLEGE PRESS

SHIR HAMA'ALOT L'DAVID
(Song of the Steps)

and

KTAV HITNAZZELUT L'DARSHANIM
(In Defense of Preachers)

by DAVID DARSHAN

translated and annotated by
HAYIM GOREN PERELMUTER

For Frank —
In friendship
and gratitude for
a precious association

HM

July 20/84

HEBREW UNION COLLEGE PRESS
CINCINNATI, OHIO 1984

COPYRIGHT © 1984
HEBREW UNION COLLEGE PRESS

Library of Congress Cataloging in Publication Data

David ben Manasseh, Darshan, b. ca. 1527
  Shir hama'alot l'David = (Song of the steps) ; and,
Ktav hitnazzelut l'darshanim = (In defense of preachers)

  (Alumni series of the Hebrew Union College Press,
ISSN 0192-2904)
  Hebrew text and translation of: Shir ha-ma'alot
le-David, and Ketav hitnatslut le-darshanim.
  Title on added t.p.: Shir ha-ma'alot le-David ; 'im,
Ketav hitnatslut le-darshanim.
  Bibliography: p.
  Includes index.
  1. Jewish sermons—Poland. 2. Sermons, Hebrew—Poland.
3. Preaching, Jewish—Early works to 1800. I. Perelmuter,
Hayim Goren. II. David ben Manasseh, Darshan, b. ca. 1527.
Ketav hitnatslut le-darshanim. English and Hebrew.
1984. III. Title. IV. Title: Song of the steps.
V. Title: Ktav hitnazzelut l'darshanim. VI. Title: In
defense of preachers. VII. Title: Shir ha-ma'alot
le-David. VIII. Title: Ketav hitnatslut le-darshanim.
IX. Series.
BM740.D2913 1984   296.4'2   84-6696
ISBN 0-87820-116-5

MANUFACTURED IN THE UNITED STATES OF AMERCIA

This book is published under the auspices of the Rabbinic Alumni Association of Hebrew Union College-Jewish Institute of Religion. A quinquennial fund to which its members contribute is set aside for the specific purpose of encouraging members of the Association to pursue studies in Judaism with the prospect of publication.

ALFRED GOTTSCHALK
President, Hebrew Union College-
Jewish Institute of Religion

P. IRVING BLOOM
President, Rabbinic Alumni
Association

WALTER JACOB
Chairman, Publications Committee
of the Rabbinic Alumni
Association

For

NANCY

"She is more precious than pearls."

יקרה היא מפנינים

CONTENTS

ACKNOWLEDGMENTS

Three great Jewish scholars who were of immense help to the author in this project, which took more than a decade to complete, were called to their eternal reward during the last few years. I recall them with gratitude, for what they represented for Jewish scholarship, and for the generous assistance they offered me along the way.

Professor Hayim Hillel Ben-Sasson, who encouraged me to undertake the translation of David Darshan's two books, saw the task as an important beginning. He advised me in the development of the methodology, oversaw the work, and examined the manuscript, except the last portion, which was on his desk but remained unread because of his sudden and untimely passing.

Professor Gershom Scholem, whom I met in 1938 while a student at the Jewish Institute of Religion in New York, when, at the invitation of Dr. Stephen S. Wise, he gave the lectures that became *Major Trends in Jewish Mysticism,* gave generously of his time and his friendship over the years, and was of enormous assistance in matters of bibliography and on questions relating to the role of Jewish mysticism that was part of David Darshan's background.

Professor Samuel Sandmel, with whom I took the "minor" in Bible for my doctorate, out of which this work grew, and whose steady friendship and encouragement were a sustaining force, is remembered with affection and appreciation.

May their memory be a blessing.

A great debt of gratitude is due Professor Ellis Rivkin, under whose guidance, in tandem with Dr. Ben-Sasson, I worked on the project. His encouragement to go forward in a field so relatively untrod within his department, his enthusiasm, and his constant encouragement meant much to me.

There are many others I must here acknowledge. They include my teacher, Professor John Tepfer, who introduced me to David Darshan and the world of itinerant preachers of the sixteenth and seventeenth centuries; Professor Alexander Guttmann, with whom I worked in my doctoral program; and Professors Eugene Mihaly and Baruch Bokser for their helpful comments on the work in progress.

The Klau Library of the Hebrew Union College-Jewish Institute of Religion was of enormous help, putting its resources at my disposal wherever I happened to be. So were the National Library of the Hebrew University, and the Library of the Graduate Theological Union in Berkeley.

I am grateful to the Catholic Theological Union at Chicago, and the Pacific Lutheran Theological Seminary of Berkeley, for the facilities of research and the agreeable atmosphere for working on the introduction to this work; to the K. A. M. Isaiah Israel Congregation for having made it possible for me, during an active rabbinical career, to continue with my scholarship, providing me with many opportunities for extended study in which to carry on my work; and to its administrative and secretarial staff for their help in typing what turned out to be a complicated manuscript.

I am particularly grateful to the British Museum and the Bodleian Libraries for having granted me permission to reproduce any or all parts of the printed books by David Darshan in their possession in the publication of this translation.

The recovered title page of *Shir haMa'alot l'David,* which involved putting together whole parts of two title pages, one in the Bodleian Library, and one in the Jewish Theological Seminary, was the work of the staff of American Printers and Lithographers of Chicago, thanks to its president, my good friend Robert Lifton.

My thanks go to my beloved comrades of the Rabbinic Alumni Association of the Hebrew Union College-Jewish Institute of Religion, for making possible the publication of this book, which represents a recovery from oblivion for David Darshan.

And finally, אחרון אחרון חביב, I acknowledge the constant patience and encouragement of my beloved wife, Nancy, and of our children, who, though it tarried, never gave up hope that the task would finally be completed.

Hayim Goren Perelmuter

Chicago, Illinois

INTRODUCTION

I

This volume is a labor of love and an act of recovery. It is designed to bring two obscure little books to life, and to make them accessible to two categories of readers.

For the Hebrew reader, to whom the world of medieval literature is a constant reservoir of discovery and rediscovery, the republication of the original texts of David Darshan's *Shir haMa'alot l'David* and *Ktav Hitnazzelut l'Darshanim* provides reproductions of texts that were popular in their time. They are now in the category of endangered species, with perhaps three copies of the former (none in perfect condition) and one of the latter extant.[1]

For the readers and general scholar, to whom the complex, pilpulistic, constantly allusive type of late medieval Hebrew represents a barrier, their translation as *Song of the Steps* and *In Defense of Preachers* unlocks a door, not often opened, to an understanding of the inner life of Polish Jewry in the late Renaissance period of its emergence as a luminous and creative center of Jewish life. It is a period that can be compared to the Golden Age of Spain or to the flowering of Babylonian Jewry and the final redaction of the Talmud.

---

[1] Copies of *Shir haMa'alot l'David* (Cracow, 1571) are to be found in the Bodleian, British Museum, and Jewish Theological Seminary Libraries. The Bodleian copy has the title page (torn and repaired) but is missing pages of the text; the British Museum copy lacks the title page, but the rest of the text is complete; the title page of the Jewish Theological Seminary copy is torn at the top, as is the last page. *Ktav Hitznazzelut l'Darshanim* (Lublin, 1574) is in the British Museum. The Juedische Gemeindebibliothek of Vienna had a copy which disappeared at the time of the Nazi occupation.

The corpus of popular Jewish homiletical literature has received too little attention from modern scholars. Yet it is literally a gold mine of information and insight into the processes whereby Rabbinic Judaism and Jewish values were transmitted to the folk, and sheds light on their needs and aspirations. It is to be hoped that more such works will find their way to translation and scholarly analysis, so that this field might be opened to a wider body of general scholarship.

We are talking about a first—the first of the itinerant Jewish scholar-preachers in Poland to emerge into the light of day with the reintroduction of the Hebrew printing press in Cracow in 1569. For *Shir haMa'alot l'David* was the first book of printed sermons for popular consumption to be published in Poland, and *K'tav Hitnazzelut l'Darshanim* (Lublin, 1574) was the first handbook for preachers,[2] providing clear evidence that the popular preacher needed a defense.

It is worth noting that the former was the second book to come off the reestablished press, while the first volume, a commentary to the *Midrash Rabbah* to the Five Scrolls,[3] bore a dedicatory poem by this *darshan* who was associated with the printer as proofreader and editor. In Italy, where the first printed Hebrew books came off the Soncino Press in 1483, fifty-nine books appeared in the next twenty-four years, including Talmud folios, Bible commentaries, and prayer books. Not before 1507 did the collection of the works of a popular preacher appear. This was the *Bi'ur* of Baḥya ben Asher (d. 1360), a homiletical classic constantly used by subsequent *darshanim* as a source book. In the years that followed (1514, 1517, 1526) the frequence of new editions indicates a growing interest in this genre of literature.[4]

In his history of Jewish preaching, Leopold Zunz listed nine books which were written as handbooks for preachers. The earliest

[2] L. Zunz, *Die gottesdienstlichen Vortraege* (Berlin, 1832), p. 428.

[3] Naphtali Herẓ ben Menaḥem of Lwow, *Perush al haMidrash Rabbah meḤamesh haMegillot* (Cracow, 1569).

[4] David Werner Amram, *Makers of Hebrew Books in Italy* (Philadelphia, 1909), pp. 139–143 and 217–223.

of these is listed as *Hitnazzelut l'Darshanim,* Lublin, 1548. This is clearly David Darshan's work, although Zunz errs in the publication year, as did Sabbetai Bass in his *Sifte Yeshenim* (Amsterdam, 1680).[5] That David was a first in this type of literature is clear.

II

The sermon as a means of communication and the *darshan* as communicator are a unique development of Rabbinic Judaism. Midrash, the process of extracting deeper meaning from the Torah text and communicating it to the covenant people, was the technique through which Biblical, prophetic, and priestly Judaism was transformed so that it could survive beyond the destruction of the first and second Jewish Commonwealths into the two millennia that followed.

The beginnings of the process, from which the preacher as a type began to appear are shrouded in mystery, but it seems rather clear that it began with the establishment of the Babylonian Jewish community, perhaps already adumbrated by Jeremiah's famous letter.[6] In any event, the process was at work in the beginning of the Second Commonwealth with Ezra, the Men of the Great Synagogue, and the quiet development of Rabbinic Judaism and its "two laws" (oral and written). It was as though the "cure were being developed prior to the disease,"[7] so that when the Jewish state collapsed under the hammer blows of Rome, the survival mechanism was at hand: canonized Bible, Mishnah, Talmud and prayer book, and a structure for community survival within a unique legal, religious, and national framework, in a diaspora setting.

As early as the time of Ezra, the *meturgeman* was there to interpret the Torah to the people as it was read to them in public.[8] The *Targum,* the earliest Aramaic translation of the Talmud, already had elements of the homiletical interpretation within it.

[5] Cf. Part IV of the introduction.
[6] Jeremiah 29:1 ff.
[7] Talmud Bavli, *Megillah* 13b.
[8] Ezra 8:1–8.

The spoken homily of the *darshan,* communicating Torah and its meaning to the people, seems to have developed in mishnaic and talmudic times. It became one of the chief means of instructing all the people—common folk, women, and children. It was a means of guiding them and strengthening their faith. It was their method, too, of reinterpreting the Bible in such a way as to give expression, often in a bold manner, to burning issues of their time.

For example, when, in times of extreme persecution in the Roman era, it became hard to believe in the premise that the righteous were rewarded in this life, the *darshanim* made bold changes. The meaning of the text "He has given food unto them that fear him, He will ever be mindful of His covenant"[9] was transformed by a play on words. Since the word *teref* ("food") could be read as *teruf* ("confusion"), they offered this reading: He has given confusion to those who fear him— in this world; He will ever be mindful of his covenant—in the next![10] It comes out all right in the end.

The vast body of homilies preached by the darshanim in mishnaic and talmudic times have come down to us in rich collections of *midrashim.* In this medium the sermons have survived in the barest of outlines. Only very occasionally do we find a complete sermon preserved, as, for example in Talmud Bavli, *Shabbat* 30b and *Hagigah* 3a.

The message was all-important, but the medium was not to be lightly dismissed. In fact, as time passed, it tended to become as important, and therein lurked a problem. For the sermon not only edified, it entertained. *Darshanim* who were dramatic and effective in their presentations attracted throngs.[11] They used every imaginable technique to seize and to hold the attention of the audience.[12] The people flocked to hear them, and even went so far, through the use of the *eruv,* as to extend the distance they could properly travel on the Sabbath to hear a good *darshan.*[13]

---

[9] Psalms 111:5.
[10] Midrash, *Genesis Rabbah* 40:2.
[11] Talmud Bavli, *Gittin* 35b.
[12] Talmud Bavli, *Pesaḥim* 117a; *Song of Songs Rabbah* 15:3.
[13] Talmud Bavli, *Horayot* 48b; Mishnah *Eruvin* 3:5.

The vast body of midrashic literature, to say nothing of the agadic material in the Talmud, preserves the traces of this rich and creative process. The classical *midrashim* probably drew the bulk of their material from the texts of countless sermons that had actually been preached in the synagogues of Palestine.

Some of the outstanding sages known as *darshanim* in the talmudic period included Sh'maya and Abatalion, Hillel's teachers, Ben Azzai and Ben Zoma, Eliezer the son of Jose the Galilean, Levi ben Sisi,[14] Joshua ben Levi, Abbahu, Elazar ben Arach, and Judah ben Pedayah.[15]

Clearly the same process that was at work when the Talmud was evolving continued into the medieval period. The Jewish communities, developing in Italy, Spain, France, and Germany's Rhineland, turned first to Babylonia for guidance, but before very long were developing their own communal structures and authority. The religious, philosophic, and mystical developments went hand in hand, and the *darshanim* continued their work of communication.

The institutionalization of the *darshan* in this role is evidenced by Moses ben Maimon's ruling that "each Jewish congregation must arrange to have a respected and wise elder who has been known for his piety from his youth and is beloved by the people, who will publicly admonish the community and cause them to repent."[16] He is, however, careful to point out that great care must be exercised to share the insights of Judaism with the masses in a way that is appropriate to their understanding. It is not wise to transmit profound ideas to those who are incapable of understanding them; as he puts it: "Instruction to the masses must be by allegory and parables, so that even women, youths, and children might comprehend, and as their understanding grows, they come to understand deeper truths."[17]

[14] Talmud Yerushalmi, *Yevamot*, chap. 12.
[15] S. Glicksberg, *haDerashah b'Yisrael*, pp. 14 ff.
[16] Moses ben Maimon, *Yad, Hilkhot Teshuvah* 4:2.
[17] Moses ben Maimon, in the introduction to his Mishnah commentary on the tractate *Zeraim*.

He is also very concerned about abuses. In his detailed discussion
on the many levels of understanding the meaning of the idea of the
"world to come" as it occurs in the last chapter of Sanhedrin, he has
this to say in his commentary to the Mishnah of that section: "Too
frequently *darshanim* are wont to communicate to the crowd what
they do not really understand and one wishes that they would
remain silent . . . or that they would say: 'We do not understand
what the Sages meant by this passage' instead of: 'This is how it is to
be interpreted.' They believe that they understand it, and they try to
submit their feeble understanding of the last chapter of *Sanhedrin*
[concerning the world to come] and other such matters, interpreting
them literally."

And three and a half centuries later in Cracow, David Darshan's
teacher, Moses Isserles, concerned with the fact that too many
unqualified people were reading the recently printed kabbalistic
books, could write: ". . . and so many of the crowd jump into study
of Kabbalah for it is tempting to the eye . . . and ordinary house-
holders who do not know their right hand from their left hasten to
its study . . . and every one who has little knowledge of it inflates
himself with it and preaches to the masses and will some day be
brought before the bar of divine justice."[18]

As the post-talmudic age merged into the medieval period, we
find the darshanic process expressed in a variety of ways. The
authors of the *piyyutim* (liturgical poems written between the eighth
and twelfth centuries) that found their way into the prayer books
had a homiletic function and expressed the folk experience. But the
darshanim, carrying on their work of communication, emerge.
Rashi's frequent references to Rabbi Moses haDarshan make us
aware of their continuing role. The homily was already an accepted
part of Jewish life in Germany in the eleventh and twelfth centuries.
A good many of the stories and ethical teachings in the *Sefer haHasi-
dim* seem to have been passages from sermons. Eleazer ben Judah
ben Kalonymos of Worms wrote: "One must preach in words more
precious than gold on the Sabbath . . . one must assemble the

---

[18] Moses Isserles, *Torat haOlah* (Prague, 1569), chap. 4.

people at that time and preach to them,"[19] while Moses of Coucy describes a journey he made through Spain giving sermons of admonition.[20] This wandering halakhist was one of the earliest itinerant preachers of the Middle Ages to emerge as an ethical teacher of the masses. From the thirteenth to the fifteenth century in Provence and Spain, *darshanim* developed, some with a philosophic bent, like Yedaiah Penini of Béziers (d. 1340) and Jacob Anatoli (b. 1194); some with a mystical bent, like Bahya ben Asher (d. 1340); and some, like Isaac Arama (b. 1420), who combined speculative analysis with the popular faith of the believers in times of stress.

Joel ibn Shuaib (ca. 1490), a *darshan* of the time of the expulsion from Spain, sums up the form and aesthetic tradition of the sermon in Spain in the introduction to his *Olat Shabbat,*[21] counseling concern with the integrity of the subject matter and the perfection of the manner of expression.

In Italy, the sermon developed in the sixteenth and seventeenth centuries among the exiles from Spain, who at the same time were nourished by Renaissance culture. Preachers like Judah Moscato (d. 1594) and Leone Modena (d. 1648) combined the forms of Jewish interpretation with the graces of the cultural rebirth inspired by a return to classical forms.

It was the Italy of the sixteenth century, the Italy of the time of David Darshan, that became a creative center. To it came the exiles from Spain and Portugal. To it came scholars from Germany, Bohemia and Poland, to study in its universities and yeshivot.

The Italian communities of the late Renaissance period were indeed a gathering center of the major Jewries from all directions, and the developing printing presses, and the stream of Hebrew books published, acted as a great catalyst. Here communities of Jews from the lands of Sefarad and Ashkenaz, as well as the indigenous Italian Jewish community, were in a creative interaction with each other and with their environment.

---

[19] A. M. Haberman, *Gezerot Ashkenaz v'Zarefat* (1945), p. 166.
[20] Moses of Coucy, *Sefer Mitzvot Gadol* (Rome, 1470), introd. 1, 2; 111:11.
[21] Venice, 1577.

It was here that our Cracow *darshan* spent some of his crucial years of development at least between 1556 and perhaps 1558, as we shall see in greater detail in the subsequent sections.

The Polish *darshanim* were influenced by their predecessors but took a different tack. The growth of Poland as a new economic frontier, between the Christian West of the Renaissance period and the Turkish-governed Islamic East, the explosive growth and expansion of its Jewish community, principally Ashkenazic, opened new economic, cultural, and social vistas.[22]

The first group of Polish *darshanim,* beginning with David ben Manasseh, Darshan of Cracow, and including such figures as Ephraim of Lunschitz (d. 1619)[23] and Yedidiah Gottlieb (d. 1645) among others, reflects a differing emphasis. The social criticism of an Ephraim of Lunschitz was particularly sharp. He violently attacked the hypocrisy, insincerity, ostentation, and intrusion of materialism into the worship service.[24] One finds preachers like David Darshan attacking the rich and greedy on the one hand,[25] and on the other attempting to justify the use of rather startling *pilpul* (dialetical tricks in hermeneutics) as a means of edifying and entertaining, as well as admonishing.[26] One finds a greater emphasis of preaching on talmudic texts and relating them to Biblical texts, because the Talmud had come under fire in Church circles and talmudic exegesis was seen as a last refuge of Judaism from Christian intervention.

Rabbi Ḥayim ben Beẓalel, a contemporary of David Darshan's, represented this view vigorously. He took sharp exception to Naḥmanides' (1195–1270) description of agadic material as "sermons," intending to downgrade passages that were hostile to Christianity in his disputations with the Church. For him, the very innermost secrets of Judaism were protected within such passages as difficult of

---

[22] For a brilliant exposition of this period, see H. H. Ben-Sasson, *Hagut v'Hanhagah* (Jerusalem, 1959).

[23] Cf. Israel Bettan, *Studies in Jewish Preaching,* pp. 273 ff.

[24] Ben-Sasson, *Hagut v'Hanhagah,* pp. 46 ff.

[25] David Darshan, *Shir haMa'alot l'David* p. 7a.

[26] David Darshan, *Ktav Hitnaẓẓelut l'Darshanim,* par. 17.

access, to shield them from intrusion by Christian scholars and theologians who had already made the Bible their own![27]

In short, the role of the *darshan* is an important factor of Jewish development that deserves deeper study. The books of printed sermons, the *Hakdamot* (introductions), indeed, the data on the title pages and the printers' comments at the end of books, all become useful grist for the mill of scholarship and cry out for continuing study.[28]

David Darshan and his works are a useful mirror of his time and his craft. Human and fallible as he turns out to be, enigmatic and fascinating, he refracts the personality and psyche of Polish Jewry at the crest of its development.

The *Shoa* of our century left Polish Jewry a shambles, and its grandeur a memory. But its influence on contemporary Jewish life, in Israel and the Western Diaspora, defies measurement. Whatever can be done to bring alive its incandescent spirit is something more than a sentimental journey. It is a pilgrimage in reverence where every name is named, and achieves, in a real sense, enduring life.

III

Wanderer, scholar, preacher, scribe, artist, healer by charms, bibliophile and reference librarian, rabbi, poet, proofreader-editor, and father of unmarried daughters—all these, and perhaps more, was David b. Manasseh, Darshan of Cracow.

He was a sad and troubled man by his own admission. He saw himself as "a man weighed down by troubles and burdened with daughters . . . the most troubled of men."[29] While travelling in Italy (1556–58), he averred that "all this I have written under pressure"[30]

---

[27] Ben-Sasson, *Hagut v'Hanhagah,* p. 38.

[28] For the student of this field, such works as L. Zunz, *Die gottesdienstlichen Vortraege,* J. Heinemann *Derashot b'Zibbur biTkufat haTalmud,* I. Bettan, *Studies in Jewish Preaching,* S. Glicksberg, *HaDerashah b'Yisrael,* and H.H. Ben-Sasson, *Hagut v'Hanhagah,* are indispensable.

[29] *Shir haMa'alot l'David,* title page.

[30] Ibid., p. 10a.

at the end of a responsum which he wrote at the request of Rabbi Jacob Reiner of Ferrara; and while writing an essay on amulets at the request of Joseph Minz to demonstrate his competence, he ended with the words: "all this I have written under pressure."[31] Troubles seemed to follow him wherever he went. He complained being buffeted from his earliest years by one setback after another.[32]

What a striking contrast is the case of Rabbi Moses Isserles, his distinguished teacher. The latter was born into a wealthy and influential family. His father, Israel, was a *Parnas* of the community and a man of substance. His father-in-law, Rabbi Solomon Shakhna, had been appointed Chief Rabbi of Poland by the Polish King (Sigismund I).[33] When, in 1556, Moses fled Cracow for temporary refuge to Szydlow, he wrote a commentary on the Purim Megillah as his gift for his father. He found the town to which he had fled dull and uncultured, "without fig tree and vine," and the book was the result of his leisure. No mention of pressure and troubles here. As he put it: "I sent it during Purim as a gift to my father Israel, head of an incomparable community . . . he is the mightiest of the mighty." So a rich man's son sent his rich and powerful father a beautiful book crafted by Vincenzo Conti in Cremona in 1559.[34]

Yes, troubles and anonymity were David's sad lot. For a long time simply a name in bibliographic catalogues and occasionally a short paragraph in an encyclopedia and in a few histories of the Jews in Poland, he emerges on reexamination with an increased stature, a heightened interest. He becomes something of a person rather than a mere cipher on a list. And he forms a wedge for the entry into a deeper insight into the life of sixteenth-century Polish Jewry, precisely because in an unself-conscious way he mirrors the forces and foibles at work among the more undistinguished masses of the people. And not through the eyes of the famous, the well-known, and the priviledged, but rather from sources which thus far have been unexamined and little known.

[31] Ibid., p. 12a.
[32] Ibid., p. 13a.
[33] *Ktav Hitnazzelut l'Darshanim,* par. 14.
[34] Moses Isserles, *Mekhir Yayin* (Cremona, 1559), pp. 2a and 24a.

When Leopold Zunz was writing his classic history of Jewish preaching, he mentioned David's book, as we noted earlier, but not his name. But in the last four decades, with efforts to delve into the social and cultural history of vanished Polish Jewry growing, an important work in this field by Hayim Hillel Ben-Sasson gave significant place to this *darshan* in an analysis of his work.[35] And not too long ago, when Asher Ziv brought out his updated scholarly edition of the Responsa of Moses Isserles,[36] significant attention was focused on David in connection with his mention on one responsum and his authorship of another.

His life-span covered a period of rich growth in Polish Jewry. A generation before his birth, there were fewer than 50,000 Jews in all of Poland. A generation after his death there were perhaps 500,000.[37] He was born a generation removed from the expulsion of the Jews from Spain, a calamity that filled his world with wandering refugees, and gave great impetus to the development and spread of mysticism. The principal direction of the movement of refugees was North Africa, Italy, Holland, and the Turkish Empire, but some made their way to Poland as an area of enormously developing economic opportunities. So it is not surprising to find, immediately after 1492, Isaac Hispanus as court physician to Kings John, Alexander, and Sigismund and to the Archbishop of Gnesen,[38] or Solomon Calahora as physician to Stephen Batory and a leading farmer of salt mines, hardly a century later.

In the land of his birth Talmud study was on the rise, having been given its first impetus by Jacob Pollack (1460–1541), who is credited with the development of Polish pilpulism. Pollack was succeeded by Solomon Shakhna, the great rabbi of Lublin and famous as teacher (and father-in-law) of Moses Isserles and Solomon Luria. It was

[35] Ben-Sasson, *Hagut v'Hanhagah,* passim.

[36] Asher Ziv, *She'elot u'Teshuvot haReMa,* (Jerusalem, 1970), notes to responsa nos. 61 and 71.

[37] S. Dubnow, *A History of the Jews in Russia and Poland,* vol. 1, p. 66.

[38] M. Balaban, *Italienische und spanische Aerzte,* in *Heimkehr* (Berlin, 1912), pp. 173, 177.

early in his lifetime that the great institution of Jewish autonomy, the Council of the Four Lands probably came into being.[39]

David Darshan was the son of the martyred scholar and rabbi Manasseh.[40] He was born, probably in Cracow, in (or around) the year 1527. In the introduction to *Shir haMa'alot l'David,* written in 1571, he refers to the fact that he collected his library of four hundred books over a period of twenty-five years from the time he was nineteen, in the *bahur*[41] stage of his studies.

The Cracow of David's childhood and youth, under the enlightened rule of the two Sigismunds of the Jagiellon dynasty, was deeply influenced by the humanism of the West and by Renaissance culture.[42] Sigismund's wife, Bona, was a member of the Sforza family. Fully one-third of the Polish nobility was Lutheran or Calvinist. It was a varied dialogue of the faiths, with the Greek Orthodox Church to the East, the Roman Church struggling to regain power, and Judaism flourishing through the burgeoning *yeshivot.* The death of Sigismund II in 1574 and the accession of Stephen Batory, a staunch Catholic, following hard on the heels of the intense work of the Jesuits and the Counter-Reformation, changed the atmosphere—especially for Jews.

The Jew, in the midst of these contemporary forces, religious, social, and ethnic, lived at a constant edge of danger, but in an expanding economy that gave him a significant role and saw his economic, and spiritual life grow in strength and influence. David indicates that he studied with Rabbis Moses Isserles, Solomon Luria, Joseph Cohen, and Isaac ben Bezalel (brother of the MaHa-RaL of Prague). The *yeshivah* of that period centered around the distinguished and respected teacher. This was especially so in the case

---

[39] Cf. Israel Heilperin, *Pinkas Vaad Arba Arazot* (Jerusalem, 1947), p. 17.

[40] On the title page of *Ktav Hitnazzelut l'Darshanim,* David is referred to as "the son of the martyred *Gaon,* Rabbi Manasseh, may God avenge his blood."

[41] This was the first stage of *yeshivah* study in the Middle Ages. The next stage was *meshuhrar,* corresponding to *licentius* in the universities. The highest level, preceding ordination and the title rabbi, was *haver.* Cf. M. Breuer, "HaYeshivah haAshkenazit b'Shilhei Y'mei haBeinayim" (doctoral diss., Hebrew University, Jerusalem, 1962).

[42] *New Cambridge Modern History,* vol. II, *The Reformation,* (1965), pp. 186 ff.

of the sages Isserles, Luria, and Cohen, who were eminent scholars, came from families of wealth and position, and could support the scholars who came to study with them. It represented a kind of inner circle of special privilege, which expressed itself in the emergence of community-authorized *yeshivot*,[43] and probably accounts for David's difficulties in getting his to endure.

David describes his difficulties in this context vividly. He writes that he was barred, against his will, from academies of Torah. There "many of the privileged in learning and in wealth" turned against him. "They prevented me from studying Torah in the proper time and I was considered a pariah among them. . . . They also made it difficult for me to make a living by preventing students from studying with me."[44]   His anger and resentment break out in one of his sermon models on the problem of how the wicked, living under a lucky star and prospering, finally get their comeuppance. In this vein he writes: "Now . . . these men of Israel who oppress their fellows are treated like the oppressing nations and have no portion in the God of Israel . . . for the moment fate smiles on them, but when the influence of their stars wanes they will stand in judgment for the enormity of their sins. *And we have seen how many individuals and families, who rule and oppress their fellows have been destroyed, they, their power and their wealth*" (emphasis added).[45] There is a bitterness and bite here, in a time of expansion and growth, that appears to prefigure the massive reaction almost two centuries later in the breakout of the Hassidic movement.

Among his fellow students at the academy of Moses Isserles were David Gans and Abraham Halevi Horowitz.[46] The former was the author of *Zemah David,* a secular historical work, and a student of astronomy and mathematics; the latter was, in his youth, a keen student of philosophy and the author of a commentary on Maimonides. Both received their prime impulse to such secular studies in Isserles' academy.

[43] Cf. Breuer, "HaYeshiva haAshkenazit b'Shilhei Y'mei haBeinayim."

[44] *Ktav Hitnazzelut l'Darshanim,* par. 14.

[45] Ibid., par. 31.

[46] I. Zinberg, *Geschichte fun der Literatur bei Yiden* (Vilna, 1935), vol. 5, pp. 58 ff.

Isserles was in fact sharply criticized by his brother-in-law Solomon Luria for permitting such secular studies. The latter complained that he had found the "prayer of Aristotle" written in a prayer book of one of the former's students. To this Isserles responded by denying the charges and asserting that if it had happened without his knowledge it was "an evil root inherited from their fathers who studied [Greek] philosophers and followed their ways,"[47] but he defended his study of Greek philosophy through Maimonides. The humanist and rationalist tendencies, eventually to be suppressed, show their traces here.[48]

At times David was a spokesman for the Haverim, rabbinical students who had passed the second phase of their studies and were ready for ordination. We find a question put to the ReMa[49] with respect to a problem concerning the placing of Hanukah candles that is submitted by David, who ends with the words: "your humble servant David submits this question with the consent of the Haverim," whereupon, in a clear indication of the intimacy of relationship, the Master responds: "My beloved friend, after you have read this please return it to me so that I may give it to a copyist that I may have it in my records." It is clear that at the time of the writing of the question he had not yet received ordination, for Isserles refers to him in the responsum without an honorific: "these are the words of David."

This responsum, which is not dated, must have been written well before 1556. For in that year Isserles left Cracow because of the plague,[50] and David was already in Italy, for in that year he copied the manuscript of the Perush haYeri'ah haG'dolah,[51] a commentary on the Ten Spheres, in Modena. It is a beautiful piece of scribal art,

[47] Moses Isserles, She'elot u'Tshuvot haReMa (Cracow, 1640), responsum 7.
[48] Ben-Sasson, Hagut v'Hanhagah, pp. 13 ff. and 39 ff.
[49] Moses Isserles, Responsa, responsum 81.
[50] See note 34.
[51] This version of the MS. is listed in G. Margoliouth, Catalogue of Hebrew and Samaritan Manuscripts in the British Museum, vol. III, no. 829. Two other versions of this commentary by the Kabbalist Reuven haZarfati (14th cent.) are in the Bodleian Library. Cf. A. Neubauer, Catalogue of Hebrew Manuscripts, no. 1949 and 2429.

written in a fine Ashkenazic style, and magnificently illustrated, with a sketch of Rabbi Akiva entering and leaving the *Pardes* unscathed, surrounded by the four creatures of Ezekiel's Chariot Vision.

We may reasonably conclude that David received his ordination sometime before this, because in the period between 1556 and 1558 there is ample evidence that this had occurred. He certified one Uri ben Shlomo haCohen as *shoḥet* (ritual slaughterer) in 1558, in Mori near Rovere;[52] he wrote a recommendation for a student Avigdor, who was related by marriage to his Italian patrons the Bordolani. Avigdor moved from Venice to Cremona to study with him, and referred to him by his rabbinic title.[53] Furthermore, he wrote a responsum and an essay on amulets for Rabbis Joseph Minẓ and Jacob Reiner to establish his credentials in Italy, where he acted as rabbi and tutored in the household of the aforementioned Bordolanis.[54]

By his own admission, he followed the practice of *yeshivah* students, moving in groups or individually from city to city, as was the general custom of university students in the Middle Ages.[55] He was sustained, he writes, "by a bounteous spirit . . . which I drew . . . from many *yeshivah* heads, namely the sages of Russia, Poland, Moravia, and Italy."[56]

At any rate, no later than 1556, and at least until 1558, we find him in Italy, where in the flourishing late Renaissance cities of the north, there were thriving Jewish communities, a creative confluence of Italian, Spanish, and Ashkenazic communities. For example, Venice and its surrounding towns had a population of 3,000 Jews, Mantua and Ferrara had 2,000 each, Padua almost 1,000, the Papal States almost 12,500; and in all there were perhaps 25,000 in all of Italy.[57]

He served as rabbi and tutor for the wealthy banking family of

---

[52] *Shir haMa'alot l'David,* p. 16b.

[53] Ibid., p. 15b.

[54] Ibid., pp. 12a and 15b.

[55] Cf. Breuer, "HaYeshivah haAshkenazit b'Shilhei Y'mei haBeinayim," passim.

[56] *Ktav Hitnaẓẓelut l'Darshanim,* par. 14.

[57] M. Shulvass, *Jews in the World of the Renaissance* (Leiden, 1973), pp. 19, 20.

Moses Bordolano, to whom the privilege of lending money at interest was restored in 1557.[58] Mirroring the prevailing custom of noble households as centers of learning and culture, they frequently maintained their own rabbi and *yeshivah*. David spent time in Ferrara and its environs with them, developing a relationship that was long sustained.

It was not uncommon for Polish Jews to visit Italy, and similarly for Italian Jews to visit Poland. In this period Poland had become an important trade link between Northern Europe and the Turkish Empire and maintained links with Italy. There was in fact a great deal of intercourse between the Jewish communities of Poland and Italy. The restored printing presses in Poland were set up by Jews who had come from Italy.[59] Polish rabbis were frequently in communication with Italian rabbis.[60] Many young Polish Jews went to Italy to study medicine, especially at the University of Padua.[61] In 1590, a Pentateuch appeared in Lemberg with commentaries in both Yiddish and Italian.[62] Many Polish Jews came to Poland via Italy, as physicians or apothecaries.[63] The famous court physician and statesman to the Turkish court, Solomon Ashkenazi followed a route that led to Turkey via Cracow. And we have already noted that a Sforza princess was Queen of Poland.

David came to Italy during a critical time for Italian Jewry. A quarrel over printing rights for an edition of Maimonides' *Mishneh Torah* had exploded with recriminations between the non-Jewish publishers in Venice. Two editions had been brought out, both with a commentary by Rabbi Meir Katzenellenbogen of Padua, a kinsman of David's teacher, the ReMa. Katzenellenbogen favored one over the other, and got Isserles to proclaim a ban on the pirated edition. This controversy, brought to the Vatican with nasty testimony

[58] S. Simonsohn, *A History of the Jews in the Duchy of Mantua* (Jerusalem, 1977), p. 211.

[59] Cf. H. D. Friedberg, *Toldot haDfus haIvri b'Poloniah* (Antwerp, 1932), pp. 1 ff.

[60] Cf. Moses Isserles, responsa nos. 10 and 69.

[61] Zinzberg, *Geschichte fun der Literatur bei Yiden,* vol. 5, p. 40.

[62] Ibid., 19. See also vol. 4, p. 69.

[63] Ibid.

by apostates supporting each publisher, resulted in the confiscation and burning of the Talmud in 1553.[64] Shortly before David came to Ferarra, a rabbinic synod had met there to decree that no Hebrew book was to be published unless approved by three rabbis and the community closest to the site of the printing press. This form of self-censorship was designed to prevent further attacks on Jewish books.[65]

This was the time also of the controversy over the printing of the *Zohar*.[66] The *Zohar*, the *Tikkunei haZohar*, and the commentary to the *Ma'arekhet haElohut* all appeared in 1558, and their appearance was enthusiastically noted by R. David. He referred especially to the latter as "a work which is adorned sevenfold . . . as is known to whomever reads it." And speaking of its author he added, "he is as his name—there is no limit to his praise!"[67] The printing of the *Zohar* was opposed by the above-mentioned MaHaRam of Padua, and as we have already noted, Moses Isserles expressed his strong reservations about the too-easy availability of Kabbalistic material.[68]

It was probably at this time that David added the Kabbalistic books to his library, as he informs us in speaking of it that "among them will be found some new kinds of books which have been hidden away for some years."[69] In his essay on amulets he quotes from the *Sefer Yezirah*, and adds: "The effectiveness of amulets becomes much better understood by anyone who has had the privilege of perusing the book *Shi'ur Koma* or the *Prayer of Nehunia ben haKaneh*, or the *Prayer of Rav Hamnuna Sava* or the book of the *Seventy-Two Names of Metatron* which are currently to be found in my library."[70]

[64] Amram, *Makers of Hebrew Books in Italy*, pp. 253 ff. See also Moses Isserles, *Responsa*, numbers 31 and 69.

[65] S. Simonsohn, "Sefarim v'Sifriot shel Yehudei Mantua," *Kiryat Sefer* 37, no. 1, (Jerusalem, 1961–62), p. 103.

[66] For a fine detailed account of this controversy, see I. Tishbi, "HaPulmus al Sefer haZohar b'Me'ah haShesh-esrei b'Italiah," in *Mehkarim b'Kabbalah, in honor of Gershom Scholem* (Jerusalem, 1968).

[67] Cf. *Shir haMa'alot l'David*, p. 12a.

[68] Cf. note 18.

[69] *Shir haMa'alot l'David*, *Hakdamah*, 1a.

[70] Ibid., p. 12a.

That his possession and dissemination of such books caused him problems in Cracow later may certainly be deemed a possibility. Clearly he may well have acquired the bulk of his library in this period. He indicates that he used money earned from writing amulets to buy books, and wrote hundreds in Posen and Ferrara, and other places. He collected them, he tells us, "from the four corners of the world" and spent a good deal of money on them.[71]

His must be considered an unusually large library for its time. We can judge this by an inventory of the libraries of the Jews of Mantua made by the Inquisition in 1595.[72] Some 20,000 books, belonging to approximately 500 owners (individuals and synagogues), were examined by the Inquisition, and among them we find only six libraries of 400 books or more, and only one with more than 1,000 volumes. Some twenty-five individuals possessed between 100 and 200 books. In one library, that of Abraham Provinziali, we find that six of his almost 600 volumes had been printed in Cracow.

In Ferrara David's credentials as a rabbi were tested by the resident rabbi of the community, Jacob Reiner, in 1557. Responding to this request, David wrote a responsum on a question concerning the validity of a marriage between two Marranos, who had married in the presence of two Jewish witnesses and affirmed their intention to return to Judaism.[73] It is interesting to note that this effort, described in his *Shir haMa'alot l'David* (1571), appeared in the Responsa of Moses Isserles without identification.[74] David must have sent it to his mentor, and it was among the Sage's responsa when they were published for the first time sixty-eight years after his death.

Rabbi Jacob Reiner was involved in the setting up of a "studium" in Ferrara. He was an Ashkenazic rabbi who came to Italy, served as rabbi of the Ashkenazic *yeshivah* in Mantua, spent some time in Verona, and came to Ferrara, where he was appointed head of the

---

[71] Ibid., p. 1a.
[72] Simonsohn, *Sefarim v'Sifriot Shel Yehudei Mantua,* pp. 103 ff.
[73] *Shir haMa'alot l'David,* p. 8a.
[74] Ziv, *She'elot u'Tshuvot haReMa,* p. 285.

yeshivah. This *yeshivah* was established with the blessing of Duke Ercole II, who exempted those enrolled in it from all tolls, observing: "This can only prove to be the honor and advantage to be derived from it by many Jewish and non-Jewish students, both natives and foreigners."[75] This he did at the request of Solomon Rivo, and David must have been one of the scholars who benefited from it. Indeed, it likely provided him with the idea of setting up a similar "studium" when he returned to Cracow.[76]

Just how long he remained in Italy, and precisely when he returned to Cracow, where he became the town *darshan,* is unclear. He was certainly in Cracow by 1567,[77] for in that year he wrote a responsum for one Elijah Galatz, who wished to know whether his wife could be compelled to testify personally in a litigation, or whether he might testify on her behalf.

The following year David was in a position to return a favor extended him by his friends, the Bordolani. They had been involved in a bitter controversy with the D'Ato family, in which the Sefardic rabbis of the area supported the latter, and the Ashkenazic rabbis, the former. The whole case caused quite a stir, and it is recorded in detail in two responsa by Rabbi Isaac di Lattes[78] and in a Bet Din transcript of the case.[79] Mutual bans were traded, the D'Atos took the Bordolani to a secular court, and Moses Bordolano came to Cracow to seek support from the rabbis of that community.

Bordolano brought with him bans of excommunication directed against Rabbi Moses di Rossi (father of the historian Azariah di Rossi), who had permitted the D'Atos to take the case to a gentile court. David wrote: "I am exceedingly amazed at you, Moses di Rossi, for pursuing, assaulting like a wild beast, and spreading venom in the midst of God's holy people, leading them to ignore

---

[75] Cf. Andrea Balletti, *Gli Ebrei e gli Estensi* (Reggio-Emilia, 1930), pp. 96–97.

[76] *Shir haMa'alot l'David,* p. 1a.

[77] Ibid. 12b.

[78] Isaac di Lattes, *She'elot u'Tshuvot* (Vienna, 1860), pp. 141 ff.

[79] Manuscript, *Sefer haProzesso.* The original is in the Leningrad Library. A microfilm version is to be found in the Hebrew University Library, where it was consulted.

the injunctions of the great scholars of the world,''[80] and added his ban to the list of excommunications.

The years of his return coincided with the struggle successfully concluded to reintroduce the printing of Hebrew books to Cracow. David was clearly involved in the process, perhaps even from the time of his Italian sojourn. The first Hebrew printing press had been introduced as early as 1534 by the brothers Helitz, who began publishing Hebrew books for the burgeoning academies and general population.[81] Three years later they converted to Christianity, but they continued to print and import Hebrew books. Perhaps as an outcome of the spread of the Reformation and the vigorous counterattack of the Catholic Church, Jews were held responsible for the backsliding and defections, and leading Jews were held responsible, arrested, and put under extreme pressure. It may be that under such pressure the Helitz brothers submitted to baptism. For whatever reason, they came under the protection of the Church and Bishop Gamrat in their subsequent publishing problems.[82]

As could be well expected, Jews refused to buy the Helitz books. Could prayer books, Bibles, and Talmud folios be purchased from such a source? To protect their interests, the Helitz brothers turned their stock over to a Christian bookseller, who offered them at a very low price, but his offer was rejected. Facing bankruptcy, the publishers begged the king (Sigismund Augustus II) to force the community to pay. A commission was set up to inventory the books— they totalled 3350, and the further importation of Hebrew books was prohibited until the bill was paid.[83] Cracow turned to the neighboring community of Posen for help, and together the money was raised, the books purchased and hidden away, and the importation of Hebrew books from Italy and Bohemia proceeded.

Cracow's academies continue to grow; books had to be imported, and they were expensive. We have already noted the existence of the relationship between Italy and Poland. Licenses to import Hebrew

[80] *Shir haMa'alot l'David,* p. 12b.
[81] M. Balaban, *Yiden in Polen* (Vilna, 1930), pp. 183 ff.
[82] Ibid.
[83] Ibid. This is one of the first inventories of printed Hebrew books on record.

books were given and renewed by the King. In 1566, King Sigismund Augustus II gives permission to Baruch Halevi to import Hebrew books for a period of four years.[84] But clearly it would be more feasible economically if a printing press were in place in Cracow.

Isaac of Prosstitz, with whom David became associated, set out to fill this need. He had worked in the printing house of Giovanni Grypho [85] in Venice, and had purchased his type fonts and equipment when he went out of business. This done he moved to Cracow. It is quite possible that David had contact with him in Venice, for he wrote a letter of recommendation in Venice for a kinsman of the Bordolano family on his way to study in Cremona.[86]

In any event, Isaac began his work in Cracow, when David was already there, with the printing of an edition of the *Ḥamesh Megillot Rabbah* with a commentary by Naftali Herẓ ben Menaḥem. The Church intervened to stop the publication, the King ordered the books seized and examined, and it appeared for a little while as if the Prosstitz effort would be aborted. Isaac vigorously carried on the battle for his rights, supported by the community leaders, and the book finally saw the light of day in the summer of that year. It was a red-letter day in the life of the community, and R. David was called upon to write a dedicatory poem. He appears to have filled the role of Cracow's poet laureate as well as *darshan*. Thus it transpires that on the last page of the very first Hebrew book to come off the presses in Cracow after the Ḥelitz debacle some thirty years earlier, we read the following: "When the poet David Darshan of Cracow beheld the beauty of the piety of the sage Rabbi Herẓ, interpreting the difficult words of the *Five Megillot Rabbah,* and when he beheld the flawless beauty of the printed edition, he spontaneously burst into song with a simple quatrain."[87] In a way it was a reaction, Cracow-style,

---

[84] Friedberg, *Toldot haDfus haIvri b'Poloniah,* p. 3.

[85] Ibid.

[86] *Shir haMa'alot l'David,* p. 15a.

[87] From the last page of *Perush al haMidrash Rabbah meḤamesh haMegillot,* by Naphtali Herẓ ben Menaḥem of Lwow (Cracow, 1568).

reminiscent of the enthusiasm of John Keats "On Looking into Chapman's Homer." David did not allow modesty to get in his way, and in the laudatory poem, well-written in the medieval style, with Bible quotations and puns, he inserted his own name in acrostic:

D iscover a book with beautiful sayings,[88] no shame in it,[89] fruit providing[90]

V erily showing, word by word, wondrous wonders, hidden phrases,

D irection giving, who can price it—breaking shells, line by line

D ared words utter, future, past, carefully crafting myriad insights

R ead words lightly in Five Megillot, saw vast depths beneath their surface

S eeking surely reputation,[91] that sage Herz, the best of scholars, expands horizons

N ow its done, day twenty-nine, of sad month Av, creating joy, in the short count.[92]

The next book to appear from his press was Moses Isserles' *Torat haHatat,* in 1570, and in the following year, in quick succession, two books in Yiddish, a folk book and a translation of a prayer book, and then David's own sampler of his works, his *Shir haMa'alot*

---

[88]

ד רשו ספר. אמרי שפר. בלתי חפר. עושה פירות.

ו דאי גלה. בכל מלה. הפלא פלא. תיבות זרות.

ד רך דרך. אין לו ערך. התיר פרך. שורות שורות.

ד בר דבר. עתיד עבר. יישב חבר. כל אפשרות.

ר אה קלות. ה״ מגילות. מצד מלות. דרש חומרות.

ש ס רב הו״א ר״ץ. גאון הירץ. גודר פרץ. ראש החבורות.

נ נגמר אומר. כ״ף ט״ת אב צר. חדווה יצר. לפרט קטן.

[89] Ibid.

[90] This line is based on a *yozer* for *Shabbat Shekalim.* Note how the poem is based on the form and content of the *piyyut*:

דבר בזה ספר. וקים באמרי שפר. למשולי עפר ואפר.

היותם נותנים כופר. בלי דופי וחפר.

[91] This is a pun on *Herz.*

[92] The Hebrew phrase חדווה יצר has a numerical value of 329, which in this case is the beginning of the Hebrew year 5329, i.e., 1568. The book was published the following year.

l'David, with its rich variety of content—sermons, responsa, sample
letters and poems, and biographical material.

David announced that he had brought a substantial library to the
community, and hoped to establish a Midrash (studium), where
ordinary folk could come to consult books, where scholars could
study, where teachers could receive instruction in educational techniques for children, and children and young people could be
taught. He would be a link to *yeshivah* heads, transmitting questions
which he himself could not handle. And he would be very careful
not to become involved in community affairs in such a way as to
interfere with existing authority: "And all of this with the clear
understanding that I will not have any interest in any aspect of office
or honor whatsoever, either in community affairs or in rabbinical
function, except those given on the occasion of a *mitzvah* at the time
of the sermon as it will be required."[93]

Finally he appealed for financial help for his project: "And the
end and core of it all is something that cannot be measured, for
whoever supports this project assures himself of a secure footing in
both worlds and will be granted long life and good fortune. . . . For
while he goes about his business and commerce, others will be occupied in the *Midrash* [Study Hall] with the holiness of the Torah. And
because of this, everything he does will prosper and it will be granted him to see the coming of the Messiah."[94] Unfortunately no help
was forthcoming, and despite the fact that he had preached and
taught, written amulets, served as a healer, acted as intermediary for
the *yeshivah* head, he had to depart for a while "until some money
will turn up and I can collect enough . . . for dowry and ornament,"
to marry off his many daughters.[95] A much more literate but equally
hapless Tevye the Dairyman indeed!

One of the projected books announced in his sampler, its introduction completed in Cracow in 1571,[96] was to be called *Maskil
l'David.* This was intended as an introduction to a book which David

[93] *Shir haMa'alot l'David,* p. 2b.
[94] Ibid.
[95] Ibid.
[96] *Ktav Hitnazzelut l'Darshanim,* par. 25.

completed a few years later in Lublin, where he went after leaving Cracow. Here he worked as editor and proofreader for a competitor of his Prosstitz employer, Kalonymos ben Mordecai Jaffe,[97] and was involved in the publishing of Isaac Duran's *Shaarei Dura,* a popular handbook on the *mitzvot* before the appearance of the *Shulḥan Arukh.* This book appeared in 1574, and its title page informs us that "it was proofread with great care by that eminent sage Rabbi David Darshan." In that year he published his *K'tav Hitnazzelut l'Darshanim* (In Defense of Preachers), which contains his introduction *Maskil l'David,* a defense of the preaching interpreter's art, and samples of interpretation of the Torah text for each Sabbath in tandem with an appropriate talmudic text, as we are informed by the title page: "He demonstrates to the student the basic principle whereby the Torah portion may be linked with the talmudic saying and the *Midrash*"[98]; and to serve as an especially useful tool for preachers, he informs the reader: "I have prepared four different interpretations for each Torah portion. . . . With this resource the preacher will be able to preach in the Temple Court every Sabbath for four consecutive years, something new interpreted in several ways, without being upbraided for repenting himself."[99]

David indicated on the title page that he intended to leave for the Holy Land,[100] where, presumably, it was his intention to complete the many writings which he had projected in his two printed books. From this source we learn that he did not succeed in setting up his Study Hall, and because there were those who derided and attacked the *darshan,*[101] he was publishing his defense now, but would expand it later. He apparently left that year, breaking off his work of editing *Shaarei Dura* as we read at the end of the latter book: "Proofread by Rabbi David, son of the martyr Manasseh, mentioned at the beginning of the book, up to the Fifth Gate."[102]

---

[97] Cf. Friedberg, *Toldot haDfus haIvri b'Poloniah.* Note especially the sections on Cracow and Lublin.

[98] *Ktav Hitnazzelut l'Darshanim,* title page.

[99] Ibid., par. 16.

[100] Ibid., title page.

[101] Ibid.

[102] Isaac Duran, *Shaarei Dura* (Lublin, 1574).

David was headed for the Land of Israel, probably Safed, which was at this time a vital center of kabbalistic creativity, where Isaac Luria, Joseph Caro, Ḥayim Vital, and Moses Cordovero were the center of an enormously influential coterie. Whether he ever reached his destination we may never know, for there is no tangible evidence of this.

One final trace of our David that long went unnoticed crops up, embedded in a short commentary to a 1609 edition of the *Talmud Yerushalmi* which was printed in Cracow by the Prosstitz press in 1609. The author of the commentary, who is not identified, wrote a brief introduction in which he indicates the importance of the appearance of this version of the Talmud, which was not getting the attention of its more widely studied Babylonian version. The second edition of this *Yerushalmi* appeared in Krotoschin in 1866, and here the title page reads: ". . . containing a short commentary by an unknown writer who concealed his name." A notation in the margin of this title page in the Hebrew University Library by an anonymous scholar who used the book reads: "Nevertheless he revealed his name in *Nazir* 54c." And here, buried in the commentary there appears the phrase: "Thus it seems to me, David Darshan."[103] On the basis of this, Professor Lieberman concluded that R. David was likely the author of that commentary. A careful comparison of R. David's style in his printed books with the style of the commentary and the short introduction seems to confirm this.

Was he then in Cracow when the book is printed? Was it a work he left behind to be published later? Or did he send it to Cracow from Safed (if he ever got there) to emphasize that the Talmud of the Land of Israel, the *Yerushalmi,* needed new emphasis in days of great messianic anticipation? There is as yet no answer to these questions. They continue to haunt and to intrigue us.

What we can say with certainty is that the two printed books he published, the manuscript he copied, the books he edited, the commentary he authored, and the library he owned, all reflect a man of talent and promise, who mirrored the deep range of Jewish culture

---

[103] Cf. Saul Lieberman, *HaYerushalmi kiPshuto* (Jerusalem, 1935), p. 8. Cf. Talmud Yerushalmi, *Nazir* 54c.

and learning in his age, a crucial period in Jewish history, and a seminal age in the history of the world. He was among the significant building blocks of the rich and many-hued stream of the developing Jewish learning and Jewish society, whose mark was deeply etched in the character of Polish Jewry in a critical period of transition.

A deeper and more carefully analytical study of his works will, it is to be hoped, yield a deeper insight into this fascinating and significant period of Jewish history, and it is to be hoped that the publication of the translation of his two little books, together with their rare texts, will contribute to this process.

For they reflect a man of his time, a Jewish scholar to whom his books and his learning meant more than anything else. They reflect a man whose dreams were not matched by the realities he confronted, and yet who reflected an unconquerable persistence, an irrepressible curiosity, always, it seems, on the wrong side of the success syndrome.

When he completed his first printed book he wrote: "I give praise and thanks to the Most High as I come to the completion of the *Song of the Steps* and to the preeminent community of Cracow, which is outstanding in scholarship and achievement. Who can adequately describe her virtues? She is indeed entitled to the complete blessings of the patriarchs, and is truly the keystone of the Jewish world."[104] Was this an effusive darshanic exaggeration, or did he perhaps touch the nerve of truth? Not the "big guns," but the "silent souls" so well described by the poet Bialik have been a shaping force that deserves to be studied and affirmed.

---

[104] *Shir haMa'alot l'David,* p. 16b.

IV
SOURCES AND LITERATURE

a

The primary, contemporary literary sources that touch on David Darshan are very sparse. Aside from his own two books, we find him mentioned as writing a poem of celebration, acting as editor in one book, signing his name on a manuscript that he copied in Italy, inserting his name in a short commentary to the Jerusalem Talmud, and a mention of him by name in the Responsa of Moses Isserles. Thus, the primary sources are:

> David ben Manasseh Darshan, *Shir haMa'alot l'David* (Cracow, 1571) and *Ktav Hitnaẓẓelut l'Darshanim* (Lublin, 1574).
> Isaac Duran, *Shaarei Dura* (Lublin, 1574).
> Reuven haẒarfati, *Perush haYeri'ah haG'dolah* (manuscript, copied and signed by David Darshan in Modena, in 1556).
> Naphtali Herẓ, *Perush al haMidrash Rabbah meḤamesh haMegillot* (Cracow, 1569).
> Moses Isserles, *She'elot u'Tshuvot* (Cracow, 1640), responsum 81.

b

The secondary literature, up to the first quarter of the twentieth century derives principally from bibliographies, whose authors saw or heard about his two printed books. None of them is aware of the manuscript he copied, or of his possible authorship of the short commentary on the Talmud Yerushalmi. They are listed herewith:

1. *Siftei Yesheinim,* Shabbetai Bass, Amsterdam, 1680.

> His information seems to come from the title pages of *Shir haMa'alot l'David* and *Ktav Hitnaẓẓelut l'Darshanim.* (Henceforth, in Parts B and C of this section, they will be referred to as *S* and *K* respectively). For *K* Bass gives an incorrect publication date of 1548.

2. *Bibliotheca Hebraea,* Johannes Christophorus Wolff, Hamburg, 1715.

Wolff follows Bass, and mistakenly identifies David Darshan with Messer David ben Messer Leon haLevi of Mantua. Cf. p. 295, no. 486.

3. *Bibliotheca Judaica,* Julius Fuerst, Leipzig, 1849.

The lengthy bibliographical account is, in good part, a collection of all the inaccuracies and errors of preceding bibliographies. He follows Bass and Wolff. He confuses David Darshan's *Tehilla l'David* (which was never published) with a book by that name published in Constantinople, in 1577, by Messer David de Leon. See vol. 1, p. 202.

4. *Catalogus Librorum Hebraeorum in Bibliotheca Bodleiana,* Moritz Steinschneider, Berlin, 1852–56.

He lists *S,* which he himself examined, and culls brief biographical details from it. He misreads the introduction, stating that David collected his books between the ages of nineteen and twenty-five, which is not the case. David writes that he collected the books for twenty-five years, from the age of nineteen. He mentions the laudatory poem in the 1569 edition of *Perush al haMidrash Rabbah meHamesh haMegillot,* by Naphtali Herz. He makes note of Wolff's errors with respect to *K,* and the confused identification with David ben Judah Leon.

5. *Knesset Yisrael,* Samuel Joseph Fuenn, Warsaw, 1886.

Fuenn lists him as David Darshan of Cracow, Darshan of Lublin. He refers to his failure to establish a study hall in Cracow, and lists the publication dates of *S* and *K* correctly.

6. *Sefer Seder haDorot,* Yeḥiel ben Shlomo of Minsk, Warsaw, 1870.

This reference contains a brief listing of David's writings as found in the title pages of *S* and *K.* He gives the incorrect 1548 date for *K.* See pp. 273b and 289a.

7. *Catalogue of Hebrew Books in the British Museum,* S. van Straalen, London, 1894.

He lists *K* as item 1966.b.23 in the British Museum Library. He is of the opinion that the chronostich on the title page is incorrect, and accepts the date of 1571, which is found in folio 5b of *K.* He lists *S* as item 1966.b.24, with the title page wanting. See p. 61.

8. *Ozar haSfarim,* Isaac Ben-Jacob, Vilna, 1880.

In listing *K* he quotes fully from the title page, and reads the chrono-stich properly, giving the correct publication date, 1574. He lists S together with the projected books mentioned on the title page, and lists additional titles mentioned by Fuerst, but raises doubts about them. See p. 248, 577.

9. *Or haHayim,* Hayim b. Yosef Michael, Frankfurt a/m 1891.

He mentions David as a contemporary of Moses Isserles, refers to mention of him in the latter's Responsa (no. 81), to the laudatory poem of 1568, to *S* and *K* (with incorrect date) giving Bass as his source (p. 323).

10. *Katalog der Salo Cohn'schen Schenkungen,* Bernard Wachstein, Vienna 1911.

The only other extant copy of *K* we could find (outside the British Museum), was in the Juedische Kultusgemeinde Bibliothek in Vienna. It was confiscated by the Nazis and then by the Russians and may now be in the Leningrad Library. Wachstein gives the correct date for *K* (1574) and takes issue with van Straalen's 1571 dating, since he points out that Moses Isserles, Solomon Luria, and Isaac Bezalel, mentioned on the title page as deceased, were still alive in 1571. He mentions the dedicatory poem of 1568 (pp. 46, 143).

11. *Bet Eked Sefarim,* H. D. Friedberg, Antwerp, 1926–30.

Both *K* and *S* are listed with the correct place and date of publication for each.

12. *Thesaurus of Medieval Hebrew Poetry,* Israel Davidson, New York, 1924–33.

The poems printed in *S* and the dedicatory poem of 1569 are listed, giving David a place among medieval Hebrew poets (Vol. I, no. 2320; Vol. II, nos. 221 and 376; Vol. III, no. 81).

c

In addition to the bibliographical references, the biographical accounts until the middle of the twentieth century, when Hayim

Hillel Ben-Sasson gave serious consideration to him in *Hagut V'Hanhagah,* are rather sparse:

1. *Ir Tehillah,* Meir Yeḥiel Malter, Warsaw, 1896.

   In this historical account of the city of Brisk, the author refers to the dedicatory poem of 1568, and parenthetically informs us that David's name is mentioned in Responsum 81 of Moses Isserles, and that he wrote *S* and *K,* both of which, he indicates erroneously, were printed in Cracow.

2. *L'Korot haYehudim b'Lublin,* Shlomo Barukh Nissenbaum, Lublin, 1899.

   This volume contains a brief paragraph on the great personalities in the history of the Jewish community of Lublin, where David is referred to as "a *darshan* in our city." He refers to his decision to go to the Land of Israel to complete his literary activity, as well as his two printed books. He uses *Or Ḥayim* (see item 9 in this section) as his source.

3. *Oẓar Yisrael,* J. D. Eisenstein, New York, 1910, Vol. 4.

   There is a brief reference to David under the rubric Darshan. He is erroneously called David ben Moses Darshan, and described, correctly, as poet and *darshan* in Cracow and Lublin. Eisenstein states that *K* was published in two editions, 1548 and 1574, his error based on the use of conflicting secondary sources, without ever having seen the book himself. See note 8 to my translation of *K.* He mentions the reference to David in the Isserles Responsum (81), the laudatory poem of 1568, the publication of S in 1571, and the reference to him as *magiha* in *Shaarei Dura,* in 1574. His sources are Fuenn (see item 5 below), and *Or Ḥayim* (see item 9 below).

4. *L'Toldot Yisrael v'Ḥakhamav b'Polin,* P. H. Wettstein, Cracow, 1913.

   He mentions the title החכם הכולל, given to David in *Shaarei Dura,* and that his father is referred to as a martyr. He mentions his teachers as listed in *S* and the title page of *K.* He accepts 1548 as the date of the publication of *K,* and sees the 1574 publication as a second edition.

5. *Encyclopaedia Judaica,* S. A. Horodetsky, Berlin, 1930, Vol. 9.

There is a brief paragraph here about David, in which he is called "preacher and liturgical poet." He repeats the theory that *K* was published in two editions. His sources include Fuerst, *Or haHayim,* Fuenn, Wettstein, Nissenbaum, and Benjacob.

6. *Toldot haDfus haIvri b'Poloniah,* H. D. Friedberg, Antwerp, 1932.

This excellent book on the history of Hebrew printing mentions David in his involvement with the publishers of Hebrew books in Cracow and Lublin. See pp. 5, 6, and 44.

7. *HaYerushalmi kiPshuto,* Saul Lieberman, Jerusalem, 1935.

In the introduction, Lieberman mentions David Darshan as author of the *Perush Kazer* to the Cracow, 1609, edition of the *Talmud Yerushalmi,* citing David's name buried in the commentary to *Nazir* 54c.

8. *Hagut v'Hanhagah,* H. H. Ben-Sasson, Jerusalem, 1959.

This is a brilliant account of the cultural, social, and intellectual life of Polish Jewry in the late Renaissance period, with a fine account of David Darshan in relation to his time. Ben-Sasson, misreading the chronostich, as did many others, gives the date of 1568 for *K.*

9. *She'elot u'Tshuvot haReMa,* Asher Ziv, Jerusalem 1970.

Some very useful comments on David Darshan in notes to responsum 62, where he identifies David Darshan as the author of that responsum (cf. *S,* 8a); and to responsum 81, where David is mentioned by name and in detail as having presented a question to Isserles on behalf of the *Haverim.*

d

A word should be said about the reproduction of the title page of *Shir haMa'alot l'David* as it appears in this volume. It is a composite of the only two available title pages, both flawed.

Of the three copies I have seen, and I know of no others in existence, the one in the British Museum, though complete in all other respects, lacks the title page. The copy in the Bodleian Library, missing several pages of the text, has a title page that was torn on the side and pasted together imperfectly. The copy in the possession of the Jewish Theological Seminary library, does have a title page, but a portion of the top is torn.

Thanks to the techniques of litho-photography, a composite could be made that restores the title page whole, as it appears here.

Song of the Steps

THIS IS
THE BOOK OF DAVID'S SONG OF THE STEPS

meaning [that of] the Rabbi David Preacher who composed sermons on all the Five Books of the Torah, each portion with four different comments, and at least two or three meanings in each comment

And let it be known in Israel as

DAVID'S GUIDE

After this he wrote some Responsa, and some of them have been addressed to the [great] sages of the age, and with them he also wrote an epistle on the Meaning of Amulets.

After this he wrote weighty letters in Aramaic addressed to world-renowned sages and leaders of the Lands, and some of them received the seal of approval from such world-renowned sages as Rabbi Joseph and Rabbi Moses Isserles, long may they live.

After this he wrote some airy letters in pure rhymed Hebrew to add wisdom to youths, and there are close to two hundred of them, including collections in rhyme and many poems, and let it be known in Israel as

DAVID'S TOWER

And after this he began to compose a mnemonic for the 613 *Mizvot* with hints and signs that will make it easy for a person to memorize them, together with the subdivisions that branch off from them, and even before it comes into being, let it be known in Israel as

DAVID'S GLORY

And in order to benefit the public, he has permitted the publishing of one or two or three [examples of each], to give the students a taste of the choice honey of their contents, and whichever of these books finds the greatest favor in the eyes of the sages of the age, we shall, God willing, publish later. That book will find favor in the eyes of the cognoscenti. Written by a man weighed down by troubles and burdened with many daughters. May God let His face shine upon you. In the year 5331 of the Creation.

Ten days [in] Second Adar *There was light to the Jews*

HERE IN THE HOLY COMMUNITY CRACOW

Seek ye out the book of the Lord,[1] and read THE HOLY
EPISTLE [so] called to water the flock, go and browse.[2]

PREFACE

Said the humble one[3] David [the] Preacher from Cracow:

Blessed be the Lord, God of Israel, in whose hand is the dominion over the heavenly and earthly, and who chose Israel to be His
people, chosen[4] [through the implanting of innate qualities], a holy
nation and a kingdom of priests,[5] only on condition that they listen
devotedly to His commandment and keep His covenant, which is
the covenant of the Holy Torah by which He adorned us rather than
the rest of the nations, in order to lead us to righteousness in this
world and the world to come.

And it is known that the cause of the exile and suffering and ca-
lamities[6] ia that we, because of our many sins, neglect [the observance of] Torah and commandments. And they make a striking parable in *Midrash Tanhuma*[7] concerning this:

---

[1] Isaiah 34:16.

[2] Genesis 29:1. The text reads רעו. Note the pun on ראו which David uses.

[3] This is an expression of humility used conventionally by scholars in this period.
For its origin, cf. Genesis 32:11 and 17:14.

[4] Exodus 19:5.

[5] David reverses the order of the Biblical quotations (Exodus 19:6). He does this
sort of thing often.

[6] Cf. Leviticus 26:16, Isaiah 65:23, and Talmud Bavli, *Baba Mezia* 8a. There
appears to be a Yiddish nuance underlying the Hebrew here. This recurs in his style.
From the earliest days of the printing of Jewish books in Cracow, almost as many
were published in Yiddish as in Hebrew.

[7] *Midrash Tanhuma* (Mantua, 1563), from the pericope *Shelah Lekha*, p. 81a. Here
is another example of reversing the order in a quotation. In the text from which the
quotation is taken, the portion about the ship's captain follows the portion about
the commandments.

The Holy One Praised be He gave the Torah to Israel to endow them with eternal life. He left nothing without a corresponding commandment. Man goes forth to plough, He commanded: "Thou shalt not sow thy vineyard, etc." . . . For example, when a man falls overboard what does the captain [of the ship] do? He throws him a line and says to him: "Hold on to the line and don't let go, for if you let go of it, you will forfeit [your] life." So here the Holy One Praised be He said to Israel: As long as Israel clings to the commandments they are alive, as it is written: "And ye who cleave to the Lord your God are alive, etc."[8]

And behold, because of our sins we are caught up by troubles as a result of the burden of the exile, of livlihood and of worries, and with the exception of one of a city and two of a family,[9] we do not have the time to grasp the life-line, and our days are wasted in vanity and our years in confusion.[10] And were it not that God's mercies are great toward us,[11] we should, heaven forbid, have perished for our sins. And it is He who rescues us from so many hardships, that every one of us may tell of His miracles and His wondrous deeds with all our soul and with all our might, as it is written: *Let them thank the Lord for His Mercy.*[12]

Therefore, it is for me to praise and to give thanks to the Lord of all,[13] Who declares the end of all from the beginning,[14] Who knew me before I was born, to be gadfly to grandees,[15] and Who gave

[8] The references from the Bible quoted in this passage, in the order that they appear in the midrash, are from: Deuteronomy 22:9, Deuteronomy 24:19, Numbers 16:20, Deuteronomy 18:13, Leviticus 17:13, Deuteronomy 14:1, Leviticus 19:27, Deuteronomy 22:8 and 6:9.

[9] Jeremiah 3:14.

[10] Psalms 78:33. Note the pun חבל/הבל.

[11] Psalms 124:1 and 117:2. The first part of the phrase is suggested by the former, and the second part by the latter.

[12] Psalms 107:8.

[13] This is a paraphrase of the *Alenu* prayer.

[14] Isaiah 46:10.

[15] נובב לגאים is a pun on נביא לגוים, Jeremiah 1:4. The meaning of נובב is suggested by its use in Zechariah 9:19 and the interpretation of the verse that is found in Talmud Bavli, *Baba Batra*, 12b. It suggests one who is inspiring and influential in the task of refashioning the stubborn sinner. David sees his mission as *darshan* akin to that of the prophet.

me a fluent tongue[16] to preach to the people in graceful style to teach them the straight path[17] in accordance with the *Halakhah* and the Torah.[18]

And the summation of it all: Blessed be the Lord of the universe, Who has motivated me to establish a Study Hall in honor of God and of Israel in whatever place the Holy One Praised Be He would provide for me. Furthermore, to honor the glory and the majesty of the God of heaven and earth, I shall bring to it more than four hundred choice books,[19] and more, all of them beautiful in form and powerful members of David's family,[20] collected with much effort for twenty-five years, from the time that I was a lad of nineteen, as is well known to the Gaon Rabbi Mattityahu of Brisk.[21] I collected them from the four corners of the world, and spent many a hundred zloty on them.

And foremost among them, I prepared a new Torah scroll with large script in order to be able to pray where we study.[22] And these books will be ready and available for all who desire knowledge and understanding of God from them. It is possible, furthermore, that among them there will be found some new kinds of books[23] which have been hidden away for some years.

And though modest my worth, I will not leave the place except on Sabbath eves to prepare for the Sabbath, always being on hand for anyone seeking to know or to delve into God's Torah, to the best of

[16] Isaiah 50:4.

[17] Ibid. 12:23, Ezra 8:21, Psalms 107:7.

[18] 2 Kings 17:34, Ezra 10:3, *Pirke Avot* 5:7.

[19] In those days this represented a substantial collection. Yehuda Ḥayyat, in his introduction to *Sefer Ma'arekhet haElohut* (Mantua, 1558), speaks of giving his two hundred books to Jews who came to ransom him after the expulsion from Spain.

[20] This is a pun on the phrase in Talmud Bavli, *Sanhedrin* 21a. In that passage the reference is to King David's four hundred sons, who were described as beautiful and powerful.

[21] Mattityahu Delacrut was a kabbalist and astrologer who was in Italy in the 1550s, and later in Poland. He is among those who introduced the study of Kabbalah to Poland. Cf. Hayim Nathan Dembitzer, *Klilat Yofi* (Cracow, 1888).

[22] Talmud Bavli, *Berakhot* 8a.

[23] David refers to books with new ideas, possibly kabbalistic,.

the ability of my modest intelligence and limited understanding. This is why Divine Providence saw fit to enable me to come by these books, and established me in this Study [Hall], despite my lowly status, in order that attachment to God might be strengthened and the life-line not be ruptured completely, heaven forbid, by the excessive weight of the anxieties of subsistence and taxes and imposts, and the uprooting and the hardships that we through our exile because of our many sins.

And there is no time [for a person] to be engaged in the study of Torah, in order to know the real meaning of the commandments.[24]

On some occasions he has the time but no book; on others he has the book, but no understanding. Thus, when he enters the Study Hall, his deficiency, whatever it may be, will be supplied. And if he understands better than I do, I shall not be ashamed to learn from him, And if there be something too difficult, both for the one who asks and for me, I shall take the trouble to consult the great scholars.[25]

And all this with the clear understanding that I will not have any interest in any aspect of office or honor whatsoever, either in community affairs or in rabbinical function, except those given on the occasion of a Miẓvah[26] at the time of the sermon, as it will be required. And I also [undertake] to be available at all times, every day for at least an hour, to instruct the simple folk about some commentator, or some decisor, or about the Bible, in accordance with their desires and at such time as they choose, which will be of great benefit to the children of the indigent. In addition, I shall outline the fine points of a book for the teachers of children, and this will be of unusual benefit for schoolchildren who learn from them.

In general, I shall not be too lazy to undertake whatever my appointed duty may be. And from this will flow many advantages for the educated and uneducated [alike]. The advantages to the totally

[24] Midrash, Genesis Rabbah 70:8. "They establish it [Torah/Halakhah] on its strength," that is to say, they arrive at a final and definitive decision. For the use of בורריין על in this sense, see Talmud Yerushalmi, Sotah 16a.

[25] As a possible example of this, see responsum no. 81, of Moses Isserles.

[26] For example, a circumcision or a wedding feast.

uneducated have already been made clear. And the advantages for those who have a little learning [are as follows]: When they come home tired and worn out from their effort to make a living, each one can take a book home with him and read it, and if he is baffled by the meaning of some text, or by some difficult word, he can jot it down on paper, even in the German language,[27] and he may send it to the Study [Hall], and the messenger need not reveal the name of the person involved. And I shall interpret it if I am able, and if not I shall make inquiry about it.

The advantage for the learned and the sharp-witted is immeasurable. For when he raises some profound problem, and sends it to the Study Hall, I shall transcribe it and send it on to the most learned and brilliant scholars, who will each offer some original interpretations [of matter]. Then I shall collate them, and bring them to the head of the *yeshivah,* and there the interpretations will be examined to see which is the keenest and most erudite, and this will provide the highest kind of intellectual and spiritual stimulation.[28]

This is not the case at the present time, for they do not know the difference between the noble and the ignoble,[29] and the young man acts insolently toward his elders,[30] and he who has a loud mouth, and is good at disputation, is adjudged the sharpest.[31]

And sometimes even a sharp-witted and expert scholar who needs to find a saying or religious law or a verse, or needs to look up some book of wisdom or Kabbalah or the like, [may], if he does not happen to be in possession of these books, write it[32] on paper, send it to the Study [Hall], and I shall take the trouble to look for it and find it.

[27] This is a reference to Yiddish, whose use was beginning to spread in Poland at this time with the large influx of Jews from German-speaking lands. A good many of the books published by the Prosstitz brothers were in Yiddish.

[28] Cf. Psalms 119:32 and Isaiah 60:5.

[29] Job 34:19. David uses the phrase in a pejorative sense.

[30] Isaiah 3:5; Talmud Bavli, *Ḥagigah* 14a.

[31] Talmud Bavli, *Nedarim* 48a, *Nazir* 49b.

[32] That is to say, his request.

And the greatest benefit of all, impossible to measure or value, will accrue to the head of the *yeshivah*, since he will not need to waste his time on petty problems, for only difficult problems will come before him. For I, with my modest intelligence, will solve the easier and less-complicated problems. And there will be times when someone of my lowly station will feel inhibited about asking questions, because he is too ill at ease to go in person before an exalted one. Therefore the great and awesome God saw fit to provide such a lowly one as I,[33] to spare him the anxiety and terror.[34]

And the end of the core of it all is something that cannot be measured, for whoever supports this project assures himself of a secure footing[35] in both worlds, and will be granted long life and good fortune. As it is written: *It is a tree of life to them that uphold it.*[36] The text does not say to those who study it, but rather those who support it. Therefore, wherever he[37] goes, his generosity[38] will precede him to clear away obstacles before him, and assure his [favorable] judgment [in the next world].

For while he goes about his business and his commerce, others[39] will be occupied in the Study [Hall] with the holiness of the Torah. And because of this, everything he does will prosper, and it will be granted him to live and see the coming of the Messiah. And he will profit in his property and his merchandise, and, together with his family, will be spared from famine, pestilence, and war. But those people who would nullify this project for impious reasons will be cut off forever, and erased from the Book of Life. And those who

[33] To act as a go-between.

[34] That is, the anxiety involved in such a visit.

[35] The phrase יחזיק לו הבנין is a pun based on his reference to Proverbs 3:18 below. It is here used as in Talmud Bavli, *Shabbat* 114b. Scholars who combine piety with good works build the world, thereby preserving its moral qualities and values. The donor will have a share in this.

[36] Proverbs 3:18. This interpretation, found in the *Zohar*, is an early example of "checkbook" Judaism!

[37] That is, he who supports the project.

[38] A word-play on צדקה and צדק.

[39] Through his help.

support the true faith will have a good end. Blessed will they be before God in their coming and their going, and their exit from this world will be as their entrance into it, they, their wives, and their offspring. Amen, he who speaks truth and righteousness, David Darshan, from Cracow. *Bet haMidrash* in numerical value equals David Darshan Cracow, minus one.[40]

And after this preface,[41] it may be that someone who is against me will say that I bring nothing with me that could make the impure pure,[42] the opposite of *what is the priest doing in the cemetery*;[43] that who indeed authorizes me to teach in a sacred study hall,[44] when I am not capable of giving a new insight to anything, and that how can I, therefore, give light to those who are in the dark in their quest for knowledge;[45] or how can I direct them to the right path?

I therefore feel compelled to bring some offerings to the Sanctuary, and to publish something, to wit *The Song of the Steps*,[46] to show the people and the leaders[47] something which at the very least will benefit the *Baḥurim*,[48] those who are beginning formal academic studies of Torah. They will be enlightened by many of its good qualities.

[40] In order to achieve equivalence he writes בית המידרש with a *yod,* which is not usual, to achieve a numerical value of 971, while the numerical value of דוד דרשן קראקא is 970.

[41] Alternate translations: "prologue," "preamble."

[42] Job 14:4.

[43] The talmudic and midrashic phrase describing the prohibition of a priest in a cemetery is used to describe inappropriateness in other areas. David's critics challenge his competence. See Midrash *Tanḥuma* (Mantua, 1563), 27a.

[44] That is, a house where the holy is study.

[45] The phrase עין באפלה is a play on עיון בתפלה, (Talmud Bavli, *Berakhot* 55a).

[46] Because of his name, he identifies himself with King David, using the title of his Psalms series. There is a double meaning for him in the word מעלות, which means "advantages" or "virtues," as well as "steps" or "ascents."

[47] Esther 1:11. He omits the phrase "her beauty" from the quotation, for he expects the reader or hearer to be able to complete it himself and get the point. This is a frequently used technique in *midrash.*

[48] This is a technical term for the first stage of *yeshivah* study. The first level is *baḥur,* then comes *ḥaver,* and then *rabbi.*

The first step is to increase their knowledge and understanding of words of wisdom,[49] to impart to them the new insights on the subject of sermons, by the modes of plain meaning, the homiletical meaning, and some matters which our forefathers could not have imagined.[50]

The second step is to increase wisdom with a few responsa[51] that will unlock the doors [to understanding]. And the weak will become strong with the epistle on *The Meaning of Amulets,* which was added to them.

The third step is for the strengthening of weak souls through these honorific letters, full of flowery phrases and golden prose,[52] worthy of being used to approach all kinds of community heads with due deference.

The fourth step is intended [to advance] the learning of young boys, [through] airy letters, and collections in rhyme, and some poems, all of these prepared with great care and well-ordered.

Now the first step as it pertains to sermons is divided into several parts:

(a) Something entertaining to amuse and bolster the morale of the weary soul.

(b) At times the sage[53] [i.e., preacher] does not attempt to use a higher level of material because of the [low level] of the understanding of the crowd, which knows absolutely nothing.[54]

(c) At times they conceal from the audience something very deep, and therefore it has been written down in a very obscure fashion.

---

[49] Proverbs 16:21.

[50] This is a circumlocution for סוד, or mystical meaning, which is the fourth of the fourfold division of the sermon: *pshat* (plain meaning), *remez* (allegorical meaning), *drash* (homiletical meaning), and *sod* (mystical meaning); in acronym it is *pardes.*

[51] David reverses the usual order and writes תשובות ושאלות.

[52] Lamentations 4:2.

[53] That is, the preacher, or *darshan,* who is here identified as חכם.

[54] Cf. Talmud Bavli, *Berakhot* 32b.

(d) At times he presents theories of single authorities, which are not accepted by all.

(e) An interpretation received [from a previous authority], based on scriptural texts from which may be derived wisdom, instruction, conduct, customs, and laws, as Rav Sherira Gaon[55] wrote as quoted in the introduction to *Menorat haMaor*.[56] He also wrote an apologia for several kinds of interpretations that are illuminating.[57]

Similarly, in his preface to the tractate *Zeraim,* the last of the *Geonim,* the Rambam, explains the matter of sermonizing in a delightful way.[58] Similarly some of the noblest saints spoke about preaching, may God bless them for doing so! So you see, there is much material on the subject. Therefore, I will let the matter rest for now. I shall explore it, if God grants me life, more extensively and with better style at the beginning of my book *Maskil l'David*.[59]

SERMON

And after all this, with the help of the Rock in whose hands are all creatures unto eternity, I shall begin to interpret this *agadah* in the chapter entitled *Four Types of Capital Punishment*.[60]

It has been taught [in the chapter   Rashi's comment:[61] *The word woe*

---

[55] He was head (*Gaon*) of the Academy of Pumbeditha in Babylonia and died about the year 1000.

[56] This is a compendium of *agadot* by Isaac Aboab, who lived in Spain about the year 1300. See his introduction to *Menorat haMaor* (Mantua, 1563).

[57] Job 31:26, Isaiah 13:10.

[58] Maimonides deals with this in his introduction to the commentary of the Mishnah, *Zeraim.*

[59] That is, his *Ktav Hitnazzelut l'Darshanim* (Lublin, 1574).

[60] Talmud Bavli, *Sanhedrin* 59b, chap. 7. This passage is considered to have great significance for kabbalists.

[61] The Rashi text as he quotes it varies slightly from the printed text. David condenses the passage, using only what he deems necessary here.

Four Types of Capital Punishment]— *Rabbi Simeon ben Manassiah says: Woe for the loss of a great servant, for had not the serpent gone astray [another version: had been cursed and become barren] each Israelite would have had two good serpents, sending one to the north, and one to the south, to bring him costly gems,[62] precious stones and pearls. Moreover, one would have fastened a thong under its tail, with which it would bring forth earth for his garden and wasteland.*

is used in the sense of pain, that is to say, a loss has been sustained by the world, and there is cause to bewail and bemoan the loss of a great servant. Sandlafon:[62] the name of a precious stone.

I find it difficult to perceive[63] why the text should say: *Woe [for the loss of] a great servant,* since this seems to imply that the serpent was great and righteous in and of himself, for this phraseology, we find, is used in connection with Abraham, of whom the sages said in the first chapter of Kiddushin: *We found a great one who served.*[64] We have found no evidence of righteousness in the servant before he went wrong, but only cunning, viz., *and the serpent was cunning.*[65] Much better that the text should have read: *woe for a good servant,* for he is good for anyone who uses him.

There is a further problem in the passage: *For had not the serpent gone astray, each man of Israel would have had two serpents, etc.* For what has the matter of the curse of the serpent to do with the Children of Israel? If Israel were worthy, they would receive the good without [the mediation of] a serpent. And if, heaven forbid, they were unworthy, even if the serpent were uncorrupted, they would not

---

[62] *Sandlafon* is the name of an angel who, tradition has it, weaves prayers for God. cf. Talmud Bavli, Ḥagigah 13b.

[63] Literally: "that which is stated is difficult for me."

[64] Talmud Bavli, *Kiddushin* 32b.

[65] Genesis, 3:1.

merit *precious stones and pearls, etc.,* because of him. Furthermore, [according to this theory which I reject], had not the serpent been cursed, would Israel neither be rewarded nor punished [for their sins]? In that case, heaven forbid, all commandments of the Torah would be null and void!

There is a further problem with the statement *they would have two good servants,* because of the implication that even before the serpent was cursed there were also evil serpents. And should you wish to interpret the word *good* as referring to the sender, it would follow that the text would then have to read at the beginning, *woe for the good servant.*

There is also a problem in the fact that north and south are mentioned, but not east and west. For it is well known to the scholars of natural phenomena, [as cited] in שערי שמים,[66] section three, article two, that the most precious stones are found in the east and west.

And [finally] there is the problem of Rashi's interpretation of *Sandlafon*[67] to mean *a precious stone.* Why would the text specify this one more than other precious stones, the more so when the text says subsequently: *and precious stones and pearls,* hence everything is included.

Let us preface [our comments on the text] with a few words of interpretation from Chapter Three, Paragraph Two of the Ethics of the Fathers,[68] besides the introductory comments already given.

> *Rav Ḥanina, prefect of the priests, said: Pray for the peace of the Kingdom, since but for the fear thereof we had swallowed up each his neighbor alive.*

[The etymology of the name] Rav Ḥanina[69] contains the allusion to the [fact that] what the prefect of the priests utters, are the many

---

[66] This was an encyclopedia of natural history by Gershom ben Solomon of Arles (13th cent.), published in Venice in 1547. It is divided into three parts: natural phenomena, astronomy, and metaphysics.

[67] Cf. note 3.

[68] David refers to it in the traditional manner as: *Perek Akavia.*

[69] The spelling of the name as חנניא is a misprint. There is a subtle pun here: חנינא/חינונים.

entreaties which man makes when he prays. Though High Priest, he is here called prefect of the priests, as it is written in the Talmud Yerushalmi[70]: *Five things were said concerning the prefect, and one of them was that he was not selected High Priest until he was made prefect.*

Pray for the peace of the Kingdom: He means to say: Let your prayer be made with good intention,[71] that you may have peace, and that the Kingdom of Heaven may have peace. The phrase *peace of the Kingdom* really means peace of the Kingdom of Heaven, as it is written: *or let him take hold of My strength that he make peace with Me.*[72] And it is known that Aaron the High Priest was a lover of peace[73] and a pursuer of peace, and he was able to direct his prayer more [effectively] than any other man, so as to make peace in the heavenly and earthly [spheres], which is why he concluded the priestly blessing with [the word] *peace.*

And this is why the *Urim* and *Thummim,*[74] which were folded into the Breastplate,[75] were placed over his heart, as it is written: *And thou shalt put in the Breastplate of Judgment the Urim and Thummim, and they shall be upon Aaron's heart, etc.* And it is known that the seat of prayer is in the heart, as it is stated in *Sifrei*[76] in the exposition of the verse: *and to serve Him with all your heart,*[77] and what is the service of the heart if not prayer?

The Ramban[78] has written that the general principle [underlying] the *Urim* and *Thummim*[79] was that there were divine names by means

[70] Talmud Yerushalmi, *Yoma* 40a.

[71] Or, proper intention.

[72] Isaiah 27:5. Verse 1 preceding this quotation has reference to the destruction of the Leviathan/serpent.

[73] Mishnah, *Pirkei Avot* 1:12.

[74] Exodus 28:30.

[75] The use of the word *kefel* ("pouch" or "fold") is from the comment of Naḥmanides to this passage (Exodus 28:30).

[76] *Sifrei* to Deuteronomy 11:1, which reads: ?ומה עבודת הלב אלא תפלה

[77] Deuteronomy 11:13.

[78] Rabbi Moses ben Naḥman (Naḥmanides), who was born in Verona in 1195 and died in Ereẓ Israel in 1270, was a talmudist, mystic, and biblical exegete.

[79] Cf. his commentary to Exodus 28:30. In the scale of revelation, this process ranks below prophecy and above the *bat kol*, the voice from heaven heard by special people in talmudic narrative. David applies these theories of the Ramban here with respect to the functioning of the *Urim* and *Thummim.*

of which the [High] Priest would be able to know the future and to inform all who came to inquire of coming events. These Names were divided into two sections. In the one case the letters [forming the names] of the tribes and embedded in the Breastplate, would, because of their inherent powers, light up. They were called *Urim,* or Lights, because they would light up before the eyes of the High Priest.

In the other case, [the Ineffable Name written down and folded into the Breastplate[80]] would, because of its inherent powers, illumine the heart of the [High] Priest [with the understanding] to combine the letters and form a word from them, so that he could be exact in his answer, etc. By way of illustration:[81] If the letters חנ"ש would light up, he would not be certain whether it should be read נחש or חשן. Therefore it was the function of the *Thummim* to make it possible for him to properly combine the letters.

The essence of the peace that the High Priest achieved on earth through this prayer is that he prayed for wisdom and for wealth. There were [in fact] two vessels in the Temple corresponding to them, the *Menorah* and the Table. The former symbolizes Torah: *for the commandment is a lamp, etc.;*[82] and Table symbolizes wealth, as we say: *Whoever*[83] *wishes to become wise let him go south; whoever wishes to become wealthy let him go north.* Your evidence for this [is] that the *Menorah* was to the south, and the Table to the north, as Rabbi Jonah[84] wrote in the first chapter of [his commentary to] *Berakhot.*[85]

As to [the essence of] the peace of the Kingdom of Heaven on high: God accepted their prayer [in this manner]: The Angel Sandlafon would wait until Israel completed their prayers, and he would make a crown for the Holy One, Praised be He, as stated in

[80] The *Thummim,* through the power of the Ineffable Name, gave the High Priest the ability properly to combine the letters.

[81] The illustration in the Ramban commentary is: יהדה. David inserts the letters in which he is interested, in order to make the point in his sermon.

[82] Proverbs 6:23.

[83] Talmud Bavli, *Baba Batra* 25b.

[84] Rabbi Jonah Gerundi, born in Verona in 1236, was a moralist and commentator of the Talmud.

[85] Cf. his commentary to Talmud Bavli, *Baba Batra* 5a. It is found on p. 3a of his commentary as found in the *M'Orat* edition of the *Talmud Bavli.*

Midrash Rabbah to the *Sidra B'shallah*[86] and as the liturgist wrote [in the] *Er'alim u'mal'ahim.*[87] You must read the prefix ב to the phrase *peace of the Kingdom* as עם, *together with,* and not *by means of,* and take it to mean: *with the peace of the Kingdom.* So it is that he will make peace below and above. For were it not for the fear of the Kingdom of Heaven, and were he not to pray to Him for wisdom and for wealth, *every man, his neighbor,*[88] that is to say, each man together with his neighbor, *would swallow him alive*—each and every one.

And here [when man is referred to], the reference is to a rich man, in the sense of *there went a man.*[89] *His friend*—the scholar, who is called *brothers and friends.*[90]

Life of the body suggests wealth, and life of the Torah suggests wisdom, concerning which Scripture says *and it is your life, etc.*[91] He would swallow up each one, that is to say, they would be destroyed, but wisdom and wealth would not be destroyed. Indeed they would not swallow up wisdom and wealth.

And after this interpretation, let us now interpret the text BY THE MODE OF THE PLAIN MEANING:[92]

It has been taught: *Rav Simeon ben Manassiah said: "Woe for [the loss of] a great servant."*[93] The real meaning of the text is: [Woe for the fact that] the High Priest, who served in the Temple which has been destroyed, [can no longer] pray for them with the Breastplate in which were fastened the *Urim* and *Thummim.* But he is not really lost,

---

[86] *Exodus Rabbah,* chap. 21:4, refers to an "angel appointed over prayers." David links this with Sandlafon.

[87] This is a reference to a *piyyut* by Amitai be Shefatiah. Cf. Ḥayyim Schirmann, *Mivḥar haShirah haIvrit b'Italiah;* see also Isaiah 33:7.

[88] That is, the rich man and the scholar.

[89] He returns to the subtext from *Pirkei Avot.*

[90] Exodus 2:1 and Ruth 1:1. See also Talmud Bavli, *Sotah* 12a, which comments on these verses as referring to Amram, the father of Moses, as a great man. It is from this that David makes his deduction. But for this, the scholar and the rich man would devour everything.

[91] Deuteronomy 30:20.

[92] Cf. note 97 in *Ktav Hitnazzelut l'Darshanim* for explanation of the four modes of interpretation.

[93] David is here concerned to relate "servant" to "High Priest."

for he is High Priest in Heaven.[94] And he uses the word חבל[95] to refer to the destruction of the Temple, as stated in *Midrash Tanḥuma*:[96] *The word Tabernacle* [משכן] *is mentioned twice to indicate that it was twice seized as a pledge on their account,* and when the Men of the Great Synagogue said: *Verily we have pledged it,*[97] they really meant that it was seized as a pledge twice.

For had not the serpent gone astray—that is to say, had not the Breastplate (חשן) been corrupted and turned into Serpent (נחש); and were the *Urim* and *Thummim* still intact . . . so that we might know how to link and combine the letters, as we have already described, every Israelite would have had two good serpents at his service. That is to say we would read Serpent as Breastplate (נחש/חשן),[98] which makes prayer efficacious for two things—wisdom and wealth.

And the precise reference *to each Israelite* [in the text] is there, because graven on the precious stones of the Breastplate were the names of the Children of Israel, as it is written:[99] *And thou shalt grave on them the names of the Children of Israel.* For this reason every Israelite would share in its powers, and would receive for himself the rewards of wisdom and wealth. That is why, moreover, there is a further interpretation [of the phrase] *he will send one to the north* as meaning that he who wishes to become rich should go north; [and the phrase] *he will send one to the south,* as meaning that he who wishes to become wise should go south.[100]

To bring him costly gems[101]—an intimation that his prayer would be

[94] Literally, "in the upper (spheres)."

[95] Pun: woe/pledge.

[96] There is a comment on the double use of the word *mishkan* ("Tabernacle") in *Midrash Tanḥuma* to Exodus 38:21. This idea also occurs in *Exodus Rabbah* 51:3.

[97] Nehemiah 1:7. There is a pun on חבל, which can mean "to harm" or "to damage" on the one hand, and "to pledge" or "to "pawn" on the other, or "rope."

[98] David makes use of *Genesis Rabbah* with reference to the consequences of Adam's fall, which will not be redressed until the coming of the Messiah.

[99] Exodus 28:9.

[100] Talmud Bavli, *Baba Batra* 25b.

[101] The word for "gem" in the Mishnah is *sandlafon*. This is Rashi's interpretation, which David does not accept. He takes the reference to be the angel by that name

acceptable with respect to the two elements of Torah [wisdom] and wealth, and [the angel] Sandlafon would weave a crown for his Creator from these two elements. This explains the plural form of [a name that is] singular.[102] This is made clear [in the text that immediately follows],[103] and these words *precious stones* suggest the wisdom of the Torah, i.e., tablets of stone on which the Torah was carved, [and the Torah is called] good;[104] and *pearls* suggest wealth. And we know that the Ephod was fastened to the bottom of the Breastplate as it is written: *The Breastplate shall not be loosed from the Ephod . . . and they shall build the Breastplate, etc.*[105]Furthermore, our sages have said in *Zebaḥim*, chapter nine: *The Ephod was the means of atonement for idolatry,* and it is further written: *without Ephod and without teraphim.*[106]

And the author of *The Akedah*[107] has written: *The Ephod was an ornament habitually worn by idolators. . . . and an example of this is the idol of Micah,*[108] *etc. . . . For this reason God commanded that they should include the Ephod in the priest's garments, but that it should be suspended behind the priest's body downward from his girdle to that low*[109] *place in man, and that is surely by way of disparagement, as one sage has said in chapter seven of Sanhedrin:*[110] *"All sneering is forbidden except the ridiculing of idols, for it is*

who weaves prayers for God. And since the plural is used, he extends that interpretation to suggest wisdom and wealth.

[102] It would be logical to counter that if "angel" were intended, the singular should be used. The use of the plural suggests a special interpretation, i.e., "wisdom and wealth."

[103] The text reads: *sandlafonim,* "precious stones and pearls."

[104] Cf. Exodus 34:14, which is an example of the use of precious stones in relation to Torah. Cf. Proverbs 4:2 for use of the term "good" in the same context.

[105] Exodus 28:28.

[106] Talmud Bavli, *Zevaḥim* 88b, and Hosea 8:4.

[107] Isaac Arama, *Akedat Yiẓḥak* (Venice, 1554), Gate 51, p. 145a. Arama (1420–94) was a distinguished preacher in Spain, whose sermons throw light on the pre-expulsion period. His *Akedat Yiẓḥak* is written in the form of philosophical homilies and allegorical commentaries on the Pentateuch.

[108] Judges 17:1ff.

[109] The Venice text of *Akedat Yiẓḥak* reads שפל. David's use of טפל may be a lapse of memory in quoting. However, it may be deliberate, possibly a Yiddishism to emphasize the distaste for idolatry.

[110] In the above text the word של is blurred, and someone corrected it to read שלי. David reads it שלך. The sense is clearly with the latter reading.

permitted to say to a Gentile, 'Take your idol[111] and [wear it on] your buttocks.'"

And the fact that the one who said:[112] *Moreover they would have fastened a thong under its tail,* that is, of the Breastplate, which is the *Ephod,* which hints at idolaters. This is why he uses the unflattering language: *with which he would bring forth soil for his garden and wasteland.* The real meaning [of this phrase] is that if Israel were deserving of the Breastplate, not only would they have wisdom and wealth, but the pagan nations would be harnessed by the reins of Israel to do their work in wasteland and in garden, as it is written:[113] *and sons of aliens shall be your plowmen and your wine-dressers.*

IN THE ALLEGORICAL MODE[114]

It has been taught, Rav Simeon ben Manassiah said: Woe for the loss of a great servant. This refers to the Evil Inclination, termed *a great king* in a phrase in *Nedarim,*[115] whom man, termed microcosm, has lost. *For had not the serpent gone wrong*—the serpent and the Evil Impulse are both essentially linked with the body,[116] and had not the body been corrupted to follow its [baser] impulses, *every one of "God's Righteous"*[117] *would have at his service two good servants,* i.e., both body and soul [would unite in] influencing[118] and driving him toward the good; for the soul would have good thoughts and opinions, and the body would have good habits. The phrase *He would send one to the*

---

[111] Arama gives the reference as Talmud Bavli, *Megillah,* 25b. The reference in later texts is to Talmud Bavli, *Sanhedrin,* 63b. This is one of the censored passages of the Talmud.

[112] That is, Manassiah.

[113] Isaiah 61:15.

[114] The use of the term *sekhel* as an equivalent of *remez* in the four divisions of the sermon represented by the acronym *PaRDeS* is found in Baḥya ben Asher, Levi ben Gershom, and Pico Del la Mirandola. In *PaRDeS, pshat* indicates the simple literal meaning, *remez* (or *sekhel*), allegorical meaning, *drash,* homiletical meaning and *sod,* secret or esoteric meaning.

[115] Talmud Bavli, *Nedarim* 32b, where it comments on Ecclesiastes 9:17.

[116] The physical as opposed to the spiritual.

[117] He reads it as מישרי אל, a pun on מישראל.

[118] Pun on נחש.

north suggests the heart, as it is written: *in my heart I hid it,*[119] as we find it stated in ספר יצירה:[120] *The heart directs the soul as the king directs the battle.* And the phrase *He would send one to the south* suggests the brain, which resides at the top of the head.[121]

To bring him costly gems and precious stones—this suggests good habits and good thoughts. And not only would the Evil Inclination have nothing to do with the body, but a *thong would be fastened under its tail*—there would be no indecent act of immorality, and it would be as though there were a leash on his tail, i.e., his genitals.

Which would bring forth earth for his garden—this means he would bring forth seed from his genitals, as it is written:[122] *and thy seed shall be as the dust.* [And this] seed is only *for his garden,* that is, his wife and bride, as it is written: *I have come into my garden, my sister and bride.*[123] Moreover, he would have intercourse with his wife only to fulfill the commandment to be fruitful and multiply [and not simply for erotic pleasure], as suggested by the phrase[124] *an enclosed garden, etc.,* a well sealed up in order that he might not be destroyed, as it is written:[125] *He created it not in vain, He formed it to be inhabited.* And the real meaning of *for his wasteland* is to rebuild the wasteland of the world.

IN THE HOMILETICAL MODE

Rabbi Simeon b. Manassiah said: *Woe for a great servant*—this means the Messiah, of whom it is written,[126] *May his name endure forever . . . as long as the sun.* And he is called *great,* as it is written:[127] *who*

---

[119] Psalms 119:11. Here the pun is צפנתי/צפון.

[120] *Sefer Yeẓirah* (Horadno, 1806), p. 68b.

[121] A pun: דר ברום/דרום, to describe the intellect, which resides at the top of the head!

[122] Genesis 13:16.

[123] Song of Songs 5:1, where we have the erotic symbolism of the term "garden."

[124] Song of Songs 4:12.

[125] Isaiah 48:15.

[126] The pun שֶׁמֶשׁ/שְׁמֹה. See Psalms 72:17. Rashi suggests that the verse refers to King Solomon. Ibn Ezra suggests that it might be King Solomon or the Messiah. David accepts the latter suggestion.

[127] Zechariah 4:7. This is not a direct quotation, but rather a paraphrase of a part of each verse.

art thou, O great mountain? This they [128] interpreted to mean the Messiah, who will be greater than Abraham and [greater] than Moses, as it is written:[129] *Behold my servant shall deal prudently and shall be exalted, etc.* And the great light that God reserved for the righteous is the light of the Messiah. For at the time of his appearance, the sun will be eight times its normal size, as it is written: *And the light of the moon, etc.*[130]

Who was lost from the world—at the time of Creation God reserved the light for the righteous, because He Who Spoke And The World Was knew in advance of the temptation by the serpent. For had not the serpent been cursed, the light of the Messiah would have shone forth at once. It is well known that the world was created solely for the sake of Israel, who was called *the first, etc.*[131]

Hence, *every Israelite would have had two good serpents*—the intended meaning being two kinds of good blessings, as we have it in Scripture: *I made divination*[132] *and he blessed me.*

He would send one to the north—that is, one blessing in the world to come that is reserved for the righteous. *And he would send one to the south*—that is, one blessing for this world in which he lives. And the main point of dwelling in this world is the restoration of the *lofty dwelling place,*[133] which is the Temple. That is the reason for the use of the term south.

Furthermore, when the text goes on to say: *He will bring him costly gems and precious stones and pearls,* it is as we find it stated in *Baba Batra,* chapter five: *Rabbi Yoḥanan sat and expounded, that in the future, the Holy One Praised Be He would bring precious stones and pearls, thirty by thirty, and set these in the Gates of Jerusalem, etc.*[134] Nor is this the only thing that Israel will have the privilege of witnessing, for they will

---

[128] See *Genesis Rabbah,* chap. 97, (p. 901 in the Soncino translation).

[129] Isaiah 52:13.

[130] Isaiah 30:26. ". . . shall be as the light of the sun, and the light of the sun shall be sevenfold."

[131] Jeremiah 2:3.

[132] This is a pun: נחשתי/נחש. Cf. Genesis 30:27. The use of the two verbs, נחשתי ויברכני, suggests two blessings.

[133] There is a pun here, דירת רם and דרום (south).

[134] Talmud Bavli, *Baba Batra* 75a.

also witness the vengeance upon Amalek and the Cutheans,[135] and of smiting them with rod and lash.[136]

And the phrase *moreover, one would have fashioned a thong* is used because it is written concerning him [Amalek]: *How he smote the hindmost of thee.*[137] And there too it is written: *Thou shalt blot out the remembrance of Amalek, etc.*[138] And it is known that the Name is not complete until he [Amalek] will be extirpated.[139] And the use of the [Ineffable] Name is to suggest Israel, for God's name is linked with ours. And the throne is the Temple, His footstool. Furthermore, when [the text] continues: *and would bring forth with it,* it means wicked Amalek; [*dust*[140]] Israel, who was as low as the dust, as it is written: *arouse thyself from the dust.*[141]

And whither shall they take them?—*to his garden,* which is in the Temple, and *to his wasteland,* for it was destroyed. And then the Name will be whole, as will be Israel and the throne—all of which refers to [the restoration of] the Temple. Furthermore, the mystical [secret] meaning of what we have expounded about Messiah and Serpent[142] is that the sin of the serpent will not be wiped clean until the coming of the Messiah, which is why they have equal numerical value.[143] Then we shall be deserving of the breastplate, which contains the *Urim* and *Thummim.* May the Highest of the High come to our aid and rescue us from our foes and our adversaries. And bring us together with all Israel to the eternal house.[144]

[135] This is a reference to their Gentile neighbors.

[136] The רצועה, (leather thong of the phylacteries), becomes the lash of retributive fury on the eve of the coming of the Messiah.

[137] Deuteronomy 25:18. Here we have a pun: זנב and ויזנב.

[138] Deuteronomy 25:19.

[139] Exodus 17:16.

[140] The sense of the sermon makes it clear that David continues his interpretation of the word עפר, which has been omitted.

[141] Isaiah 52:2.

[142] This is a paraphrase of the saying in *Genesis Rabbah* 12:6 (cf. Theodor edition, p. 104), which deals with the consequences of Adam's fall, which will not be redressed until the Messiah's coming. It is repeated in Talmud Bavli, *Baba Batra* 17a, and *Shabbat* 95b. There the phrase is עטיו של נחש, which David paraphrases as נחש חטאו של.

[143] The three words משיח, נחש, and חושן have the same numerical value, 358.

[144] That is to say, the Temple in Jerusalem. This synonym for the Temple is found in the Talmud Bavli, *Sukkah* 5b.

ANOTHER SERMON

MISHNAH, BEGINNING OF OUR CHAPTER

The law of covering up the blood [145]*applies both within the Holy Land and out-*
side it, both during the existence of the Temple and after it, in respect of unconse-
crated animals or birds, but not consecrated birds. It applies only to wild animals
and birds, whether they are at one's disposal or not. It applies also to a כוי[146] *for*
it is an animal about which there is a doubt. It may therefore not be slaughtered
on a festival; and if it was slaughtered thereon, one may not cover up its blood.

One may also raise the question as to why it is necessary to say
[specifically] *applies.* Let us simply say: *They cover the blood within the*
Holy Land and outside it. And further, why use [the term] בפני הבית [to
designate] the time of the existence of the Temple rather than use the
term בזמן הבית?[147] And why mention the word *applies* three times?

It is fitting [however] to begin with themes of the portion of the
week.

He tethers his ass to a vine[148]—Here the text makes clear the identity
of the righteous who will be worthy of [witnessing] Shiloh, i.e., the
Messiah. These are the righteous who are compared to a vine, as
Onkelos[149] renders it. And it is they who with their mind have mastered their body, which is called a *city*,[150] as we find it stated in *Neda-*
rim:[151] *a "little city" means the body, etc.* In so doing he tethers the Evil
Inclination within him, hence the text reads: *He tethers his "city" to a*
vine.

[145] Cf. Mishnah, *Ḥullin* 6:1.

[146] In translations of the Mishnah, the word is not translated, but is read in trans-
literation as *koy.* We shall see evidence later in the sermon that David chose to pro-
nounce it as *kvi.* The *koy/kvi* כוי was thought to be a species of cattle found in a wild
state, like the bison, yak, deer, buffalo, or wild antelope.

[147] He raises the question in order to suggest the reading בְּפִנֵּי ("in the corners
of") instead of בְּפְנֵי.

[148] Genesis 49:11.

[149] He was a first-century proselyte to Judaism, thought to be related to the
Roman emperor, Titus. He translated the Pentateuch into Aramaic.

[150] The pun is עַיָר and עִיר. In the form עירו, it can mean either "his foal" or "his
city."

[151] Talmud Bavli, *Nedarim* 32b. This passage is influenced by Ecclesiastes 9:14–25.

His purebred[152] *to the choicest stem.*[153] This is an intimation of that time when the prophecy *I shall whistle for them and gather them together* will be fulfilled. And the construction will be out of the body, which is the Temple of the Soul, and the Temple is called איתן in the Book of Ezekiel, according to Rashi's interpretation. This also is the sense of the Targum, with its translation—*They will build His Temple.* And since there is a hidden reference to the resurrection of that which is material [body], that is, חומר,[154] it is referred to by the use of אתן, as a word for *donkey,* which is a synonym for [the word] חמור. Then he goes on to explain that he will also merit the world to come [and] the hidden good referred to in the statement:[155] *All the prophets prophesied only in respect of the Messianic era; but for the world to come, "The eye hath not seen, O Lord, beside thee, what he hath prepared for him that waiteth for Him." . . . What does "The eye hath not seen" refer to? Rabbi Joshua ben Levi said: To the wine*[156] *[set aside on the Day of Creation for the righteous] still [maturing] in its grapes, etc.*[157]

One may well raise the question where he [Joshua] sees a hidden reference to wine. It is possible to see this in the statement *the eye hath not seen,* for the letter ע[158] has the same numerical value as the word *wine,* which has not yet been seen, for it is still in its grapes [for the Righteous]. And the essential meaning is this: that, after the righteous man has guarded himself, and has not been drawn after the four humors, which incite and stir him up to base desires, as the

---

[152] The pun here is אתן ("donkey") and איתן ("Temple").

[153] The pun here is שרקה ("choice stem") and אשרקה ("I shall whistle"). Cf. Zechariah 10:8.

[154] A double set of puns: חומר/חמור and איתן/אתן.

[155] Talmud Bavli, *Sanhedrin* 99a. This is an excerpted quotation. Cf. also Isaiah 64:3.

[156] This is the יין המשומר, the wine set aside at the time of the Creation for the righteous as their reward in Heaven.

[157] The "etc." refers to the portion of the quotation which he omits from the Talmud Bavli, *Sanhedrin* 99a passage, namely: "that is to say, Eden." This is an example of his practice of quoting only half of the verse, because he expects his audience to know the second half.

[158] This is a pun here, עין ("eye") and ע (the name of the letter). The numerical values of the letter ע and the word יין are both 70.

natural scientists well know,[159] and such lusts increase with the plethora, which resembles wine, it is appropriate that he merit the hidden wine, measure for measure; and *after he covered his blood,* that is to say, after he so behaved as if he were not of flesh and blood, he overpowered his Evil Inclination so that it was not visible. It is appropriate that he likewise merit something not visible, i.e., the wine [set aside for the Righteous in the World to Come] still [maturing] in its grapes.

And the reason why the text says *in wine he washes his garments* is as follows: Because of the reward which is his for washing his garment, which is body,[160] the garment of the soul, as in the text *wash your hearts of guile,*[161] and has not followed the humors, he will be rewarded with the wine.

His robes in the blood of grapes—Rashi's commentary [describes] *suto*[162] as a kind of garment, like *k'suto.* That is to say, because he has covered the blood and does not appear as [merely] flesh and blood,[163] he will be rewarded with that which *is still [maturing] with its grapes,* which is [also] invisible. And let this passage be interpreted by transposition: [when] *he washes his garment* [he will be rewarded] *with the blood of the grapes.* And the reason for the omission of the letter כ from סותה is [to emphasize] the idea of incitement,[164] for the blood incites man to lust.

And this is why, it seems to me, that the law of the covering of the blood is in the Torah, as the text reads: *And whatever man there be of*

[159] David was a physician of sorts, writing amulets and treating a variety of ailments. Cf. *Shir haMa'alot l'David* 16b. He shows a knowledge of the medical theories of his time as based on Pythagoras, Galen, Hippocrates and Aristotle. They spoke of four elements (earth, air, fire, water), four qualities, (dry, hot, cold, moist) and four humors, (blood, phlegm, yellow bile, black bile). It seems to be a vague foreshadowing of endocrine and general biological aspects of human physiology. Cf. F. H. Harrison, *History of Medicine* (Philadephia, 1929), pp. 88–89.

[160] Literally, "matter" or "the material."

[161] Jeremiah 4:14.

[162] There is a pun by assonance here: כסותה/סותה.

[163] He continues along these lines with the imagery of controlling the passions, a frequent theme of the itinerant preachers of the time.

[164] There is a triple pun here: כסות/סותה/הסתה.

the Children of Israel, or the strangers that sojourn among them, that taketh in hunting any beast or fowl that may be eaten he shall pour out the blood thereof, and cover it with dust.[165] And it seems to me that the phrase *whatsoever man of the Children of Israel* alludes to this matter [control of lust] as well. That is to say, every single Israelite should overcome his inciting[166] impulse, which incites like a man, which is why the text continues, *or of the strangers who sojourn in their midst,* meaning the inciter in their midst, i.e., the Evil Inclination *That taketh in hunting any beast or fowl,* i.e., who has been ensnared by the Evil Inclination, as it is written: *and built snares against it.*[167]

Taketh in hunting any beast or fowl—a reference to the qualities of insolence and pride. *Which may be eaten*—which destroys man. *And he shall pour out the blood thereof*—the [Evil] Inclination incites him also to emission, and he is drawn by the four humors that come out of the plethora,[168] to fulfill his bodily desires. And my new interpretation of *he shall cover it* is that the individual should be strong enough to overcome it, as though he were something more than [mere] flesh and blood. *With dust*—he shall do so [overcome the Evil Inclination] precisely because [of the fact that he is] dust. *Because dust thou art and to the dust thou wilt return.*[169] And, . . . *whither thou goest,* etc.[170] And this, generally speaking, is the sense of the Mishnah.

IN THE ALLEGORICAL MODE[171]

Covering up the blood—[this injunction] is meant to tell us what is required to cover[172] the humors that come from the plethora, that

---

[165] Leviticus 17:13.

[166] Note the pun החגרה/מן הגר הגר. The second איש in the text (Leviticus 17:13) is taken to suggest a personification of the Evil Inclination.

[167] Ecclesiastes 9:14.

[168] That is, bodily lusts.

[169] Genesis 3:19.

[170] Mishnah, *Pirkei Avot* 3:1. Here we have another example of the use of an incomplete quotation, where the omitted portion לחקום עפר רמה ותולעה, is to be filled in by the reader or hearer, and if he cannot do that, he misses the point.

[171] See note 55 in the preceding sermon.

[172] That is, control.

man not be drawn after them. Now these humors are attracted to the four elements of the body, which are like leaders,[173] and therefore he uses the term *applies within the [Holy] Land*—that is to say, in the lowest element—earth. *And outside the [Holy] Land*—that is to say, the other three elements which revolve around it,[174] as is known to the natural scientists.

During the existence of the Temple,[175] [i.e. within the House], the inference here is that man should cover over the baser drives[176] that originate in the four elements, as it is written: *And behold there came a great wind from across the wilderness, and smote the four corners of the house, etc.*[177] The reference is to the four elements of the body, which is compared to a house. And you have to read here [in the Mishnah], *in the corners of the house.*

And after it[178]—literally, [outside the House]. This refers to the base drives that originate in the mind. But it subsequently makes it clear that it is not good completely to repress the desires, as our sages of blessed memory have said: *Three things let the left hand push away and the right hand draw near—impulse, infant, and woman.*[179] And that is why our text [in *Hullin*] says *in respect of unconsecrated animals or birds,* i.e., with respect to those things which are permitted, concerning which there is no command [you cover the blood, that is, exercise restraint]. *But [it does not apply] to consecrated [animals or birds]*—that for which there is a positive command, for example, the fulfillment [of the command] to be fruitful and to multiply, and the like, as we say, *man should always sanctify [himself] at the time of sexual intercourse,*[180] and as another example, Kiddush on the Sabbath.

---

[173] This is a pun: חנהיגים/נהג.

[174] Or, surround it.

[175] Here David reads it as בְּפְנֵי ("in the corners of") and not בִּפְנֵי ("before the time of"). He completely transforms the meaning of the Mishnah from a law applying before and after the time of the Temple to an internalized view of personal morality.

[176] The phrase גסות רוח has the force of presumptuousness or aggressiveness. Cf. Mishnah, *Pirkei Avot* 4:7, and Talmud Bavli, *Sukkah* 29b and *Baba Batra* 78b.

[177] Job 1:19.

[178] His reading of the text is: "And not in the corners of the house."

[179] Talmud Bavli, *Sanhedrin* 107b.

[180] Talmud Bavli, *Niddah,* 70a. There is also a reference to this in *Baalei Hanefesh* by Abraham ibn Daud, p. 112, Jerusalem, 1954.

And then [the text] speaks of the three principal guides of the body,[181] whose acronym is מל״ך, which is why the phrase *applies to wild animals* is used, an allusion to the heart, where vitality resides.

And to birds—alludes to the mind,[182] for it elevates itself and soars upward to cleave to the Active Intellect, as [Scripture says]:[183] *And one of the Seraphim flew unto Me.*

Whether they are at one's disposal, etc. This means that one should make a distinction in one's heart and mind between those who are destined for eternal life, like the believers in the *Thirteen Roots*; [184] *or not*[185]—and those who are not destined for the world to come, like the deniers [of the root] and heretics, as [in the verse] *that ye go not about after your own heart and your own eyes.*[186] What the verse really means is *after your speculation,*[187] which has to do with the mind.

And it applies to a כוי, in the sense of כְּוִיָּה[188] [burning], an allusion to the desires of the liver, which control the plethora which burns in man, as you find it stated in *Bekhorot: much blood much warmth.*[189] The word שחין clearly means warmth as you find it [used] in *Yoma,* in the prayer of the High Priest: *a year of warmth and rain, etc.*[190] It means that with respect to mind and heart, whatever confusing and misleading thoughts are [inspired by the Inclination], they must be

---

[181] The initials מל״ך stand for מעים ("kidneys"), לב ("heart"), and כבד ("liver"), the three principal guides (מנהיגים) to moral, emotional, and ethical conduct. This suggests why the verb is used three times.

[182] There is a pun here, עוף/מעוף, to characterize the soaring quality of the mind or intellect.

[183] This is a medieval philosophical term for God. Cf. also Isaiah 6:6.

[184] That is, root principles. The term עיקר ("root") is used to express the idea of a fundamental principle of Judaism, e.g., Isaac Albo's ספר העיקרים, and the thirteen עיקרים of Moses ben Maimon. When in Talmud Bavli, *Ḥagigah* 15a, the apostasy of Elishah ben Abuyah is referred to, it is described as "cutting the roots."

[185] The term מזומן is used in this Mishnah to apply to fowl raised domestically. By a pun, David uses it in the sense of "invited."

[186] Numbers 15:39.

[187] There is a pun here: עיוניכם/עיניכם.

[188] David's pun כויה/כוי is evidence that he pronounced it *kvi,* and not *koy,* as in the usual readings. Cf. note 2.

[189] Talmud Bavli, *Bekhorot* 44b.

[190] Talmud Bavli, *Yoma* 53b.

completely cast aside. But that which relates to the כוי, i.e., the liver, namely eating and drinking, is impossible to set aside completely.[191] Because that is a need which requires just enough fulfillment in order to survive, but no more. Now this applies definitely for the remaining days of the year,[192] for there is no positive command with respect to the enjoyment of eating [on these days]. But with respect to Sabbaths and festivals, concerning which there is reference to pleasure and rejoicing, it is permissible to eat more. This is why the text reads: *It may therefore not be slaughtered on a festival*; its intention is to suggest that [the desire to enjoy eating and drinking] is not to be suppressed.[193] *And if it was slaughtered [thereon] one may not cover up its blood,* for he will be called to account for it.[194]

IN THE HOMILETICAL MODE

It is the intention [of this text] to show explicitly and implicitly how it will be when the Messiah comes, and the Holy One Praised Be He will slaughter and destroy wicked Amalek, shedder of blood, as well as the sinners of Israel, who committed many sins which are red as blood.[195] And the use of the term *covering of the blood* stems from the phrase in chapters two and three of *Ḥullin*:[196] *I did not eat meat [of an animal] about which one says "Cut! Cut!"* This is Aramaic[197] for ritual slaughter.[198] That is to say, God will slaughter shedders of blood. This measure [of retribution] *applies within the land,* i.e., the

[191] He rejects the extreme asceticism of the Lurianic kabbalists. One ought to control and suppress fantasies, but not natural instincts. However, he stops short of hedonism.

[192] That is, days that are neither Sabbaths nor festivals.

[193] Here he interprets the word *kvi*, by means of a pun, to say that inclination or passion is not to be "slaughtered" on a festival.

[194] He will be called to account because he did not observe the command to rejoice on the festival by enjoying what he eats and drinks.

[195] Isaiah 1:15.

[196] Talmud Bavli, *Ḥullin* 37b and 44b.

[197] David uses the term *targum*.

[198] That is, *sheḥitah*. By means of a pun, he relates the word כוס (root נכס) to the word כסוי, just as, at the beginning of the sermon, he utilizes Rashi's pun of סותו/כסותו. Cf. *Shir haMa'alot l'David*, p. 6a.

peoples[199] who dwell in the earth; *and outside it,* i.e., the rulers of the peoples who are beyond the lower world, which is on earth. As it is written:[200] *The Lord will punish the hosts of the high heaven on high, and the kings of the earth.* And it is written:[201] *For the Lord hath indignation against all the nations, and fury against all their host; He hath utterly destroyed them, He hath delivered them to the slaughter.* And it is written: *For my sword hath drunk its fill in heaven, behold it shall come down upon, etc.*[202] And the word *applies*[203] is specifically used, for we find it used [in Scripture] in that sense in connection with the punishment of the Gentiles [i.e., the Egyptians]: *and made them to drive heavily.*

In the corners of the Temple: Here [the text] intimates how the Holy One, Praised Be He, would also destroy the sinners in Israel, until only a tenth would remain and even from that tenth he would exterminate the sinners. As it is written: *And if there be yet a tenth in it, it shall again be eaten up.*[204] And the phrase *during the existence of the Temple* occurs here because we find it used in connection with the tithe, as you find it in the chapter [One Who Engages] Laborers,[205] and the first chapter of *Gittin:*[206] *R. Jannai said: "Tebel*[207] *is not liable to tithes until it sees the front of the house,*[208] *for it is written,*[209] *"I have brought away*

---

[199] Note the use of the term ישראל, in contrast to the term אומות, which is used to denote gentiles, who he suggests are governed by evil astrological forces.

[200] This is probably a reference to his view of the Church as the enemy of the Jewish people in Poland and in Rome. Cf. also Isaiah 24:21.

[201] Ibid. 34:2.

[202] Ibid. 34:5. Edom, which is a term for Rome, or the perennial enemy of the Jewish people, is the concluding word of the verse, and David omits it. It is his way of expressing his hostility to the government. Could this have been a reason for the Jewish establishment in Cracow keeping him at a distance?

[203] The word נוהג is seen here as being used in the sense of punishment, because of its usage in Exodus 14:25. The pun נוהג/ינהגנו has reference to the chariots of the Egyptians, mired in the Red Sea.

[204] Isaiah 6:13.

[205] Talmud Bavli, *Baba Meziah* 87b.

[206] Tamud Bavli, *Gittin* 81a. David is incorrect in placing the quotation in the first chapter of the tractate.

[207] These are fruits from which one is permitted to make an improvised meal in the field without separating out the priestly or levitical share.

[208] Here the phrase is read בִּפְנֵי הבית.

[209] Deuteronomy 26:13.

hallowed things out of mine house." And Israel has been compared to the harvest, as it is written: *Israel is holy unto the Lord, the first of His harvest.*[210]

And outside the Temple—The letter פ[211] is read with a *dagesh*, to exclude the tithe, that is to say, that portion that is destroyed before the tenth part is reached. And it does not matter which comes first [i.e., nothing is excluded from retribution].

In respect of unconsecrated [birds] or [animals]—precisely those upon whom the holiness of Heaven does not rest[212] will be dealt with like *unconsecrated birds and animals* with respect to destruction and extermination.

But not consecrated [birds]—those upon whom the holiness of Heaven rests will have site and survival,[213] as it is written there [in Scripture]: *as a terebinth as an oak whose stock remaineth, when they cast their leaves, so the Holy Seed shall be the stock thereof.*

And after this, the text explains further the measure of destruction which God will inflict upon the nations of the world, even those whom He brought on to enslave Israel, because they sinned in oppressing them more than was necessary, as it is written in Zechariah: *And I am very sore displeased with the nations that are at ease, for I was but a little displeased, and they helped for evil.*[214] So then the text says: *It applies to wild animals and birds,* it refers to the Rulers of the Gentiles, as it is written in Daniel:[215] *And four great beasts came up from the sea, etc.,* for they prey like animals and attack Israel with their claws like birds [of prey]. *Whether they are at one's disposal*—as I have explained earlier.[216] *Or not*—all the more! After that, interpret it [to mean] that when He has finished off the sinners, the Holy One Praised Be He would guide Israel, as it is written: *and He will guide us*

---

[210] Jeremiah 2:3.

[211] Here he reads it as בְּפֶנָה.

[212] That is, those who do not observe the commandments of the Torah.

[213] The literal meaning of the Hebrew מצב וקיום is: "a place to stand and survival." Cf. also Isaiah 6:13 as here quoted.

[214] Zechariah 1:15.

[215] Daniel 7:3.

[216] Psalms 48:15.

eternally.[217] and whom will he guide? Those who wept[218] in exile, as it is written in [the Book of] Jeremiah:[219] *They will come with weeping, and with supplications will I lead them.* And when the text reads *and it applies to a k'vi* [בכוי], you must read the letter ב with a *kametz* in the sense of weeping.

And after that the text explains why it is in doubt, because [the Jew's] life is in a state of suspense and in doubt in exile, as to whether he might at any moment die for the Sanctification of the Name, as it was inflicted upon us, because of our many sins, in the many pogroms in which so many righteous ones were slaughtered and burnt, as it is further explained.

It may therefore not be slaughtered on a festival—that is to say, it is not seemly for the Amalekites to slaughter Israel, the mourned one,[220] on their festival,[221] when they make every day that festival! Why? *And if they slaughtered [it] they do not cover his blood*—that is to say, they ought to remember that when they slaughter Israel, *they do not cover his blood,*[222] for the Holy One Praised Be He will take his vengeance of them, as it is written:[223] *I will avenge their blood and I will not clear the guilty.* What it means is that [God in effect says]: "Even though I will forgive the Gentiles all their other sins, I will not forgive them for the sin of shedding Israel's blood, but I shall take vengeance of them." And when will this happen? As the end of the verse[224] states: *for the Lord dwells in Zion,* that is, when he will cause His Presence to dwell in Zion. And through whom will God take vengeance for *covering the blood?* Through the Messiah son of David, who comes

[217] Note the pun: בכו/בכוי.

[218] Jeremiah 31:9.

[219] When it suits David's purpose to make a pun with פְּנֵיה, he pronounces the word in his Mishnah text כְּוִ, but when he needs a pun for the verb בכו, he pronounces it כוי.

[220] This is pun on בכוי as above.

[221] Here we have a probable reference to Easter, which all too frequently for the Jew of that time was a season of pogroms. He adds the ironic comment that in this way they manage to make every day a holiday.

[222] That is, the crime cannot be concealed.

[223] Joel 4:21.

[224] Joel 4:21.

from Judah, as it is written:[225] *What profit is it that we slay our brother and cover his blood?* And by virtue of this act,[226] he would become ruler of the whole world, as it is also implied in [this] Mishnah.

The covering of the blood—this refers to the Messiah who comes from Judah,[227] as the Scripture passage reads: *and cover his blood.*[228]

Applies—he will be a leader.[229] *In the corners of the Temple*—they who still live on earth. *And outside*—that is to say, he will also lead those who have departed from the earth and are dead. For in that time the resurrection of the dead will take place, as it is stated in *Midrash Rabbah,* [Genesis] portion *Vayeḥi,* in the name of Rabbi Ḥelbo: *Why did the Patriarchs long for burial in Ereẓ Israel? Because the dead of Ereẓ Israel will be the first to be resurrected in the days of the Messiah and to enjoy the years of the Messiah.*[230]

Both during the existence of the Temple and after it—that is to say, those who died during the existence of the Temple, [and those who died] when the Temple was not in existence, for example, the [generation] of the wilderness and the [generation] of the exile.

In respect of unconsecrated [animals or birds] but not consecrated [birds], that is to say, precisely those who are love-sick,[231] for God will have remnant and resurrection, as it is written: *for I am love-sick.*[232]

But not consecrated [birds]—this refers to the wicked, of whom it is written that *they sanctify themselves to go into the gardens.*[233] And the word *applies* is used three times in this *Mishnah,* corresponding to the three times it is found in Scripture as referring to the Messiah: In *Kohelet*:[234] *My heart still guiding me with wisdom*; in Isaiah: *And the spirit*

---

[225] Genesis 37:26.

[226] The act whereby Judah spared Joseph's life.

[227] He deliberately spells Judah יודא to avoid writing down the Ineffable Name as it is found in יהודה.

[228] It is Judah who speaks the words in Genesis 37:26.

[229] A pun: מנהיג/נוהג.

[230] Midrash *Genesis Rabbah* 96:5.

[231] Note the pun: חולי/חולין.

[232] Song of Songs 5:8.

[233] Isaiah 66:17. The meaning he intends is found in the second half of the quotation, which he omits, and which reads: "eating swine's flesh."

[234] Ecclesiastes 2:3.

of the Lord will rest on him, the spirit of wisdom,[235] *etc.*, [culminating with the verse] *And a little child shall lead them;*[236] [and thirdly] *Give ear, O Shepherd of Israel, thou that leadest Joseph like a flock*[237]—this is the heart [of the matter], for it implies that the Messiah, with God's help, will lead Israel, who are like sheep, because of that which was said concerning Joseph: *What profit is it if we cover his blood?*[238]—And after that it is made clear that through him[239] [the verse] *they shall put forth their hand on Edom and Moab,*[240] etc., will be fulfilled.

And when the text says *It applies to animals,* it refers to the Cutheans,[241] as it is written: *The swine will denude it of forest.*[242]

And to birds—a reference to Moab, as it is written in Isaiah, chapter sixteen: *For it shall be that, as wandering birds, as a scattered nest, so shall the daughters of Moab be,*[243] etc.

Whether they are at one's disposal—that is to say, the aforementioned would always be provided with sustenance from their occupation.

Or not at one's disposal—as it is written concerning David:[244] *A nation that I knew not will serve me.*

And it applies to a כוי—there is a difference of opinion in chapter five [of *Ḥullin*][245] between Rabbi Eliezer and the sages whether the כוי [is the offspring] of a he-goat that copulated[246] with a gazelle. That is to say, the Messiah would be a leader[247] of Israel, who are too feeble

---

[235] Isaiah 11:2.

[236] Ibid. 11:6.

[237] Psalms 80:2.

[238] Genesis 37:26.

[239] That is, through the Messiah ben Joseph.

[240] Isaiah 11:14.

[241] He uses the talmudic term for Samaritans to designate what he sees as the hostile Gentiles around him.

[242] Psalms 80:14.

[243] Isaiah 16:2.

[244] 2 Samuel 22:44.

[245] Talmud Bavli, *Ḥullin* 79a. Note the pun צבי/תיש.

[246] The Hebrew הבא makes it possible to use the verb in the sense of coming to the Land of Israel.

[247] Note the pun: מנהיג/נוהג.

and weak[248] to come unto the gazelle,[249] which is the Land of Israel, which is the gazelle of all lands.

About which there is a doubt—because he has endured more than the full measure[250] of exile and deserves redemption, as in the case of the poet who composed [a liturgical poem] for Ḥanukah which reads: *[Despite the fact] that he was filled with sufficiency of sin, yet the Almighty showed His mercy, etc.*[251]

It may therefore not be slaughtered on a festival—for at that time all of Israel will have a [great] festival, with the fulfillment of the promise: *He will swallow up death forever.*[252]

And if it was slaughtered [thereon] one may not cover up its blood—that is to say, even though the sinners are slaughtered, neither their blood nor their bodies are covered, so that [their sight] might be an [object of] abhorrence to all flesh, as it is written at the end of Isaiah: *And it shall come to pass, that from one New Moon to another, and from one Sabbath to another, shall all flesh come . . . and they shall look upon the carcasses of the men that have rebelled against Me,*[253] etc. And may Heaven save us from those upon whom such punishment is destined to come. And may we be privileged to be among those who behold it!

Amen.

---

[248] The pun here is: תיש/חלשים ותשים.

[249] Another pun: צבי/ארץ הצבי/צבייה.

[250] Still another pun: ספוק/ספק.

[251] This quotation is taken from a *piyyut* (liturgical poem) for a *yoẓer* for the first Sabbath of Ḥanukah by Yosef bar Shelomo. Cf. S. Baer, *Avodat Yisrael* (Jerusalem, 1937), p. 638.

[252] Isaiah 25:8.

[253] Isaiah 66:23.

A RESPONSUM[254]

The Gaon, our Teacher and Rabbi, Jacob Reiner,[255] head of the academy, examined me with this question in the year [5]317 [1557] in the holy community of Ferrara. He is at present head of an academy in Germany.

QUESTION: Mr. Bibber[256] converted and married Miss Bitter,[257] who also converted, and he took her while they were in their Gentile status and betrothed her according to their laws. She gave birth, and in the status of Gentile produced a daughter, whom they raised among them. They betrothed her to a man who was also a trouble-making apostate.[258] They bore a son (who remained) uncircumcised. The waters of baptism[259] were poured on his head, and he was raised among them, ate their bread, drank from their cup,[260] and worshipped their god. Father and son were totally assimilated among them.[261]

[254] This responsum appears in the Responsa of Moses Isserles which were printed in Cracow for the first time in 1640, some sixty eight years after his death. It was attributed to him and included as responsum number 62. As we can see here, David wrote it in 1557, probably sending it to his teacher, who kept it among his papers. By 1670, responsa attributed to Solomon Luria were removed, but other extraneous material was left in.

[255] Rabbi Jacob Reiner taught at a *yeshivah* set up in Ferrara by Solomon Riva with the warm approval of the Duke of Este, who saw it as an asset to the community. Cf. Cecil Roth, *History of the Jews of Italy* (Philadelphia, 1946), p. 214, and A. Balletti, *Gli Ebrei e gli Estensi* (Reggio-Emilia, 1930), pp. 96–97.

[256] Pun משקה/שקה. His prejudice shines through by the contemptuous names he gives the two characters in the responsum.

[257] This is a pun from the Talmud Yerushalmi, *Megillah* 3a, which reads: תמר תמרורית בתמרוריה עומדת. Perhaps there is also a pun on Mary, through the Hebrew word מרי, which means "apostasy" of "revolt."

[258] This could also be rendered as: "a trouble-making renegade."

[259] This term was widely used in the sixteenth century to describe baptism. See, for example, the introduction to Isaac Abarbanel's *Zevah Pesah* (Modena, 1557), p. 1a.

[260] That is, took communion.

[261] For the use of נטמעו in the sense of total assimilation, see Talmud Bavli, *Kiddushin* 70b and *Ketubot* 14b.

And when the son grew up, it was made known to him by a vision that he was of the seed of Israel and that his baptism was to no purpose.[262] He therefore determined to return to his ancestral heritage,[263] and so informed his friends. But he did not have himself circumcised, nor did he yet give up his former ways to worship in the vapid house of their god.[264] But in his heart he had good intentions.

One day he cast his eyes on a maiden in the same situation, the daughter of two apostates who were also *halting between two opinions,*[265] and they agreed together to return to their ancestral faith.[266] They would whisper [about this] together, and would discuss the matter every day, but it was all just talk, and no action emerged from it. So that the daughter of the apostate and the aforementioned son of the despicable [one], whose spirit had moved him to return to his former faith,[267] decided to wed. Thus they made a marriage agreement, and then sent for two Jews to act as witnesses for the marriage. Thus the son of the despicable one married the aforementioned maiden in the presence of witnesses with a ring, in accordance with the laws of Moses and Israel. And now let the Master instruct us whether this marriage is valid or not. For at the time, neither of them had converted, while the woman [on the other hand], who had been betrothed, converted to Judaism according to the Halakhah only after the passage of some time. And the groom has not yet converted and has gone to a distant land where no Jews live.

RESPONSUM:[268] The master tests us with a deep matter, but in my humble opinion, it is quite clear that we have to take into considera-

---

[262] Another rendering might be: was a lie. Cf. *Midrash Exodus Rabbah* 3:2, commenting upon Job 15:31.

[263] Literally: his father's possession.

[264] Cf. Talmud Bavli, *Ḥagigah,* in reference to Jeremiah 49.

[265] Cf. 1 Kings 18:21.

[266] The literal meaning is: "to return to the worship of the Lord, the God of their fathers."

[267] That is, to Judaism.

[268] The question is in Hebrew and the responsum is in Aramaic.

tion that the legal act of betrothal has taken place, because we know for certain that both of them, the groom and the bride, are of the seed of Israel. For we read at the end of the first chapter of *Yevamot*:[269] *Rav Judah said in the name of Rav Assi: If at the present time a Gentile betroths [a daughter of Israel], it must be taken into consideration that the legal act of betrothal has taken place, since it may be that he is of the Ten Tribes. But surely anything separated [from a heterogeneous group] is regarded as having been separated from the majority.[270] [Rav Assi's statement refers] to places where they have settled, and where do we find reference to settled places? As it is written: "And he put them in Ḥalaḥ and Ḥabor, on the river of Gozan and the cities of the Medes. . . ."[271] When I mentioned the matter in the presence of Samuel, he said to me: "'Thy son'[272] means 'thy son,' and your son, descended from a Gentile woman is not called 'thy son' but 'her son.'"*

Rashi's commentary to *"it may be he is of the Ten Tribes"* [is]: *For they married Gentile women, and it is held that in the case of a Gentile woman who bore the child of an Israelite, that child is a bastard, and we must be concerned about [the legal validity of] a bastard's betrothal. [And precisely] "in places where they are in a settled condition," that is, the children of the Ten Tribes. For all that is in a settled condition is considered as half to half . . .[273] "Thy son" implies that he who is descended from a Jew and a Jewess may be called "thy son" [i.e., is considered a Jew], but thy son who is descended from a Gentile woman is not called "thy son" but "her son"—we deduce this [from the verse]: "He will turn away thy son," for it is not written: "She will turn away thy son," consequently it [the verse] does not say: "Thou shalt not take his*

---

[269] Talmud Bavli, *Yevamot* 16b. David's quotation varies slightly from the text. He cites the text as quoted by Nissim in his commentary on Talmud Bavli, *Kiddushin* 28a. His own change in the text is to use the term גוי in place of עכו"ם.

[270] If it is not known to which group a person from a mixed multitude belongs, the assumption is that he comes from the majority. Since the Ten Tribes in exile were a minority, it should be assumed that the betrothal was made by a Gentile. However, the principle of a "settled place" is not the assumption of majority, but rather half and half, and on that basis it would not be correct to assume the person to be Jewish.

[271] 2 Kings, 17:6 and 18:11.

[272] Deuteronomy 7:4.

[273] That is, it is not automatically regarded as a majority, hence identity as fit and unfit cannot be automatically assumed.

daughter for thy son," for in that case, if a child were born to a Gentile woman [of a Jewish father], he would not be called "thy son," and we do not read "she will turn away thy son from after me," for they are completely Gentile, and therefore he is not called "thy son," but rather "her son." Thus far Rashi's text.[274]

From this it may be concluded, that in the case of the groom, we do not take into consideration whether he has become converted to Judaism or not, for here the word "Gentile" is used, and the only area of doubt is whether he stems from the Ten Tribes, in which case he is of the seed of Israel. With respect to that son of a troubler, [i.e., the groom], we know for certain that he is of the seed of Israel. Now as to the principle *"Thy son" [who stems from a Jewish woman] is called "thy son," while "thy son" who stems from a Gentile woman is not called "thy son" but "her son,"* we know for certain that this groom, the son of a troubler, stems from the seed of Israel.

We find it also stated in the text: *But surely there were also daughters? And Ravina has said, from this it may be inferred that thy daughter's son born [from a union with] a Gentile is called "thy son." There is a tradition that the wombs of the women of that generation were cut to render them sterile* [and therefore descendants of the Ten Tribes could not have had Jewish mothers].

[To this passage] Rashi's interpretation reads: *But surely there were also daughters* [i.e., of Israel] *who were taken captive and betrothed Cutheans [Gentiles] and bore children from them. And Ravina has said: "Thy daughter's son who is born from a Cuthean is called thy son. . . .[for it is written], "That he will turn thy son away from following Me," and since it is not written that "she will turn away," it rests on the principle that "thou shalt not give thy daughter to his son." It is stated thus because of the possibility that she would bear him a son and the father "would turn him aside from following Me," and hence he is termed "thy son," and it is necessary to be concerned*

---

[274] David abstracts the Rashi, which reads in full as follows: ". . . consequently he does not repeat the phrase 'you shall not take his daughter for your son,' for in that case he should have said that the Gentile woman would turn him aside. Deduce from this here too: a son born to a Gentile woman is not called 'your son,' and we do not read in the text concerning her 'that she turn aside your son,' hence they are complete Gentiles."

about the validity of that marriage. For that generation of the Ten Tribes was sterilized, [that is] their wombs were split [obstructed] so that they could not receive semen, and they were rendered barren. Thus far Rashi's comment.

The logical conclusion here also is that had they not been made barren, we would have to be concerned about [the validity] of the betrothal, despite the fact that his father is clearly a Cuthean. This applies even more so to the case of this son, the troubler, whose father and mother are clearly of Jewish origin. And despite the fact that it is stated there: *Some say: When I mentioned the matter in the presence of Samuel, he said to me: "They did not move from there until they declared them to be complete Cutheans, as it is said in the Scriptures: 'They have dealt treacherously against the Lord for they have begotten uncircumcised children,'"* we are in this instance speaking only [i.e., this only applies] of a Jew, who has intercourse with a Gentile woman, in which case the child is a stranger, and is not called "thy son" (that is, he is considered a Gentile), as it is explained by Rav Nissim[275] in chapter three of *Kiddushin.* But in the case of a Cuthean who has intercourse with a Jewish woman, no one will dispute the fact that he is called "thy son" (that is, is recognized as a Jew).

On the basis of the above we may deduce that the betrothal of Troubler, i.e., the groom, is valid. And the deduction in his case applies to her [as well], in that the betrothal of the daughter of the apostates is valid. Since we have cited the *Halakhah* in the latter version,[276] let us say a word about the two statements [that is, the permissive attitude of Rav Assi, and the stricter position of Samuel] according to the interpretation of Rav Nissim. And we see clearly in the first instance that there is no one who differs in the case of those [Israelite] daughters [taken captive and married by Gentiles]; the *Halakhah* is clearly handed down that *the son of thy daughter stemming from a Cuthean is called "thy son,"* for we find this cited quite plainly in many places in the Talmud, as we read in chapter two of *Yevamot*[277]

---

[275] Nissim ben Reuben Gerundi was a commentator of the Talmud who flourished in Barcelona between 1340 and 1380.

[276] That is, Talmud Bavli, *Yevamot* 16b.

[277] Ibid. 23a.

and chapter three of *Kiddushin*,[278] with reference to a Gentile woman whose child is [Gentile] like her. We learn this from the passage: *Rabbi Yoḥanan said, on the authority of Rav Simeon bar Yohai: Because Scripture states, "For he will turn away thy son from following me," thy son by an Israelite woman is called thy son, etc.*[279] And even though you will find versions of [this text in] the *Gemara* [which read] *"Thy son" who comes from an authentic Jewish woman is called "thy son."*[280] Nevertheless the commentators all agree that *"thy son" who comes from thy daughter is called "thy son"* even when the father is a Gentile. And the *Halakhah* has already been determined that when a Cuthean and a slave have intercourse with an Israelite woman, the child is legitimate, and it is stated in chapter four [of *Yevamot*]. He would even be eligible for the priesthood, adds the RIF.[281]

From the language of the *Maggid Mishnah*,[282] chapter four, *Hilchot Ishut*, we see that he [that is, RAbaD], also bases his view on the principle contained in the Talmudic passage: *But surely there were also daughters!*[283] [that is, that the son of an Israelite woman by a Gentile is a Jew], for he wrote concerning the Israelite apostate as follows: *And from the discussion of the first chapter of Yevamot, it appears to me that if his progeny, born after his conversion, married a Jewish woman, the marriage is valid, and [this applies] only when a Jewish woman bore the child, and even if she is an apostate. But if the child is born of a Gentile mother, there is no proper marriage to be considered, for we know that even in the case of an authentic Jew who has intercourse with a Gentile woman and begets a son from her, that child is not called "his son" but rather "her son," [that is, he is not a Jew], and this is clear.* Until here is his language.

Now that phrase, *and [this applies] only when a Jewish woman bore the child and, lo, even if a Gentile who has intercourse with a Jewish woman, the*

[278] Talmud Bavli, *Kiddushin* 68b.

[279] Talmud Bavli, *Yevamot* 23a.

[280] Talmud Bavli, *Kiddushin* 68b.

[281] Isaac Alfassi, talmudist and codifier of *Halakhah*, lived in Fez, Morocco, in the eleventh century.

[282] This was a critical commentary to the *Mishneh Torah* of Moses ben Maimon by Abraham ben David (RaBaD) of Posquières, 1125–1198.

child is legitimate[283] is included only to emphasize the point that follows to wit: *but if he begets [a child] with a Gentile woman, etc. [that child is not Jewish].*

A similar idea is expressed by Mordecai at the end of his comment in chapter four of *Yevamot.* I quote:[284] *And it seems to me that since, in chapter four of Yevamot, the Halakhah is that [in the case of] "a Gentile or a slave who have intercourse with an Israelite woman, the child is legitimate" even though he be uncircumcised, and has not gone to the ritual bath to become a Jew, his betrothal is valid nevertheless, if he marries [a Jewish woman]. But [in the case of] an Israelite who has intercourse with a Gentile woman, the child is [Gentile] like her. [This applies] all the more so [to] an apostate whose child is from a Gentile woman, since we have ruled [that in the case of] a Cuthean or a slave who has intercourse with an Israelite woman, the child is legitimate, and it makes no difference whether she is single or married. Furthermore, a married woman who apostasizes and bears a child to a Cuthean, the child is legitimate, and his betrothal is valid, and it is forbidden to loan him money at interest.*[285] *Abiasaph.*[286] Until here is his language.

In the same vein we find it stated in the responsum attributed to the Ramban (Naḥmanides), paragraph 142:[287] *Question: [In the case of] an apostate who betrothed a Jewess, his betrothal is valid; it is even so [in the case of] a Gentile, who proselytized and relapsed, as we find it stated in Yevamot,*[288] *"Why were the sages not concerned with the danger of her becoming an abandoned wife?"* And toward the end of the responsum [he states]: *And yet if he betrothes, his betrothal is valid. And in the case of a Jew who betroths [a woman who is] an apostate, the betrothal is valid in her case, and if she returns [to Judaism] she is forbidden [to marry] his kin, and he is forbidden [to marry] her kin, and she requires a divorce from him [in order to*

---

[283] Talmud Bavli, *Yevamot* 23a.

[284] Cf. Mordecai's commentary to Talmud Bavli, *Yevamot,* in the M'orot edition of the Talmud (New York, 1959), p. 3a.

[285] That is, it is forbidden to take interest from him because he is a Jew.

[286] This is the name of a book by Eliezer ben Joel Halevi (ca. 1160–ca. 1235). He was Mordecai's great-grandfather. Cf. H. D. Friedberg, *Bet Eked Sefarim* (Antwerp, 1928), p. 1.

[287] I have been unable to locate this quotation.

[288] Talmud Bavli, *Yevamot* 47b.

be able to remarry]. Should she bear a son, even from a Gentile, he is a true Jew of proper lineage, as we find it stated at the end of the first chapter of Yevamot: "And were there not daughters?" That is to say, daughters who apostasized and bore children to Gentiles [are Jews] in accordance with the statement of Ravina: *"Thy son" of thy daughter fathered by a Gentile is called "thy son,"* and all the more so if he is fathered by a Jew. Until here is his language.

From all the foregoing we may deduce that there is really no difference of opinion between the two versions of the views of Samuel, since we have seen that the greatest of the sages are in accord with the principle [derived from] *and were there not daughters?* Hence, I would say that it is impossible to find a true distinction between the two traditions. And what we would really find distinct is that, according to the first tradition, despite the fact that it holds: *"Thy son" is called thy son, but the child fathered on a Gentile woman is not called "thy son" but "her son,"* I may in any case argue that Rav Assi is not concerned with this aspect, because he was concerned with strictness [of ruling] in considering problems of marriage, as we read in chapter four [of *Yevamot*], concerning a proselyte *immersed and emerged,*[289] *is immediately a Jew to all intents and purposes. What legal consequence arises from this statement? Rav Jose, the son of Hanina,*[290] *explained [the legal consequences are] that if he relapses, he is to be seen as an apostate Jew. [And secondly], that if he marries a Jewess, his marriage is valid.*

Logically we are obliged to state that Rav Assi paid no attention to this, for if you will not understand it in this way, it is hardly conceivable to suggest that Rav Assi was ignorant of several *Mishnayot*. For in chapter two of *Yevamot* we have an explicit *Mishnah:*[291] *Whoever has a son from any origin whatsoever, his son absolves his father's wife from the obligation to levirate, and he is his son for every purpose except for those born to him from a female slave or from a Gentile woman.* In a similar vein we have the *Mishnah* in chapter three in [the tractate] *Kiddushin,* that *the*

[289] Talmud Bavli, *Yevamot* 47b.

[290] The attribution of this statement to Jose ben Hanina is omitted from the Talmud text I have examined.

[291] Talmud Bavli, *Yevamot* 22a.

child of a Gentile woman traces his genealogy from her only.[292] Hence it is certain that Rav Assi did not attach importance to the aspect of genealogy, for even though he is genealogically linked to his [Gentile] mother, when it comes to marriage he is still considered a Jew.

This understanding is also found in the opinion of Rabbi Eliezer of Metz as quoted in *SeMaG*,[293] Positive Commandments, paragraph 162, to wit: *Rabbi Eliezer of Metz*[294] *has stated that if he were a deliberate transgressor of one of the commandments of the Torah, and did not repent, you are not required to help sustain him, or to lend him money [without interest], for it is written,*[295] *"And thy brother shall live with thee," and as it is written;*[296] *"from one of thy brothers." Since he has deliberately transgressed, he has put himself beyond the pale of brotherhood, until he shall have [been punished by] flogging, as the Talmud states in chapter three [of tractate Makkot],*[297] *"Then thy brother should be dishonored before thine eyes" [that is] when he has taken his punishment, he is thy brother, "but prior to that he is not thy brother." Now even though it taught in chapter two of Avodah Zarah, that [the Scripture text] "with every lost thing that is thy brother's"*[298] *meant to include the apostate, he was included only with respect to the return of his lost object. We may not deduce that we must help him from the property of others. And with respect to what emerges from chapter four of [tractate] Gittin,*[299] *that Rav Ami wished to redeem an apostate [from servitude], who was willfully eating nonkosher food—this he did above and beyond the call of duty. Furthermore it is forbidden to lend him money at interest. However, in the case of a defiant apostate, it is permissible to lend him money at interest, for in the formulation [of the prohibition of lending] on interest, Brotherhood is expressly stipulated: "If thy brother be waxen poor, etc., . . . take not from him interest*

---

[292] Talmud Bavli, *Kiddushin* 62b.

[293] *Sefer Miẓvot Gadol*, Moses of Coucy, is a collection of the commandments incumbent upon a Jew. He was a thirteenth-century talmudist and codifier.

[294] Eliezer ben Samuel of Metz (1175–1238) was a student of Rabbenu Tam and taught Torah in Mainz. He was the author of *Sefer Yerei'im*.

[295] Leviticus 25:36.

[296] Deuteronomy 15:17.

[297] Talmud Bavli, *Makkot* 23a.

[298] Talmud Bavli, *Avodah Zarah* 26b.

[299] Talmud Bavli, *Gittin* 47a.

or increase."[300] *And the statement of Sanhedrin: "Though a man has sinned, he does not cease to be a Jew,"*[301] *pertains only to matters which do not have a stipulation of brotherhood, for example, matters of marriage and divorce, as stated in chapter one of Yevamot:*[302] *"If at the present time a Gentile marries a Jewess, it must be taken into consideration that the legal act of betrothal has taken place, since it may be that he is of the Ten Tribes."* Until here is his language.

And since the Talmud is hesitant [to conclude] that Rav Assi may have said what he said despite the fact that he had heard Samuel's statement but did not agree with him because there is no explicit scriptural reference, and it was proper to take a stricter position in the matter of marriage; therefore they found it necessary to quote the tradition: *Others read when I mentioned the matter in the presence of Samuel he said to me: "They did not move from there until they had declared them to be totally gentile, as it is said in Scripture: 'They have dealt treacherously against the Lord, for they have begotten strange children.'"*

Now surely if Rav Assi had heard this statement, he would not have disagreed with it. In the first place, it is an explicit command from Scripture, and secondly, the phrasing *they did not move from there* indicates a finally formulated legal decision as we have it in chapter eight of *Baba Batra.*[303] Our Rabbis taught: *The halakhah may not be derived either from a theoretical conclusion or from a practical decision unless one has been told that the halakhah is to be taken as a rule for practical decisions.*

And Rabbi Nissim has written: *However, whenever it is stated in the Mishnah that "they did not move from there" until they established the law in accordance with his position, you have no stronger formulation of a halakhic ruling than this. You will find it so stated in the first chapter of Pesaḥim.* Until here is his language. And the reason for their not having made a distinction as well between the tradition of *others read,*[304] and that

---

[300] Deuteronomy 22:3.

[301] Talmud Bavli, *Sanhedrin* 44a.

[302] Talmud Bavli, *Yevamot* 16b. He indicates the end of the quotation with the initials עכ״ל, which stand for עד כאן לשונו ("thus far his words").

[303] Talmud Bavli, Baba Batra 130b.

[304] This is the view of Samuel in Talmud Bavli, *Yevamot* 16b.

of *surely there were daughters,*[305] may be explained by the fact that because nothing new was essentially stated there, the Talmud did not take the trouble to point this out.

There is, moreover, reason to examine closely why some of the greatest of the decisors did not omit the law [concerning] the betrothal of a female apostate. It is clearly evident that there is no problem with respect to the betrothal of a male apostate; his betrothal is valid even though his status [as to validity of acts and status as a Jew] is weakened from another aspect, as we do recognize his offspring as a Jew.[306] The betrothal is valid all the more so in her case, for her standing [as a Jewess] is much stronger, even when she marries a Gentile, with respect to her offspring being recognized as a Jew. Were we not loath to challenge the opinion of Rav Nissim that [the sense of the verse] *"For they have begotten strange children,"* compels *the view that a Jew who has sexual intercourse with a Gentile, her child is to be considered a Gentile,* we could have well understood the talmudic passage of *others say* without any difficulties whatsoever.

This appears to be, likewise, the view of *Tossafot,* for they raised a question about Rashi's commentary [to this talmudic] passage: *"If at the present time a Gentile betroths [a daughter in Israel] note must be taken of such a betrothal, etc."—it is the view that if a Gentile woman bore a child to a Jew, this child is [considered a] bastard, and we must scrutinize a bastard's betrothal closely.*

Now this is [somewhat] strange, for it is evident from several *mishnayot* that he derives his status [of descent] from her. And they [the *Tossafists*] resolved [the problem they raised against Rashi], that it seems that Rav Assi's reasoning is based on the principle of *thy daughter,* and he does not accept the thesis that *the daughters of that generation had their wombs cut, etc.*

According to this, we must conclude that Samuel failed to understand Rav Assi's argument in answering: *"Thy son" is considered thy son, and "thy son" from a Gentile woman is not considered "thy son" but her son.* It is difficult to assume this [that Samuel did not understand the

[305] This is the view quoting Ravina in the same passage.
[306] Lit., "we do not assign his offspring to his lineage."

sense of Rav Assi's statement]. And this [the above-mentioned difficulty] is the reason that the *Tossafists* have used the term *strange* though they had a resolution [for the problem they raised]. Rashi, for his part, felt himself compelled by Samuel's statement to comment as he did. For this reason he had to quote: *Others say they did not move from there until they declared them to be completely heathen, etc.*—even [those that come] from the females.

Hence Samuel's answer was proper, and indeed, there was no need for the Talmud to ask: *But were there not daughters?* Because of this, it was necessary to state: *They did not move from there until they declared them to be completely Gentile, etc.*, even those descended from the daughters. This necessarily relates to the descendants of the Ten Tribes, for the verse *They have dealt treacherously with the Lord* refers to them. The objection cannot be raised that in relation to Judah, we have [it] also [stated]: *Judah hath dealt treacherously,*[307] for this is entirely different, since we do not have there: *She hath dealt treacherously with the Lord, etc.*

A similar case is found in chapter three of *Kiddushin,*[308] and chapter two of *Avodah Zarah.*[309] The Talmud, in raising a question about *for he will turn aside* [i.e., the prohibition to marry a Gentile because he would influence the Jewish mate in the direction of idolatry], suggests that this applies to the Seven Nations.[310] In this instance, it is that the Seven Nations were more apt to lead them astray than others. Here too, in the case of the Ten Tribes, because their betrayal was greater than others, the text rules against [the legitimacy] of children even from [Jewish] daughters.

The situation is totally different in our time, for we do not consider the Gentiles in our age to be idolaters, but only that they practice the customs of their forefathers. This idea is found also in the notes of Mordecai, where he writes: *Furthermore we find it stated there that Rav Assi says: "When a Gentile marries in our time, we must take this marriage into serious consideration, for he may be descended from the Ten Tribes."*

---

[307] Jeremiah 3:8.
[308] Talmud Bavli, *Kiddushin* 68b.
[309] Talmud Bavli, *Avodah Zarah* 56b.
[310] Cf. Joshua 3:10.

And it is explained there [that it relates] to places where they are permanently settled, like Ḥalaḥ and Ḥavor, etc. When I mentioned this in the presence of Samuel, he said: "They did not move from there until they declared them to be completely heathen." Rav Ḥananel decided that we do not accept Rav Assi's view even in places where they are permanently settled. But an apostate who marries, his marriage is fully valid according to the Torah, as we are taught in chapter four of Yevamot.[311] There is some evidence in the decision of Rav Hananel that we do not accept Rav Assi's view even in places where they are in a settled condition, [that the meaning of the phrase] *they did not move from there until they declared them completely Gentile* relates to the Ten Tribes only. Similarly we find it stated in chapter eleven of *Sanhedrin*:[312] *Rabbi Akiva says: "The Ten Tribes will never return." Rabbi Elazar says: "As the day darkens and lightens, so their darkness will turn into light for them, etc."*

These two methods of resolving that I resolved in my imperfect intelligence, will stand according to all decisors, if anyone will look into the matter. The most troubled of men, David Darshan from Cracow, who is at this time in the holy household of Bordolani[313] here, Ferrara.

THE MEANING OF AMULETS

I composed this essay on the meaning of amulets in Ferrara, in the year [5]318 (1558), when the head of the academy Rabbi Joseph Minẓ[314] required me to write some novella about amulets by way of examination.

---

[311] Talmud Bavli, *Yevamot* 47b.

[312] Talmud Bavli, *Sanhedrin* 110b.

[313] This was a prominent Jewish banking family in northern Italy. Moses Bordolano's banking privileges were reconfirmed in Mantua in 1557, after having been rescinded ten years previously. Cf. S. Simonsohn, *History of the Jews in the Duchy of Mantua* (Jerusalem, 1977), pp. 219, 258.

[314] The term *Gaon*, here used as a term for academy head, was a title for the heads of the major academies in Babylonia. Joseph Minẓ was a grandson of Judah Minẓ (1478–1579) and brother-in-law of Rabbi Meir Katzenellenbogen (Maharam) of Padua. This was one of the most distinguished of the Ashkenazic rabbinic dynasties in Italy. Since David here writes מהר״י מינץ, we cannot be certain whether he was referring to Joseph or Judah. Since the latter was eighty in 1556, it might well have been him.

Since one may never refuse [the request] of a great man, I shall express my inadequate view.

It is stated in chapter six of the Mishnah *Shabbat*:[315] *A man may not go out with a nail-studded sandal, nor with a single [sandal] if he has no wound on his foot, nor with phylacteries, nor with an amulet if it is not from an expert, etc.*

Rashi's commentary to this passage reads: *"Nor with an amulet"— which he wears for the purpose of healing. "If it is not from an expert"— however, an amulet from an expert is permitted, for it is an ornament for the sick person like one of his garments.*

We find it [further stated] in the *Gemara*:[316] *Rav Papa said: Do not think that both the man [issuing it] and the amulet must be recognized as expert, but as long as the man is expert, even if the amulet is not approved, [it may be worn on the Sabbath].*

Rashi's commentary [to this passage] reads: *"As long as the man is expert, even if the amulet is not approved, [it may be worn on the Sabbath.]" For example, a man prepared an amulet for three people, whereupon this man becomes an expert healer because he healed three people; and the amulet [is considered] approved, because this amulet has healed three people. For that matter, if this man wrote three amulets for three different kinds of illnesses for three different people, then the person is approved [as a healer] with respect to all amulets that he might prepare at any time, and the amulet which had been prepared for three people is approved for this sick man; and the amulet is now considered approved, whether it was writtetn by this healer or by someone else.*

The *Sefer haTerumah*[317] and the *SeMaG*[318] and the *SeMaK*[319] hold with Rashi's opinion, [who stated that] if he healed three different kinds of diseases with three different amulets, the [healer] is considered approved for all kinds of amulets, [and] also for other illnesses. However *Tossafot* and the *R'osh*[320] disagree.

---

[315] Talmud Bavli, *Shabbat* 60a.

[316] Ibid. 61a.

[317] This book was written by Barukh ben Isaac of Worms (Venice, 1521). It is a compilation of the positive and negative commandments.

[318] This is an abbreviation by which the *Sefer Mizvot Gadol,* by Moses of Coucy (13th cent.) was commonly known. It was first printed in Rome in 1470.

[319] This is an abbreviation for *Sefer Mizvot Katan,* by Isaac of Corbeil, who lived in France in the second half of the thirteenth century.

[320] That is, Asher ben Yeḥiel (1250–1328), eminent talmudist and codifier, author of the *Arba'ah Turim.*

This is what the *R'osh* writes: *Rashi's commentary [which states] that if he healed three kinds of illnesses with three kinds of amulets, the man is [deemed] expert for all types of amulets for other illnesses, does not appear reasonable to me. For if he were expert in three types of amulets, should he thereby be deemed competent [to write] other amulets in which he has no expertise? It therefore appears to me that the phrase "the man is expert" can be explained in the following manner: If he wrote one formula*[321] *on three prescriptions,*[322] and the three of them were effective, the man is considered expert for that particular formula, whenever he writes it. But this does not apply to other formulas. Furthermore, the amulet is not approved if someone else wrote it, whereas an amulet that healed three times is approved for everybody.

Now, three amulets for three people three times is explained thus by Rashi: *If he wrote three copies of one amulet, and each one was effective for three people, or three times for one person, the healer is [deemed] expert for this amulet everytime he writes it down, and these amulets are approved for every person.*

Tossafot and the *Tur*[323] hold a similar opinion [to the *R'osh*], and we find that they all disagree with Rashi in the interpretation of *the man is expert* and *the amulet is approved*. According to Rashi's interpretation of *the man is expert,* we conclude that he is [deemed] expert for every type of amulet that he might write; while according to the others (*R'osh, Tur, Tossafot*), he is only deemed expert for those amulets that are of the proven formula, but not of other formulas. According to Rashi's interpretation of *the amulet is approved,* this holds even if it is copied on another prescription, even if it were written by someone else. But according to those [who disagree with him], it holds only for that particular amulet, and not for any other [document] on which this formula is written, even if the same man wrote it, unless the man is [deemed] expert.

And even though the words of the *R'osh* and *Tossafot* are perfectly

---

[321] The term לחש refers to a spoken incantation or formula which becomes an amulet (קמיע) when written down.

[322] David uses the term אגרת, which can mean letter or epistle, or any type of written document.

[323] Cf. note 7 supra.

clear, and require no corroboration, I see fit to support their position. For in my own experience, the facts in both cases[324] were in accord with their opinion concerning Rashi's [position] that *the man is [deemed] expert* means that he is expert for every amulet that he might write. It is well known by this time, in all regions through which I have traveled, that I was successful with[325] many kinds of amulets against witchcraft, madness, the plague, children's phobias,[326] and many others. The best-known place where I tested [them] was here in Ferrara. Similarly, I tested [them] by the hundreds, in the holy community of Posen, when I was in my *Baḥur* status [at the *yeshivah*], when I was supported by the exalted grandee, Reb Meir Levi, long may he live. And in the case of the plague, I tested thousands, all this in the famous holy community of Cracow.

The upshot of all this is, that despite the fact that I had good success a great many times, sometimes, I tried to do something new that I had not done before,[327] and it did not come out right. So I discovered that the words of Rashi did not make sense.

Even in the text of the Talmud Yerushalmi,[328] the opinion expressed there is at variance with Rashi's, for it states: *A man is believed when he says, "With this amulet I healed three people,"* and it does not state, *A man is believed when he says "I am an expert."* Furthermore, in the interpretation of [the principle] *the amulet is approved,* according to Rashi, this formulation holds even if written by someone else. This too is not so, for we have seen, on many occasions, that some of the greatest scribes copied amulets that had worked hundreds of times, but they did not work for them.

---

[324] That is, the facts with respect to the healer deemed expert and the amulet considered efficacious.

[325] The meaning of this phrase, שעלו לידי, is made clear by its use in *Shir haMa'alot l'David,* p. 11a, line 9, which reads ולא עלה לידם.

[326] The technical name for this ailment (פחד התנוקות) in the medical books of that time was *pavor puerorum.*

[327] That is, a new formula for an amulet.

[328] Talmud Yerushalmi, *Shabbat* 8a, where we read: "Rabbi Abbahu quoted Rabbi Yoḥanan as saying: 'This amulet is efficacious, for with it I healed a first, second, and third time.' "

Now the sense of the matter, as it appears to me in a logical interpretation of *the man is [deemed] expert* [is simply this]: that he is [deemed] expert only for amulets of that particular formula. [Let me explain it] by means of a metaphor: We see [an instance where] the king gives permission to one of his subjects, because of his integrity, to do three things, one after another, in matters which he has hitherto decreed should not be done. Would we conclude, because of this, that he might dare to transgress in more grievous matters, like robbery and murder? In that case nobody would be safe.[329] And if, applying this metaphor to amulets, he were to be [deemed] expert for all amulets that he might write, were we to follow Rashi's position, he would be able to resurrect the dead and to perform many miracles which it would be impossible to imagine!

Similarly, in the case of the interpretation [of the phrase], *the amulet is approved,* only that particular formula is approved, but no other, even though it be the same formula, written by the same person, unless, of course, that person is [deemed] expert. For example, the king gives Reuben permission, for a limited time, to sign the king's name to a document with his own hand. He shows it to the tax collector, who excuses him from the tax. He does this three times, and [by this time] the tax collector is familiar with the document, and excuses the tax for whatever [person] shows it to him. Have we grounds to conclude that anybody could sign the king's name to a document, show it to the tax collector, so that ultimately the whole tax would be abrogated?

So it is with amulets according to Rashi's interpretation. For if this formula is valid even if another man writes it, according to him it is conceivable that all the amulets in the world, written by any person, are approved, because it is possible [to imagine] every amulet tested three times, and whatever is in the realm of possibility, it is not impossible to [imagine it] happening. Were this not so, the possible would be impossible, as the logicians well know.

It is my view, on the subject of amulets, that it is reasonable to conclude that he whose mental capacity is better developed, who is a

---

[329] The literal meaning: "no living creature would remain alive."

whole person, and has developed his wisdom to a great extent, such a man is apt to have more success in the matter of amulets [than others], and he is, in very truth, on the path to the attainment of the ultimate gift of the level of prophecy in man, as Maimonides describes it in part two, chapter thirty-two [of the *Guide*]:[330]

There are three opinions among men concerning prophecy. The first opinion—that of the multitude of the pagans . . . is that God, may He be exalted, chooses whom He wishes . . . whether this individual is a man of knowledge or ignorant . . . on condition that *. . . He turned him into a good man and endows him with prophecy.*[331] *. . . The second opinion is that of the philosophers, It affirms that prophecy . . . is not achieved in any individual from among men except after a training that makes that which exists in potentiality . . . pass into actuality. . . . it is not possible*[332] *that an individual should be fit for prophecy, and prepared for it, and not become a prophet. The third opinion is the opinion of our law. . . . It is identical with the philosophical opinion except in one thing. For we believe that it may happen that one who is fit for prophecy and prepared for it should not become a prophet . . . as it is known from the history of Baruch, the son of Neriah. For he followed Jeremiah, who trained, taught and prepared him. And he set himself the goal of becoming a prophet, but was prevented. . . . Thereupon he was told through Jeremiah: "Thou shalt say unto him: Thus sayeth the Lord; Seeketh thou great things for thyself? Seek them not!"*[333] *As for its being fundamental with us that the prophet must possess preparation and perfection in the moral and rational qualities, it is indubitably the opinion expressed in their dictum: "Prophecy*[334] *only rests upon a wise, strong and rich man."*

[330] The excerpted quotation, as David gives it, is found in translation on pp. 360–61 of the Shlomo Pines edition of the *Guide of the Perplexed* (Chicago, 1963).

[331] This is David's summary of the text which reads: כי בני אדם עד עתה לא אמרו שישרה השם שכינתו על אדם אלא שיחזירהו למוטב.

[332] David writes אי אפשר, while the text reads ולא יתכן. He seems to be quoting from memory. In the text the phrase "it is not possible that any individual should be fit for prophecy . . . and not become a prophet" follows "it is not possible that an ignoramus should turn into a prophet." Similarly, the order of the phrases "as for its being fundamental with us . . . upon a wise, strong and rich man" and "thereupon he was told . . . seek them not" are reversed in the quotation here.

[333] Jeremiah 45:3.

[334] Talmud Bavli, *Shabbat* 92a and *Nedarim* 38a.

In a similar vein, Rashba[335] writes in paragraph 413 of his Responsa as follows: *As to the writers of amulets [about whom] they stated that "the healer is approved [for all amulets]," what they mean is that the success of the amulets showed him to be under an auspicious star so that his amulets work, and they are at pains to do their work at a time propitious for the stars, on a fixed month and fixed day, and they write it upon a special parchment. Likewise, with respect to those psalms whose use is approved by the eminent leaders in Israel, it is universally agreed that they must be used at a time[336] that is known to be propitious.*

Here too it is clear that we are not dealing with some ignoramus, for he precisely states: *And they take great pains to see to it that their work coincides with [the influence] of a special star, etc.* Now where would an ignoramus know anything about astrology?

And should you counter [with the argument] that we have already seen several amulets that worked that were copied by an ignoramus, that happens to be because it is an *approved amulet*.[337] This is attested further in a statement by the Rashba [in the responsum cited above]: *Similarly we depend upon the experts of cures, in the cases of those cures which are not explained by ordinary logic. (See Aruch,[338] letter Kaf.) And it is not only upon experts in Torah and experts in healing that we are permitted to rely as experts in amulets; but upon ordinary folk, for whom these amulets worked. In such instances, too, we are permitted to accept them as writers of amulets, whether they be of herbs or written.[339] But the sages did not specify for us which written amulets or which herbal [amulet].*

The Asheri[340] has comments along these lines as well, and I quote: *When an expert healer prepares a new amulet for a sick person, that amulet only is permitted, and if someone else copies it it is not [deemed] efficacious, even though it healed three times at the hand of the expert. It is possible to say that the healer's horoscope was favorable, and hence its success. However,*

---

[335] Rabbi Solomon ben Adret, *She'elot u'Tshuvot* (Responsa) (Bnai B'rak, 1958), vol. 1, p. 147.

[336] That is, astrologically proper.

[337] That is, one that has worked many times.

[338] This was the earliest Aramaic dictionary, compiled by the lexicographer Nathan ben Yeḥiel, who died in 1106.

[339] That is, a written formula.

[340] Asher ben Yeḥiel. Cf. note 320 supra.

when an amulet from an unapproved person heals three times, it becomes
approved no matter who writes it. In this instance it cannot be linked to the
healer's horoscope, since he was not approved when he did it.

I am greatly surprised at the Narboni[341] in his commentary to the
Guide, section 40,[342] chapter 62, wherein he expresses the opinion
that it is not possible for amulets and names to be effective [to heal
or do wonders]. He thus exposes himself in all his nakedness to a
total ignorance of the Talmud's insight, as we have already
explained it. For even though he devised his conclusions from the
words of the *Guide,* he did not correctly understand that its venerat-
ed author spoke only [negatively] of those [ignorant and wicked]
who just dreamed them up. But he did admit that there was something to the fact that there were those who knew how to combine
[letters], and the proof of this is that he did not express his disagree-
ment when he dealt with the subject of amulets in his talmudic code,
as we find in mentioned it the Laws of Sabbath [in the Code].

Furthermore, the Midrash tells us that Bezalel[343] knew how to
combine letters with which the heaven and the earth were created, as
it is stated in *Sefer Yeẓira.*[344] And especially after we were illuminated
by the wisdom of the Kabbalah, that divine light which is replete
with the choicest examples of the combining of letters into Names,
as the Ramban[345] states in the introduction to his Torah commentary, and I quote: *We have yet another mystic tradition, that the whole*
Torah is comprised of Names of the Holy One Blessed Be He, and that the let-
ters of the words group themselves into divine Names when divided in a dif-
ferent manner, as you may imagine by way of example, that the verse of
בראשית *divides itself into these other words* בראש יתברא אלקים. *This principle*
applies to the whole Torah with the exception of the combinations and numeri-
cal values of Holy Names.

---

[341] Moses ben Joshua of Narbonne, who died after 1362. He was the author of a
commentary to the *Moreh Nevukhim* (*Guide of the Perplexed*) of Moses be Maimon.
Cf. J. Goldenthal, *Der Commentar des Rabbi Moses Narbonensis zu dem Werke More Nebu-*
chim des Maimonides, (Vienna, 1852).

[342] This seems to be in error. The pertinent passage is in sec. 1, chap. 62.

[343] Talmud Bavli, *Berakhot* 55a.

[344] One of the earliest kabbalistic books, published between the second and sixth
centuries.

[345] Moses ben Naḥman. See his introduction to the commentary of Genesis.

It is remarkable that he should write thus, despite the fact that his lifetime preceded the appearance of that wonderful, divinely inspired book of the *Zohar,* as we learn from the author of the מנחת יהודה[346] at the beginning of his commentary to the book מערכה,[347] a work which is adorned sevenfold with combinations and permutations [of sacred letters], as is known to whoever reads it. He is, as his name, there is no limit to his praise!

Furthermore, the effectiveness of names and amulets becomes much better understood by anyone who has had the privilege of perusing the book שיעור קומה[348] or the *Prayer of Rav Neḥuniah ben haKaneh*[349] or the *Prayer of Rav Hamnuna Sava,*[350] or the book *The Seventy-Two Names of Metatron,*[351] which are currently to be found in my library, with God's help. Now the book *The Seventy-Two Names of Metatron* is mentioned in the *Tossafot* to the first chapter of *Yevamot,* in connection with the statement: *This the Master of the World declared.*[352]

And from what I have seen in the book אגרת חמודות, it appears that Maimonides did not apply himself to the study of Kabbalah until toward the end of his days, for the author there quotes him as saying: *When I came to the Land of the Hart,*[353] *I encountered an old man who*

---

[346] The commentary by Judah ben Jacob Ḥayyat to the ספר מערכת האלהות was published with that book in Ferrara in 1557. This is an example of how David kept up with new books in the field.

[347] This was a kabbalistic book by Pereẓ ben Isaac haCohen Gerundi, who lived in Spain in the thirteenth century.

[348] Literally, "The Measurements of the Body." This was an ancient tract of Merkaba mysticism, with frank and almost provocative anthropomorphisms. Cf. G. Scholem, *Major Trends in Jewish Mysticism* (Jerusalem, 1941), pp. 62 ff.

[349] This was a kabbalistic prayer from the geonic period, preserved in manuscripts. I received this information from Dr. Scholem in Jerusalem.

[350] This is another magical prayer from the geonic period.

[351] G. Margoliouth, *Catalogue of Hebrew and Samaritan Manuscripts,* vol. III (London, 1909), MS. 752, p. 93; and A. Neubauer, *Catalogue of the Hebrew Manuscripts in the Bodleian Library* (Oxford, 1886), no. 229.

[352] Talmud Bavli, *Yevamot* 16b.

[353] I have learned from Dr. Scholem that this account of Maimonides and the Kabbalah was published in Ferrara in 1556 by Shemtov ben Shemtov and in the הסגות of Moshe Askar. David may have seen the former, though he quotes it from the above-named book. Cf. also the article by Scholem in *Tarbiẓ,* 1935, on this aspect of Maimonides.

initiated me into the wisdom of the Kabbalah. And had I known it in my
younger days, I would not have written many of the things I wrote.

Similarly Abarbanel writes at the end of chapter three of נחלת
אבות[354] concerning Maimonides, and it is possible that the reference
in מגדל עוז[355] in the ספר המדע both refer to this event which took place
toward the end of his life.

> And all this, as it appears to me, I have written under pressure,
> says the humble one, David Preacher from Cracow, who
> sojourns for the time being at the household of those grandees,
> the Bordolanis.

A BAN OF EXCOMMUNICATION

> In the year 1568, His Excellency, Moses Bordolano, passed
> through the holy community of Cracow, and in his possession
> were scrolls upon scrolls from the scholars of Italy and the
> scholars of Russia, pronouncing a ban of excommunication
> upon Rabbi Moses di Rossi for having permitted the d'Ato
> family to sue the Bordolano family in a Gentile court of law. In
> view of the fact that I recognize them as authentic, I follow the
> footsteps of these great scholars.[356]

> ד All you who dwell all over the world,[357]
> May your well-being increase!
> Heavens have put on gloom,
> And the shining stars are dimmed.

> ו Woe to the ears that must hear this,
> All eyes will shed tears.

[354] This book was first published in Constantinople, in 1505.

[355] Shemtov ben Shemtov, in his comment to Maimonides' observations on the
study of the Kabbalah, indicates that he saw an ancient manuscript that reported
that Maimonides had studied the Kabbalah in his later life. Cf. מגדל עוז to ספר המדע,
chap. 1, of משנה תורה.

[356] The contemporary record of this trial held in Ferrara in 1558 is found in MS.
ספר הפרוצטו, the original of which is in the Leningrad Library, and a microfilm copy
is in the MSS. collection of the Hebrew University Library. There is also reference to
the conflict in the Responsa of Isaac di Lattes, published by M. H. Friedlander
(Vienna, 1860), pp. 141–146. See also Simonsohn, *History of the Jews in the Duchy of
Mantua*.

[357] Each line of the anathema is an acrostic of David Darshan of Cracow.

ד My entrails have become twisted,
And what is usually quiet[358] has become turbulent,
Because there has arisen amidst Israel,
That brazen one

ד Who refuses to obey the words of the Torah,
And the outer doors[359] have got hold of him.

ר He ran sixty laps to derive shame from "rags,"[360]

ש For he brings in the legal case of a Jew
Before those that are against them,
And adds glory to the name of their god.

נ This teacher, Moses di Rossa, is not worth the food of his
belly,
May his fat become lean![361]

מ He attempts to bring an elephant through the eye of a
needle,[362]
To permit to the sons of d'Ato what is prohibited.

ק In the end they will inherit the flame of Gehinnom,
And about them it was said:

---

[358] The use of the term שייפא is zoharic. Occasionally David shows a tendency to imitate Zoharic style, which was not infrequent, e.g., משרי קטרין by Abraham b. Eliezer Halevi (Constantinople, 1510); and Joseph Caro's מגיד מישרים.

[359] This is a reference to the gates in the ascent of the mystic in *Hekhalot* literature, gates which shut in the face of unworthy aspirants.

[360] See Midrash, *Song of Songs Rabbah* to 1 Kings 6:15 and 1:17. The priests ran on a floor of cypress in the course of their proper duties. Moses di Rossi is condemned for running in the wrong direction!

[361] This is a pun on the name di Rossi, ירזה/דרזה.

[362] Talmud Bavli, *Baba Meẓia* 38b, Midrash, *Numbers Rabbah,* chap. 10, and Midrash, *Leviticus Rabbah* chap. 5.

From the day that I knew you,
you have been rebellious.[363]

ר Evil upon evil they compound with their teachers.
In some there is no evil that is hidden from them.

א They obey Moshe of the "brazen generation,"[364]
The helper and the helped one will come to be burned in
the fire.

ק The faulted ways of the Arameans,[365] they
applied to body and property
Of those sainted men, the members of the Bordolano
family.

א Who have in their heart the fear of God on high,
The nail of the Bordolano is more worthy
than the belly of the d'Atos.[366]

I am exceedingly amazed at you,[367] Moses di Rossi, for pursuing,
attacking like a wild beast,[368] and spreading venom[369] in the midst of
God's holy people, leading them to ignore the injunctions of the
great scholars of the world. You obviously find it difficult to comprehend the verse:[370] *If there arise a matter too hard for judgment, etc.,* . . .
thou shalt not turn aside from the sentence which they shall declare unto thee,

---

[363] Deuteronomy 9:24. He reverses the order in quoting.

[364] This is another pun on di Rossi, דור עוזי.

[365] He uses the word Aramean in the sense of deceiver (רמאי). Cf. Midrash, *Genesis Rabbah* 63:4.

[366] Midrash, *Genesis Rabbah* 45:7.

[367] His use of the phrase הפלא ופלא can be linked to Deuteronomy 17:8, which insists on judgment in a doubtful case before a Jewish court, and begins with the words כי יפלא.

[368] Here we have another pun on the name di Rossi, דרס.

[369] Cf. Talmud Yerushalmi, *Terumah* 3:22: יודע הוא אם הטיל בו ארס.

[370] Deuteronomy 32:31.

etc., . . . and *the man who doeth presumptuously in not hearkening unto the priests, etc., . . . even that man shall die.*

Now it is just your ignorance and stupidity that save you, for the rebellious elder,[371] who deserves death as commanded in the Torah, must be a scholar who has attained the rank of judgment, and knows everything except a matter too hard for judgment, as we find it stated in chapter ten of [Tractate] *Sanhedrin.* And now, even that which young schoolchildren understand is too hard and too opaque for you, *for their rock is not as our Rock, even our enemies themselves being judges*[372] testify against you, for you bring the holy to the home of the impure one, to be judged in the circus-houses[373] and theaters of worshippers of other gods[374] [i.e., idols]. And there is ample shame and wrath[375] upon you, that you exalted yourself above the Master of Heaven, and rendered homage to the gods of silver and gold. Nor did you turn to the God in whose hands is your soul, neither did you turn all your paths to him. There may my king cleanse you,[376] and remove your sin in righteousness and justice. And you will return justice to Sinai and judgment to the One that dwells on it.[377] Then will you be rescued from the decree of excommunication,[378] and there will be healing to your tranquility. So speaks in truth and justice, David Darshan from Cracow.

[371] For the law on זקן ממרא see Talmud Bavli, *Sanhedrin* 84b and 86b, and Talmud Yerushalmi, *Shabbat* 1:3d.

[372] See Midrash, *Sifrei* to this passage (Deuteronomy 32:31).

[373] In the Talmud circus-houses are usually referred to in a derogatory manner, symbolizing Roman secular power and excess. Cf. Talmud Bavli, *Megillah* 6a, *Ketubot* 5a, *Avodah Zarah* 18b. In Midrash, *Lamentations Rabbah* to Ruth 3:13, there is a favorable reference.

[374] There is a pun in the use of אחרים, *other* gods. It evokes the memory of Elisha ben Abuyah, the most famous apostate in the Talmud, who was known as *Aḥer.*

[375] Esther 1:18.

[376] Daniel 4:24, where the actual verse reads: "Wherefore . . . let my counsel be acceptable to thee and break off thy sins by almsgiving . . ."

[377] The authentic judge "sits" on Sinai, i.e., he bases his decisions on proper *Halakhah.*

[378] נח״ש stands for שמתא, חרם, נדוי. The initials represent the word "serpent." A very strong term for excommunication.

I wrote about this problem in the year 1567, when His Excellency Elijah Galatz came to me with reference to a dispute he had with a certain judge concerning his wife.

QUESTION: Reuben sued the wife of Simeon, and Simeon appeared in court in place of his wife and said: "My teachers! You know full well that no man wishes to see his wife humiliated through appearance in court.[379] Therefore I have come to represent her here, for whatever she deals with from our household[380] is mine, for she has no possessions of her own, such as estate in my usufruct,[381] and the like. Therefore, should she lose the litigation, the payment would have to be made from my resources. You are also going to hear the claim of Reuben, the plaintiff, and you will see that she has nothing to do with him in this claim. But if you deduce from this claim that the case cannot be decided without her presence, I shall bring her to court." And a certain judge replied: "Reuben need make no statement whatsoever, until your wife comes to court. For the law in this instance is perfectly clear." And they debated this point.

RESPONSUM: The law is not that simple, for, from what the *Tur* (*Ḥoshen Mishpat*, par. 124) states: *And so [in the case of] worthy ladies, Rav Alfas[382] did not excuse them from [testifying] in this law-suit, but [he directed] that court clerks be sent to them to take their deposition, and not to allow others to plead their case for them, and the R'osh concurs, etc.,[383]* it might be possible to say that this refers to women who have no husbands, or to conclude that the husband is not capable of pleading their case, therefore *others* (i.e., court clerks) are specified. For with respect to his wife, the husband is never referred to as *other,* for the

---

[379] Talmud Bavli, *Ketubot* 37b.

[380] For usage of this phrase, see Mishnah, *Demai* 8:5.

[381] This is property owned by the wife, income from which may be used by the husband. Such property is known as נכסי מלוג.

[382] Isaac Alfassi, an eminent talmudist and codifier, born in Fez, Morocco, in 1013.

[383] The prohibition of "others" representing the wife in court is not to be interpreted as referring to the husband.

husband is as his wife. Please try to understand for yourself the statement in chapter four of [Tractate] *Gittin,*[384] as well as what is cited in *Ḥoshen Mishpat,* par. 122, that if the husband enters into litigation with a second party who has seized his wife's property, it requires her authorization, but if there is usufruct from the property, he does not require authorization.

From this [reference],[385] one must conclude that even though *he has the right to use only the usufruct [from her estate],* he may plead [the case] without authorization with respect to the capital. All the more so when the matter at issue concerns them both, for the property belongs to him, and he may plead the case. Nor may his opponent say: "My case is with her."[386] And even when he says that the case will not be resolved without her, for he [the husband] will, therefore, bring her to court, it is also the case [that the husband may represent her.]

And in *Tossafot,* at the beginning of the chapter,[387] though they speak [of the necessity of her presence] for taking the oath as witness, in the actual litigation her arguments may be presented by another. Further, it is possible to turn him aside [in his argument that she appear], by saying even if he refers to that practice [of compelling her appearance], it is not the sense of the legal decision [in the text]. In any case one may not confuse the sense completely, for we must say that the use of the word *other* is not precise enough, and it should have stated *her husband* precisely, [and it is so stated] in order that there be no conflicting opinion among the decisors.

Now Mordecai [in his comment on the matter] in chapter five of *Baba Kama*[388] says the same thing and I quote:

Rav Eliezer ben Nathan[389] *handed down the following decision: Since*

---

[384] Talmud Bavli, Gittin 48b.

[385] See supra.

[386] Literal translation: "You [addressing the wife] are the one with whom I am dealing."

[387] Talmud Bavli, *Gittin* 48b.

[388] Talmud Bavli, *Baba Kama* 49a.

[389] He was a liturgical poet and halakhist who was a contemporary of Rashi, and perhaps a fellow student of his in the *yeshivah.* He was the great-grandfather of Asher ben Yeḥiel.

women are frequently involved in carrying on business these days, it is as though their husbands appointed them to be their agents, and if there are witnesses [to the wife's liability] the husband is required to pay for the sake of the stability of the market, so that they deal with them [i.e., the women]. If there are no witnesses, she must appear and testify under oath. And with respect to those who say that no man wishes that his wife be humbled in court—this refers to a vow, for she must appear personally in court to free herself from a vow, but here it is possible [for her to testify] by means of a court-appointed representative, and further, it is better that she be subjected to embarrassment than to [be in a position] of having committed a felony, etc.[390]

Now we should pay special attention to the use of the phrasing *and if there are witnesses the husband is required to pay*—for you would have expected the text to say: *she is required to pay from her husband's funds.* It is clear [from the phrasing] that he is appearing on her behalf and *all glorious the queen's daughter within.*[391]

There is, it would seem, another meaning to [Mordecai's] statement *and if there are witnesses she must appear and testify under oath,* etc., up to *here it is possible by means of a court-appointed representative, etc.,* [to wit] the case which you cite is not analagous,[392] for you cannot have a court-appointed representative for the purpose of taking an oath [on behalf of the litigant]. But in my view, the problem is resolved as follows: First, he [the plaintiff] declared that the husband was liable, and he meant to say that he was pleading on her behalf. Therefore [Mordecai] wrote: *by means of a court-appointed representative.* Hence all the more so by means of her husband. And with respect to the other [part] of Mordecai's statement: *if there are no witnesses she must testify under oath,* he added: *let her be humiliated, etc.*[393] [This is intended to show that] she is obliged to come to court, and precisely in that matter in which they are both involved, in which instance he [the

---

[390] That is to say, it would be better for her to appear in court to defend her integrity than to be spared public embarrassment.

[391] Psalms 45:14. This passage is used in talmudic sources to speak of a woman's right to privacy. Cf. Talmud Bavli, *Shevuot* 30a, in connection with a woman's participation in court litigation. Cf. also Talmud Bavli, *Gittin* 12a, *Yevamot* 77a; Midrash, *Leviticus Rabbah* 4:6 and *Numbers Rabbah* 2:26.

[392] Literally: "The case under discussion is not parallel to the evidence."

[393] And not be put in a position where she might become guilty of a felony.

husband] had wished to appear on her behalf previously. And if she is required to appear for the purpose of taking oath, he must bring her.

And with respect to Reuben's argument that he did not wish the case tried without the presence of [Simeon's] wife, because she would not dare to be brazen in his presence and in the presence of the court, this is no argument. For when they send court clerks to present the claims [and take their testimony,] [the possibility of brazenness] is not a matter of concern. All the more so in this case, that if they understood[394] his arguments that she must come, she would be sent for. And he would be able to argue his case in her presence, and she would not have the audacity to be brazen. Nor is there any reason to make a distinction between the former and the latter encounter, since she knows nothing of the first presentation, not having having been there. It is as simple as that.

In any case, her absence [in that instance] is not sufficient reason for Reuben not to state his claim according to the directive of the decisors, for *here is a community in which everything can be found,*[395] and there are found there great men, heads of *yeshivot* who have examined this matter more than I have. And these views of mine have been written under pressure; weighed down with sorrows am I, the teacher of children,[396] the humble one, David Darshan of Cracow.

WEIGHTY LETTERS

a

The King by justice establisheth the land, but he that exacteth gifts overthroweth it.[397]

Come and see,[398] when God created the higher world, He established everything properly. And He took out the best of the lights on all sides, and it all was one.[399] And he created the upper heavens and

---

[394] Alternate translation: "if they were persuaded by."

[395] Talmud Bavli, *Ḥullin* 56b.

[396] That is, he was a *melamed*!

[397] Proverbs 29:4.

[398] This is a zoharic phrase. David uses a psuedo-zoharic style in these letters.

[399] See the *Zohar* to Genesis 1:1.

the upper earth to establish it all at once, for the benefit of the lower [regions].[400] And these lower [regions] establish the earth according to the laws of truth which they fulfilled, as is stated in the verse: *The King by justice establisheth the land.* This refers to David the King, of whom it is written: *And David did justice and righteousness, etc.*[401] And thereby he sustained the earth, and out of his merit it was sustained after this.

But he that exacteth gifts overthroweth it—this refers to Rehoboam. Come and see! The Holy One, Praised Be He, is on the side of the righteous. For [with respect to the righteous], even though divine retribution has been decreed for the world, it is suspended because of them, and does not have dominion over the world. All the days of King David, the world was sustained for his sake, and even after him it was sustained for his sake, as it is written: *For I will defend the city to save it, for Mine own sake and for my servant David's sake.*[402]

Similarly, all the days of Jacob, and all the days of Joseph, evil dispensations held no sway on earth. Nor is there a single generation without someone like Jacob, David, and Joseph, who knows God's ways to follow them, in that they strive [to fulfill] the Torah day and night, and perform the law of truth, like the sons of the holy and the exalted, the great scholars of Frankfurt, who know how to establish the ways of the Holy One Praised Be He, and they do not turn aside from[403] the words of the redeeming Torah. Their portion is in this world and in the world to come, because the earth endures for their sake by virtue of the Law of Truth, which they constantly fulfill. Fittingly to them apply the words: *The King by justice establisheth the land*—the word King means our sages.

And the secret [meaning] of the matter is that the numerical value of the [phrase] *the King by justice establisheth the land* is the same as *these*

---

[400] See *Zohar* 1, 240b, for the idea that creation on the upper plane is reflected in the lower plane. Cf. Gershom Scholem, *Major Trends in Jewish Mysticism* (Jerusalem, 1941), pp. 218, 219, and 229.

[401] 2 Samuel 8:15.

[402] Isaiah 37:36.

[403] See *Targum* to Isaiah 45:14. ‏(עדי) יעדון‎.

are the sages of the community of Frankfurt.[404] Because of this, we the undersigned have come forward to register a charge against a certain eminent gentleman who is presently located in your jurisdiction. He is known by the name of Rabbi Mordecai, a master of alchemy, and his behavior toward his family is very unrighteous. For he has four superb daughters who are still unmarried, the youngest of whom is eighteen years old. He has been absent from them for eight years, and has left them penniless.[405] He has not sent them a penny and has left them as a public charge on the resources of our holy community of Cracow. Such a person can, heaven forbid, cause the destruction of the earth, and the verse *but he that exacteth gifts overthroweth it* can be applied to him. The secret meaning of the verse *but he that exacteth gifts overthroweth it* is—the corresponding numerical value [equals the numerical value] of the phrase *Our teacher Rabbi Mordecai the Alchemist.*[406]

We therefore direct our request to you, though not to burden you [with it], to find a just solution to this affair, to get him to pay, first by gentle persuasion,[407] and failing that, by compulsion, sparing him no expense.[408] Further [we request that] you forward the funds to us, so that we may marry off his daughters with dowry, apparel, and wife's settlement.[409] And all we want from him is his money, as the saying goes: *his taste and not his substance;*[410] for he is known here-

---

[404] Actually the numerical value of מלך במשפט יעמיד ארץ is 946, and of אלו גאונים מן קהל ורואנקבאורט is 947.

[405] Lit.: "naked without a penny."

[406] The numerical value of the verse is 1,699 and of the phrase, 1,716! He gives him the honorific title of מה״רר.

[407] His use of the pun פה רך ("gentle speech") and פרך is from Midrash, *Exodus Rabbah,* to Exodus 1:13.

[408] טרשא—a price higher than the seller would take if he sold for cash. פשיטין וטרשין—lit. "small coins or large."

[409] מהר—originally, purchase price for a wife, later, a legal term for wife's settlement.

[410] That is, money and not his person. Cf. Talmud Bavli, *Avodah Zarah* 67a. He reverses the sense of the talmudic quotation which suggests that "taste without substance is forbidden." He skillfully uses this phrase and the next as rhyming puns to describe the kind of rogue that Mordecai really is, thus: רב מרדכי and טעמו ולא ממשו קב רשו.

abouts as Reb Mordecai-Who-Never-Pays-His-Bills![411]

And we trust that the authorities will confer [on the matter], and mete out such punishment, may heaven protect us, on this Rabbi Mordecai, that the whole town will quake with fear. For he has not occupied himself with the *Duties of the Heart*,[412] and by virtue of his preoccupation with alchemy has caused his daughters much grief. His daughters' rights[413] do not concern him,[414] and instead of trying to betroth them,[415] he does audacious and forbidden things with his mind [in alchemy]. It is known that God's wisdom is in your midst and you do good deeds; and you will know how to bring blessings to the place as required, and will act in accordance with your great wisdom in the case of this individual without delay. And you will assist in marrying off and redeeming four *openers of the womb*.[416] Thus you will merit [the rewards of] the verse: *And I will betroth thee unto me in faithfulness, justice, righteousness, mercy, and compassion*.[417] Amen. He who speaks with truth and justice. David Darshan from Cracow.

b

Hope deferred makes the heart sick but desire fulfilled is a tree of life.[418]

---

[411] Talmud Bavli, *Sanhedrin* 29b, where we find the phrase, that is to say, a man who has a *kab*-full of indebtedness, *kab* being a unit of measure for grain or flour. Here we have reference to a man who pretends to be overwhelmed by debt to avoid paying his obligations.

[412] This is the title of a popular ethical guide written by Baḥya ibn Pakudah (11th cent.). He uses the title of the book as a way of referring to personal and moral responsibilities.

[413] Used in the sense of גר ויתום; cf. Deuteronomy 24:17, that which is one's due by right.

[414] Literally, "do not occur to his mind."

[415] This is a clever pun, ארס/הרס. He uses the verb הרס in the sense of audacity to do an unseemly thing. Cf. Exodus 19:21, in the instance of the Golden Calf.

[416] Exodus 13:2, that is, maidens or virgins.

[417] Hosea 2:21–22. David, probably quoting from memory, puts verse 22 before verse 21, and omits the word לעולם.

[418] Proverbs 13:12. He bases his interpretation on Rashi in Talmud Bavli, *Berakhot* 32b and 55a, where תוחלת ממושכה is taken to mean "drawn-out prayer." It is these passages that contain the substance of his ideas. Perhaps this is why he refers only to Talmud Bavli, *Rosh Hashanah* 16b.

This [verse] teaches us that one ought not to scrutinize[419] God's purposes to see whether they come to pass or not. Why should this be so? Because if one scrutinizes the extent to which his Divine Judge[420] makes them come to pass, [one ought also] to scrutinize all his [own] deeds. And the inner meaning of this is that this process of scrutinizing in that prayer causes his sickness of heart. Why sickness of heart? For it is as though he were to entice[421] someone to try to direct the heavenly and the earthly, as the sages[422] maintain in chapter one of *Rosh Hashanah*:[423] *Three things call a man's integrity to mind,* and one of them is: *the scrutinizing of prayer,* as Rav Nissim interprets it in that context.[424]

But desire fulfilled is a tree of life—We learn that whoever desires that God listen to his prayers should apply his efforts to Torah, for it is a tree of life, and in this sense *desire is fulfilled.* Who is this desire? He is the Angel[425] in whose hands are all possible prayers, and he brings them before the Supreme King, and it [the prayer] comes before God to fulfill the wish of that person [uttering the prayer]. By way of example, there are powerful men in the world[426] who do not respond sympathetically to the petitions of a person, because they are so insensitive,[427] and are always seeing the worst in people.[428] Woe to those who bore them!

---

[419] This is used in the sense of reflecting on forbidden things. See *Tosefta* to Talmud Bavli, *Ḥagigah* 2:7, and Talmud Yerushalmi, *Ḥagigah* 2:1. David bases his comment on the statement of Rav Ḥiyya bar Abba: "If one prays long and looks for the fulfillment of his prayer, in the end he will have vexation of heart, as it says: 'Hope deferred, etc.' "

[420] Literally, "their opponent in the case," that is, בעל דין.

[421] Literally, "who stands constantly over one to . . ."

[422] The use of חברייא for חכמים is interesting. The first half of this letter, as well as the first half of the preceding one, is zoharic style.

[423] Talmud Bavli, *Rosh Hashanah* 16b.

[424] See Rav Nissim's commentary to this passage.

[425] דרגא means "ladder" or "stage." But here David is thinking of the role angel *Sandlafon.* Cf. *Shir haMa'alot l'David,* p. 4a. Hence I have chosen to translate it in this way.

[426] Literally, "men of evil armament."

[427] Literally, "their hearts are stuffed, and their flesh is stuffed."

[428] Literally, "always turning people aside [to sin]."

[Conversely,] there are those who respond to the petitions of others, because they are saintly men, masters of the secret lore, who constantly apply themselves to the study of Torah, and who give a person the benefit of the doubt.[429] Blessed are they in this world and in the next![430] The secret meaning of the verse *hope deferred* is that it is the numerical equivalent, no more and no less, of the phrase: *These are indeed "uncircumcised of heart and uncircumcised of flesh."*[431] And they make the heart sick because they are destroyers of the world by binding the sacred person of a Jew in chains and captivity, and for this reason it is useless to petition them. [Contrariwise,] there are pure souls who cling to the right side,[432] which is the side to which the holy community of Israel clings, who do righteous deeds like those holy lights—good are they[433]—and wise ones who concern themselves with Torah and do good deeds—they are [the sages of] the holy community of Ofen.[434] And the secret meaning of [the phrase] *tree of life* [corresponds] in numerical value to *the community of Ofen*—no more and no less.[435]

Desire fulfilled—for it is a prayer that is not drawn out, and it is fitting to place the request before them, and assuredly the petition, which we the undersigned earnestly desire will come [before them],[436] and our request be granted by these saintly ones, with God's help. Amen.

We have heard tidings that make our entrails tremble,[437] how one of your brethren has been taken captive by the Gentiles. He is

---

[429] For דחלפין זכו read זכות. This is pseudo-zoharic for the Hebrew, that is seeing the favorable side in people.

[430] It is good for them in this world and in the next.

[431] The *gematria* is not exactly equal. The words from Proverbs have a numerical value of 1,255, while the other has a value of 1,254. In the second case he pads the quotation from Ezekiel 44:7 with the words הלא זו הם to achieve the relative equivalence.

[432] See *Shir haMa'alot l'David,* p. 4a.

[433] יינון is pseudo-zoharic for אינון.

[434] An earlier designation of Budapest.

[435] That is, 234.

[436] That is, the leaders of Ofen (Budapest).

[437] Habakkuk 3:16.

known by the name of Isaac Moses Delos. In his case, one of the curses [of Deuteronomy] has been fulfilled—there is none to ransom[438] and none to redeem. It would be a sacrilige that the life of a single Jew be lost. Now, we have heart that his money is in your hands. We beg your excellencies not to spare any of his assets, and to put forth every effort in his behalf, to the fullest extent of your power, even if he should not be left with a single penny of his own. In any case, do not procrastinate, for his mother and his wife make a great clamor on his behalf, [and are letting it be known] that they are willing to strip themselves[439] [of all they have], by selling everything they possess, their known as well as their hidden assets. They will not abandon him no matter what it costs. We, the undersigned, are especially prepared to help. Perhaps God will have compassion upon him and restore him [to freedom], and not leave so many bodies and souls in anguish, and especially his wife, widowed [though her husband is] alive.[440] In truth *hope is deferred* in her case, for the blessing is missing from her house.

Therefore, do not procrastinate in your efforts to perform this important commandment[441] without blemish or distortion, but rather lovingly and joyfully, and pursue your search for his whereabouts. By virtue of this, God will protect you from on high,[442] and bring you, together with all Israel, out of captivity and exile, and in your case, the blessing and not the curses will be fulfilled.[443] Amen. David Darshan of Cracow—who speaks in truth and in righteousness.

c

To cause those who love me to inherit substance [יש][444] *and that I may fill their treasuries.*

People in the world who apply themselves to Torah are worthy.

[438] Deuteronomy 28:68.

[439] Ezekiel 16:22, where the reading is ערום ועריה. David reverses the phrase, as he often does.

[440] Literally, "widowed alive" or "in living widowhood."

[441] He is here referring to the commandment for redemption of captives.

[442] Zechariah 6:19.

[443] Deuteronomy 28 ff.

[444] Proverbs 8:21. In Mishnah, *Ukzin,* 3:12, it is noted that the numerical value of

They are beloved in heaven and on earth, and each day of their lives they build up their inheritance in the world to come. As it is written: *To cause those who love me to inherit* יש. And what is יש?[445] It is the substance of the world to come, where the good man receives limitless rewards from heaven, which others do not achieve.

Now this particular [interpretation of] יש, as found in the teachings of the sages in chapter eleven [of *Sanhedrin*],[446] is descriptive of those holy luminaries,[447] the sages of Italy, who occupy themselves constantly with the Torah and derive no personal benefits from it, love heaven and earth, and by their righteous deeds, earn their rights to [the rewards of] the world to come. Indeed the verse *To cause those who love me to inherit* יש most appropriately applies to them.

Moreover, the hidden meaning of the phrase *to cause those who love me* is that its numerical value is identical with *these are the sages of Italy*.[448]Furthermore, its elders and its leaders are indeed worthy,[449] for God has given them the knowledge to understand the hidden paths, and has instructed them in many mysteries and heavenly treasures, and [has led them through] many heavenly gates[450] because of the righteous judgments which they make in this world. Because of this, their treasuries will be filled with that good that is brought to the world to come. Therefore [the phrase] *I will fill their treasuries* applies to them, and the secret meaning of [the word] *and their treasuries,* is that it has the same numerical value as *the circle of the elders and leaders.*[451]

We direct a complaint to you, you saintly ones, young and old, community leaders and men of trust, against a man who has

the word יש is 310, and suggests the promise that the righteous will inherit 310 worlds. Cf. Talmud Bavli, *Sanhedrin* 100a and also *Baba Batra* 13a.

[445] The accepted translation for *yesh* (יש) is "substance," but I use the word untranslated, because of David's play on it, and its *gematria*.

[446] In the text, David refers to it as פרק חלק.

[447] That is, those who reach the highest forms of Torah study are rewarded 310-fold.

[448] Not exactly! The respective numbers are 764 and 763.

[449] זכאין is used in the sense of צדיקים.

[450] Literally, "many city gates that open to above."

[451] That is, 764.

betrayed his *fruitful vine*.[452] His name is Dan bar Tuvia, and he also goes by the surname Don Reina. He is a teacher of young boys and is [a man] of medium height.[453] He grew up in Cracow, the capital [city], and has abandoned his wife in our midst as a widow [with a] living [husband], and in great distress. He has left her as an abandoned wife[454] for more than twelve years, and has not remembered her with a letter[455] or any financial support, for *the seven abominations of his heart*[456] are concealed. He has been contacted many times with warnings of excommunication if he does not return to the wife of his youth, but he warded off the representatives with glib talk, and turned them aside with a vague reply, so that the authorities might not see the letters of excommunication, and thus repair the breach.

We therefore request of you that wherever our bans reach you, you will search for him to bring him to strict justice, and that you will seize both his person and his money, until justice will be done by you. Keep him in prison until he [agrees to] return to her or divorce her. Blessed is he who produces and brings a bill of divorce to Madam Beilah, daughter of David Halevi, a modest and virtuous woman in all her deeds and of unblemished reputation. Beilah is not averse to being "bailed out" of her plight![457] She is well-born and eager to do what is right, and generally there is nothing bad in her. The failings and drawbacks are his. He walks in darkness and blindness, and by his evil deeds *covers the Lord's altar with tears, with weeping and groaning*[458] because he has betrayed the wife of his youth. It is thus described in the Book of Malachi.

---

[452] That is, his wife. Cf. Psalms 128:3.

[453] Literally, "neither tall nor short." See Talmud Bavli, *Yevamot* 106b.

[454] That is, an *agunah,* who could not remarry unless her husband were proven dead or gave her a divorce.

[455] That is, of divorce.

[456] Proverbs 26:25.

[457] There is a pun on her name and a passage from Talmud Bavli, *Ḥullin* 63b, which deals with בילה or "mingling." The passage reads: "For Rav Zeira stated: whenever proper mingling is possible, the mingling is not indispensable (אין בילה מעכבת)." The significance of the pun, which I have attempted to translate with a pun, is: Beilah will not be against receiving her due. He had dealt with the previous portion of the passage, with respect to "covering the blood," in his second sermon. Cf. *Shir haMa'alot l'David,* p. 5b.

weeping and groaning[458] because he has betrayed the wife of his youth. It is thus described in the Book of Malachi.

Therefore, we the undersigned irrevocably decree a severe ban of excommunication until he satisfies the claim of this woman. Let him be under this ban in every land, if he does not repair the breaches, either to return to or to divorce his unhappy abandoned wife, whose skirts are unstained.[459] Let all who see our ban heed it with trembling, to cut him off from the community of Israel who keep their laws, until such time as he straightens that which he made crooked.[460] Then they will merit all the blessings which are provided in the Torah. He that speaks with truth and righteousness. David Darshan of Cracow.

AIRY LETTERS

a

A letter[461] [of recommendation] on behalf of the *Baḥur*[462] Avigdor, who went from Venice to Cremona to study [Torah].

Avigdor, more precious than pearls[463] in his knowledge,
Venerable in wisdom, tender in years.[464]
In the midst of the land,[465] a blessing,
God blessed his strength and favored the work of his hands.[466]
[Deep] in the Eden[467] of the mind, he planted a garden
   to bring forth ancient[468] [truths],

---

[458] Malachi 2:13.

[459] A reverse pun based on Lamentations 1:9, "her uncleanness is on her skirts" (טומאתה בשליה). The text reads תומה, which would mean "her innocence."

[460] Isaiah 40:4.

[461] The first part of the poem is a double acrostic of the student's name, with the same letter of the name at the beginning and middle of each line. In the translation, I have evolved a single acrostic, to illustrate the idea.

[462] *Baḥur,* the first stage in *yeshivah* study. See Introduction to *Shir haMa'alot l'David,* note 8.

[463] Proverbs 3:15.

[464] Midrash, *Genesis Rabbah* 90:3. Here there is a comment on Genesis 41:43, where Joseph is described as אברך.

[465] Isaiah 19:44.

[466] Deuteronomy 33:11.

[467] Genesis 2:8.

[468] Leviticus 26:10. Note how David compresses the reference.

> Opening the door to the Garden of nuts
>   to pluck the lily.[469]
> Ramparts he casts up as he builds a bulwark,[470]
> He exposes and reveals the fine points of learning.
> His mind dwelt in the depths of the sea [of Talmud].
>   for four hundred repetitions [of Text].[471]
> Here in Cremona, in a brief hour, he consumed the
>   kernel and cast away the husk.[472]
> He poured a spirit from on high upon him in glory;[473]
> May relief and rescue accompany the valued *Baḥur* Avigdor.[474]

Who is it, and what sort of a person is it who presumes to approach him [his excellency] in writing or in person?[475] [Is it not written of the idols]: *They cannot utter speech, they have hands and feet not.*[476] For he is mightiest of all his peers in tongue and speech, as is suggested by the fact that the numerical value of his name Avigdor is identical with the word *mightiest.*[477] But I base my plea upon the dictum of the sage: *If I show myself wise, you will praise me, and if I show myself foolish, you will teach me.*[478]

Now here is the reason for leaving my niche: Thus far I have not attained *resting place and portion*[479] [i.e., I am still unmarried]; however, my greeting is accompanied by good tidings. My

[469] This is a reference to the study of Kabbalah. Song of Songs 6:11.

[470] Ezekiel 17:17.

[471] Here we have a series of skillful puns of Exodus 12:40. מצר ים/מצרים and שנה/שונה.

[472] A pun on Talmud Bavli, *Ḥagigah* 15b, כרימונע/כרימונה. The pomegranate is a symbol for kabbalistic study.

[473] Isaiah 32:15.

[474] Esther 4:14.

[475] Literally, "in writing."

[476] Psalms 115:7. David revises the order of the phrases as they appear in the Bible, for the purpose of his rhyme.

[477] הגבור and אבגדור have the same numerical value (216).

[478] Midrash, *Samuel* to *Pirkei Avot* 1:17.

[479] Deuteronomy 12:9.

esteemed brother Jacob is thriving in a moist garden[480] (i.e., is well married), for to his good fortune, God has provided him with a blessed portion, [a woman] *who fears the Lord, she is to be praised,*[481] and her title is truly *the Mistress of Kingdoms,*[482] who is none other than the daughter of the eminent, the princely, and the famous, sister of Meir Bordolano[483] who repairs the breach[484] [i.e., a benefactor and defender of the Jewish people]. Happy is he and it is well with him[485] to be blessed with such good fortune.[486]

Furthermore, my teacher, that giant in scholarship[487] Rabbi Joseph Minz has gone forth to seek healing for his illness,[488] and has moved to the holy community of Casa Maggiore.[489] I was therefore compelled to exchange my currency [i.e., move on], so that no obstacle will prevent me from continuing my studies.[490] I encountered a man whom I found trustworthy in all the deep learning, widely known, Rabbi David Darshan of Cracow, who teaches Torah in the household of the princely and distinguished Bordolano family. He is like a prepared table providing understanding in place of food [lit., "breasts"][491] and suckling [students] like me with

---

[480] Cf. the medieval poet Isaac bar Reuven, in אזהרה טובה, as cited in E. Ben-Yehuda, *Dictionary* (New York, 1958). The pertinent quotation is: הכין גן נעול לכלתי גן נעול רטוב. See also Job 8:16. Could he be thinking in Yiddish, viz., *schmaltzgrub?!*

[481] Proverbs 31:30. He omits the word אשה from the quotation.

[482] Isaiah 47:5.

[483] See note 59a to *Shir haMa'alot l'David,* p. 10a.

[484] For usage in this sense, see Talmud Bavli, *Berakhot* 19a. Also Ezekiel 22:20.

[485] Psalms 128:2.

[486] See Leviticus 16:9, Joshua 18:11, and Judges 1:3.

[487] David uses the term *gaon.*

[488] This is from the prayer for Yom Kippur Eve, כי הנה כחמר, which reads: כן אנחנו בידך ממציא למזור תרף. For purposes of rhyme, David reverses the words, and on the surface it does not seem to make sense. His meaning is to be understood in relation to the whole question, which he expects his readers to know.

[489] A town north of Cremona.

[490] In the *yeshivah,* the teacher was the central figure. When he left, it was necessary to become part of another group.

[491] In Talmud Bavli, *Berakhot* 10a, it is stated that the breasts of King David's mother were high up in her body, where her heart (here referred to as בינה) was, so that when he suckled, he would not behold her pudenda (ושעשה לה דדים במקום בינה).

knowledge, understanding, and insight. Who can sing his praises in matters of knowledge, for his light shines upon the Talmud and legal decisions, teaching from them commandments and laws, scaling the wall[492] with understanding and creating a firm foundation on earth with his interpretation and homiletical [skill]. And he has become proficient in the techniques of research to distinguish between good and evil, truth and falsehood. He also knows his way [in the intricacies] of dialectics and with insight and logic can distinguish between the simple conjugations and the complex [ones] and is strong [in his understanding] of them. Thus one gets to understand tradition, text and grammar. His mind is like a sapphire when it comes to the Hidden Way, the way of truth and Kabbalah which is shut and locked. [Not only that but] when it comes to the art of the scribe, he makes the letters radiant.[493] [As it is written:] *And David had great success in all his ways and God was with him.*[494] Blessed is he whose lot is thus in this world. Therefore, I beg of you, sir, if it be not too much trouble, that you grant me this small request, to show me your open hand [whose authority] is known throughout the land, to write, [on my behalf] on parchment, in square script, with your seal and signature, *to show the peoples and the princes the beauty*[495] of your magnificent handwriting. It will not depart from between my eyes[496] [i.e., I will have it in my possession at all times], so that it will always be my testimony and my protection. And I, the lowly one, am prepared, with no drawbacks whatsoever,[497] to be at your

Hence David here describes himself as שלחן ערוך עשות בינה במקום דדים (a prepared table providing understanding as the breast provides milk) reversing the quotation, as he often does to make his points.

[492] This is a pun, based on Genesis 49:22, which is itself a pun. See Stanley Gewirtz, "Of Patriarchs and Puns," *Hebrew Union College Annual,* vol. XLVI (Cincinnati, 1975), pp. 33 ff. There the pun is on שור, here David's pun is בינות/בנות.

[493] This is a pun on Genesis 6:16, תבה/תיבה.

[494] I Samuel 18:14.

[495] Esther 1:11.

[496] He uses the phraseology about phylacteries (Deuteronomy 6:8) by way of saying that he would have the letter of recommendation in his possession at all times, like a passport.

[497] Literally, "without adversary and evil occurrence." See 1 Kings 5:28, where the phrase אין שטן ואין פגע is used to inform King Hiram of Tyre that there were no drawbacks to the building of the Temple.

service at all times and at a moment's notice. Even though the coming of the Messiah is far off, the hearts are close and pressing.[498]
Thus speaks the youth who is led by the word of his teachers, the son of your aunt, *Joshua, a young man who departs not out of the tent*[499] [i.e., who constantly studies Torah].

b

A COMPOSITION AND POEM

He lights up the world and sparkles[500]
He spreads light and brightness and joy[501]
To the bulwark for the needy who cries out.
Ye great luminaries, leaders heads and rabbis,
Greet this poor man warmly.[502]
Give light to the weary
Compassion to the toiler
Grant your largesse according to the burden.[503]
Light is scattered for almsgiving[504]
To load him with gifts according to law and custom
Without delay or postponement.
Let your words be a doorway for light[505]
To lade him with a gift in secret
That subdues anger[506] and malediction.
Let it illuminate the road for him
To bring him home safely through the storm

---

[498] See Talmud Bavli, *Yevamot* 62a, for use of the term גוף by transference, as the fictitious storehouse of souls that must be emptied (that is, sent to earth) before the Messiah can come, viz., אין בן דוד בא עד שיכלו כל נשמות שבגוף.

[499] Exodus 33:11.

[500] This is a pun on the name of his uncle, Meir, who is mentioned in the poem: המאיר המאירי מאיר.

[501] Job 31:26.

[502] Ibid. 31:17.

[503] This is an amusing pun on Talmud Bavli, *Sotah* 13b.

[504] A pun on Psalms 97:11.

[505] Ibid. 119:130.

[506] Proverbs 21:14.

Who bears the burden from his youth.[507]
They [who walked in darkness] saw a great light[508]
For the pauper full of poverty
And for the poor man separated from the good
Much blessing and light
Will accrue swiftly and speedily
To him who aids the hard-pressed in his trouble
To wit, that wandering Cohen, Meir ben Eliezer
Who fulfills God's commandments
Without dilution or admixture.
How numerous are his good qualities
Both his and those of his forebears.
He lacks possessions and wealth
He has arranged for the marriage of his daughter.
And as to the dowry, believe him that he cannot afford it![509]
Oh you generous ones, open the gate[510] [of your generosity].
And rescue him from this trouble
With the help of young and old.
Especially since he is advanced in years.[511]
Favor him[512] with a good eye

---

[507] Lamentations 3:27. David uses the word מנעוריו instead of בנעוריו.

[508] Isaiah 9:1.

[509] See Tosefta, *Ketubot* 2:20: "If a woman says she is married, believe her; if she says she is not married, believe her; for the mouth that permits is the mouth that forbids." He uses the last phrase, הפה שאסר, to suggest the quotation, and the need to believe his request.

[510] Psalms 118:17. Proverbs 20:29 commands the favoring of the elders; it is also reminiscent of the opening portion of the Neilah prayer on Yom Kippur.

[511] Proverbs 20:29, where we read, פתחו לי שערי צדק.

[512] This is a delicate play on Proverbs 20:29, which commands the favoring of elders; while Exodus 23:3, and Leviticus 19:15 forbid favoring either rich or poor in a court of law.

To his gain and not to his loss
Pile the gifts on him
And you will fulfill the command of giving[513]
And merit the [reward of] *as the bridegroom rejoiceth*[514]
May God lift up [his countenance] upon you
And let his face shine upon you[515]
And rebuild the Temple in your day.
May he who stumbles be strengthened
By the Creator and Ruler.
Close to the year 1571.[516]
Amen. He who speaks in truth and righteousness
David [the] Preacher, from Cracow,
A disciple of the *Gaon* Rav Isaac [ben] Bezalel,[517]
    who is secure in the shadow of God,[518]
And disciple of the *Gaon* Rav Solomon of Ostrog,[519] who pays
    out rich coinage in his discourses,[520]
And not to turn my back on my own kin
My mother's brother Meir.

---

[513] He expresses the idea of the command by the use of the two words from Deuteronomy 15:10.

[514] He expresses the idea of the reward for giving charity with the use of the phrase כמשוש חתן, from Isaiah 62:5.

[515] Numbers 6:24 ff.

[516] The numerical value of the word אשל ("oak") is 331, that is, the year 5331, or 1571.

[517] Isaac ben Bezalel, who was a brother of Lowe ben Bezalel of Prague, the creator of the Golem.

[518] בצל אל/בצלאל is, of course, a pun on the name.

[519] Solomon Luria (1510–1573), one of David's teachers and brother-in-law of Moses Isserles.

[520] אסטרא/אסטירא is an interesting pun, and a double use of the verb, in the sense of "pay out" and "discourse." In Talmud Bavli, *Shabbat* 22a, we find the phrase מעות מרצה used in the former sense, while in Talmud Bavli, *Avodah Zarah* 36b, it is used in the latter sense. To the word מעות David adds the pun on the sage's place of residence, and the coinage represents the master's teaching.

A POETIC CERTIFICATION FOR RITUAL SLAUGHTER[521]

יתד וארבע תנועות[522]

I sing a song to One who shows no favoritism,[523]
    who is forgiving of the humiliation[524] of
    multitudes who slumber,
Who gives [forth] Torah with might and with
    strength, and guides properly in
    all times and seasons.
His good will, in his boundless mercy,
    is to show love, whose *eyes are as doves*[525]
He commands us to purify our souls, that our eyes may behold
    the good things that are hidden away for us,[526]
To slaughter [for one's food] with compassion for [His]
    creatures, domestic and wild animals and birds, as
    commanded twice in the Torah[527]
He made as His free-will gift the study
    of ritual slaughter, without reversing
    the doctrine in recognizing the
    signs [that would render the meat forbidden].
There is no limit to his excellency in
    removing falsehood and strengthening
    the essence with the choicest of
    pearls[528] [His Torah],

---

[521] This is a poetic certification of authority to act as *shoḥet* (ritual slaughterer for kosher meat). It is intended for Uri ben Shlomo haCohen, whose name is woven into the poem in acrostic fashion.

[522] A short vowel and four long vowels. See Ḥayyim Schirmann, *HaShirah haIvrit b'Sfarad uProvence* (Jerusalem, 1960), vol. 4, pp. 707 and 710.

[523] Deuteronomy 10:7.

[524] Rav Meir, in Mishnah, *Avot* 6:2.

[525] Song of Songs 1:15.

[526] Psalms 31:20, where we are informed of the hidden blessings that are the rewards of the righteous in the world to come.

[527] This is a reference to Talmud Bavli, *Ḥullin* 63b. See also Deuteronomy 14:7 and Leviticus 11:4.

[528] Strengthening the עיקר, the essence (of Judaism).

My Rock gave [me] David my light,[529]
    when He brought to me the
    Bahur named Uri of the lineage
    of priests.
His surname is Lipman, in
    understanding as sweet as manna;
    in all times and seasons he
    seeks out the learned.
He has demonstrated [his ability] to
    me in ritual slaughter according
    to the Torah.[530]
He has already done the slaughtering
    well, performing it three times
    in a row without fainting,[531]
    and he has [shown an ability]
    to examine knives [for defects].
I herewith grant him authority, to
    perform ritual slaughter on his own;
    and for all who may want him
    and invite him [to perform].
I have given him [this certificate] on
    condition that it praise him and
    not condemn him. Whosoever
    has leisure [to inquire further] I
    shall elaborate in person.

Since he is [a human being] in the image of God, if he wants to know a subject in depth, he must review it many times. For this reason I grant the authority to this bright neophyte,[532] Uri ben Shelomo Cohen, whose name appears [in acrostic] in this poem, sur-

---

[529] There are two puns here: ארי/אורי and מתוק מן/ליפמן.

[530] He uses the clipped phrase בהשחיטות סיני, that is, *shehitah* in accordance with the revelation at Mount Sinai.

[531] The feminine form נתעלפה is used for the purpose of rhyme.

[532] פעוט is Aramaic for קטן. Frequently used by scholars as an expression of humility.

named Lipman from Rovere, to perform ritual slaughter for himself
and for anyone who might desire to eat meat. [I grant him this
authority] on condition that he review the pertinent laws of ritual
slaughter once a day for the first month; once a week for the second
month; and thereafter once every six months for the rest of his life.
Thus rules the tiny gnat,[533] David [the] Preacher from Cracow, on
the fourth day of the Second Adar, 1558, here at Mara near Rovere.

THE AUTHOR'S APOLOGIA

I give praise and thanks to the Most High[534] [as I come to] the
completion of the book *Song of the Steps* and to the preeminent community of Cracow, which is outstanding in scholarship and achievement. Who can adequately describe her virtues? She is indeed entitled to the complete blessing of the patriarchs[535] and is truly the
keystone [of the Jewish world]. And this will become apparent when
I describe the advantages that have accrued to the holy community
because of my presence there, even though I am the least of them.[536]
Think of the advantages that accrue from its giants and scholars!

First and foremost in the matter of sermons—every Sabbath I had
something new to say, preaching with plain language and clear
speech, so that even women and children would understand. And
this achieved acclaim in all the lands and provinces, this beauty of
eloquence that impressed rabbis and community leaders in all corners [of the world]. I was also available at all times, with my modest
intelligence, to anyone with questions with respect to the teaching of
the God of Israel. I was also available at all times, for young and
old, for joyous occasion, or heaven forbid for some misfortune.[537]

---

[533] A reference to self in an extreme expression of humility. It is a synonym for
"humble one." See Talmud Bavli, *Sanhedrin* 38a, and also the Yemenite liturgical
poem, שמע האל: לפניך אני נחשב כעין יתוש קטן קדמני תחלה.

[534] He uses the medieval technical term "first cause" (עלות העלות) which was frequently used. See, for example, Yehuda haLevi, *Cuzari* (Vilna, 1914), 1:1, and Baḥya
ibn Pakuda, *Ḥovot haLvavot* (Vilna, 1923), 5, foundation 5.

[535] David uses the phrase from the grace after meals, using the variations of the
word כל as they appear concerning the patriarchs. (Cf. Genesis 24:1, 27:33, and
33:11.)

[536] See Talmud Bavli, *Avot d'Rabbi Nathan* 24a, where it is related that Hillel had
seventy disciples, and that Yoḥanan ben Zakkai was the least of them!

[537] 1 Kings 5:18–19.

On occasion there were those who came to me in the middle of the night, crying: *"Why are you asleep?"*[538] Arise and stop the bleeding." And there were those who would come [in the night] and say: "Arise and whisper a charm for a woman in labor, for she is in great danger." Or they would come and say: "Arise, for my sinfulness has caused a bone to lodge in the throat of my son!" Or they would come and say: "Arise in the blackness and darkness of the night, for my child is seized with terror, panic, or fright!" And there were occasions when someone went berserk, and my presence was urgently required. And I did so many things like this, I tell you without fear of contradiction, without any fee or reward. Only when I wrote an amulet in all purity against a plague or some other calamity [was I reimbursed], but I did not use this money for any other purpose other than to buy books, so that they might be available for all who sought wisdom, as I have indicated in the Holy Letter in the introduction [to this book].

But, woe is me, that, because of my many sins, I have nothing but daughters, and I must therefore depart from this honored community for a while, until some money will turn up,[539] and I can collect enough zlotys and coins for dowry and ornament, and marry them off to appropriate [grooms]. And may God bless all who help. He who speaks with truth and righteousness, David the Preacher from Cracow, who, with the authority of our teachers, leads with honor; and they are the *Geonim* Rabbi Joseph [Minẓ] and Rabbi Moses [Isserles], the great sages of [our] generation.

Says Isaac of Prosstitz, the person who has been given the authority to establish a printing press here in the Holy Community of Cracow. Praise and thanks to Whom thanks are due, that we completed printing this little book. From the beginning to this point these are the words which came forth from the mouth of Rabbi David [the] Preacher, may God protect him. It was completed on Thursday, the day of Purim, in the year 331 [1571] in the abbreviated reckoning.

---

[538] Jonah 1:6.

[539] This is an amusing pun on Job 39:1. God tells the suffering Job, "Where were you when the wild goats of the rock were born?" (הידעת עת לדת יעלי סלע). David uses סלע in the sense of "coin," and not "rock." He sees himself as a Job with daughters!

In Defense of Preachers

A BOOK
IN DEFENSE OF PREACHERS[1]

Which is the introduction to the Book DAVID'S GUIDE,[2] *that has been seen
and praised by the great sages of the world, such as his teachers Rabbi Isaac
Beȥalel, Rabbi Solomon Luria, and Rabbi Moses Isserles, all of blessed
memory,[3] who left [a legacy of] life to all Israel. In addition, many more giants
of the generation, may God protect them all, have praised it effusively. It was
written by that*

*erudite scholar Rabbi David Darshan from Cracow,
son of the martyred sage
Rabbi Manasseh, may God
avenge his blood,
presently
preaching the good
[way] to his people
in the splendid
community of
Lublin.*

He permitted it to be published after he did not succeed in setting
up a Study [Hall] in these provinces, as has been mentioned in the
Introduction to the book *Song of the Steps.*[4] He desires to fulfill his
vow to direct his footsteps to the Holy Land, and there, God willing,
he desires to compile these three treatises, namely the book *David's
Guide,* and the book *David's Tower,* which he has already written; and
the book *David's Glory,* which is still incomplete.[5] And since he
finds that some people deride preaching, he has published some-

---

[1] Yedaiah (Penini) of Béziers at the end of his אגרת התנצלות writes: תם ונשלם כתב
התנצלות.

[2] משכיל can mean "instructional poem" (Psalms, 32, 42, 52, 88, and many
others); or it can mean "guide." Since that is the purpose of the book I use the latter nuance.

[3] These sages died in 1571 and 1573.

[4] See *Hakdama* (Introduction) to *Shir haMa'alot l'David.*

[5] He had not yet given them all as sermons. Cf. Jeremiah 5:13 for usage of the
word דיבר. Cf. also Eliezer Ben-Yehudah, *Dictionary,* vol. 2, p. 8.

thing novel, the Introduction to *David's Guide,* the most precious of pearls, and it is, in fact, *A Book In Defense of Preachers.* May the mouths of the scoffers be stopped up, for they are headed straight for perdition. He has brought evidence from the whole Talmud and *Midrash* [to show that] preaching is divided into several categories, each of them as clear as midday, when the heart is directed to our Father in heaven. Then he demonstrates to the student the basic principle whereby the Torah portion can be linked with the [talmudic] saying and the Midrash. He has taken the first verse of the Torah and deduced many new ideas from it with brevity. And they are all linked to the saying which is the subject of the interpretation, by way of clarification and explanation. It will be as sweet as *spiced wine,*[6] the wise will hear and *increase his learning.*[7] And in the second part we have noted briefly the innovations.

> Let them be examined by
>   whoever so desires.
> Printed shortly after Shavuot
> in the year [1574][8] *God is close*
> *to hasten salvation,* here
> in the capital [city] Lublin.

---

[6] Song of Songs 8:2.

[7] Proverbs 1:5.

[8] The use of the abbreviated form for the Ineffable Name of God in the chronogram קָרוֹב יי for the date misled some scholars, who on the basis of the numerical value of the letters (318) set the date at 1568. Others, seeing קרוב at the end of the line came up with 308, or 1548. Since Moses Isserles and Solomon Luria are referred to as dead on the title page, and they died in 1572 and 1573, the above datings represent a problem. If one takes the numerical value of the four letters of the Ineffable Name as 26, we come to 334, or 1574, which is the date of publication. Many early bibliographers, such as S. Bass, J. C. Wolff, J. Fuerst, Yeḥiel ben Shlomo, and L. Zunz, give the date of 1548. H. M. Ben-Sasson gives the date 1568, while S. van Straalen cites 1571, becausef it is given by David as the year he completed writing the introduction. Cf. *Ktav Hitnaẓẓelut l'Darshanim,* par. 14.

TABLE OF CONTENTS FOR NOVEL INTERPRETATIONS IN THE INTRODUCTION

[9] Proverbs 16:20.

[10] Wherever he here uses the term *ḥakham,* he means *darshan,* and I therefore translate it "preacher." It is about and for the preacher that he is writing.

[11] That is, a kabbalistic idea that must be presented with great caution and reserve.

[12] Yedaiah (haPenini) ben Abraham of Béziers, who died in 1340. His retort to Solomon ben Adret's ban on philosophic studies and his attack on the allegorical interpretations of the sages of Provence appeared in the latter's responsa, first published in Vienna in 1548. It was reprinted in Warsaw in 1881 under the title: אגרות הרשב״א ויכוח אשר היה בין חכמי פרובינציא עם אגרת הבדרש.

[13] Talmud Bavli, *Sanhedrin* 34a.

14. Apologia by the author David, [whose name] has the numerical value of 14.
15. The reason for *no end to the making of books*.[14]
16. The intention of the author to interpret sayings from the Talmud and the Mishnah in a number of ways not found in the earlier [homilists].
17. Clear evidence that it is possible to take the name even of an unworthy human and say that it is an allusion to God, either in a scriptural passage or a passage in the Talmud; and that it is also possible [to assert that] it is an allusion to the Evil Inclination.
18. Some nice reasons why one does not refute a homily.
19. Homilies which rest on a Biblical text affirm that the Bible can never lose its literal sense.[15]
20. Precisely because our knowledge is imperfect, we may explore and interpret the secrets of the *agadot* (i.e., homiletical and allegorical portions of the Talmud) and this [process] does not involve denial[16] or heresy.
21. Most of the *agadot* have a hidden [mystical] meaning and also transmit [ideas] of philosophy.
22. A nice dialectic [to show] why it is permissible to deduce more than one meaning [from a rabbinic saying] when it is alleged that the man who said it meant only one thing.
23. Proof that most of the sayings of the Talmud are metaphors.
24. The preacher may make infinite[17] interpretations on a *Mishnah* or a saying [from the Talmud] in order to strengthen the true faith; and he certainly may bring evidence [for this purpose] from scriptural verses or from the Talmud and *Midrashim*.
25. Why the author chose these three divisions: plain meaning, allegorical [meaning], homiletical [meaning].

---

[14] Ecclesiastes 12:12.

[15] Talmud Bavli, *Shabbat* 63a. Nevertheless, its meaning can be extended by methods of interpretation.

[16] In Judaism the term corresponding to atheism is כפירה בעיקר, or "denial of the essence."

[17] Talmud Bavli, *Erubin* 21b.

TABLE OF CONTENTS OF NOVEL
IDEAS IN THE TREATISE

---

[18] Proverbs 16:20. Note the pun משכיל/אשכילה.

HE THAT GIVETH HEED UNTO THE WORD SHALL FIND GOOD.[18]

ד   1. *I will give heed unto the way of integrity,*[19] *[since] the path of life goeth upward for the wise;*[20] to ascribe greatness unto the Creator,[21] *who fashioned the whole world in its place,* not with toil and exertion, but with a word. As it is written: *By the word of the Lord were [the heavens] made.*[22] And at the end [of the Creation story] he succeeded fully, as it is written: *And God saw all that he had done and behold it was good.*[23] And it is all included in the verse: *He that giveth heed unto the word shall find good.*[24]

ו   2. *And they that are wise will shine as the brightness of the firmanent*[25] in holiness, especially those that are wise in the fivefold books of the Law which God revealed to Moses, together with the Oral Law, which is divided sixfold; and the Ten Commandments, which are the foundation, with each commandment and utterance graven on stone. *The law of Thy mouth is good unto me,*[26] [as] *an inheritance for the congregation of Jacob.*[27] This too can be derived from the verse: *He that giveth heed unto the word shall find good.*

ד   3. The knowledge and the wisdom *to receive instruction*[28] and to conquer the [Evil] Inclination was given to sinners by their Creator; so that He might punish them here and in the hereafter with a time of anguish, or reward them with good and with treasure, as it is written: *The Lord preserveth the faithful.*[29] And it is known that the word *dibbur* (speaking) is used in the sense of extreme and severe rebuke, [so that the sinner might repent] to enable him to merit God's good for Whom noth-

[19] Psalms 101:2. He uses these two separate verses in Biblical-style parallelism.
[20] Proverbs 15:24.
[21] This phrase is from the *Aleinu* prayer.
[22] Psalms 33:6.
[23] Genesis 1:3.
[24] The word משכיל is found in the first two quotations, and טוב, in the second two.
[25] Daniel 12:3. High praise indeed for *darshanim.*
[26] Psalms 119:72.
[27] Deuteronomy 33:4. He uses these two verses to state that the Torah is indeed a good thing for the Jewish people.
[28] Proverbs 1:3.
[29] Psalms 31:21.

ing is impossible. This too can be understood from the short verse: *He that giveth heed unto the word shall find good.*

> Now I shall first explain the
> methods of preaching whose main
> goal is severe reproof to the
> masses of the people.

ר   4. Unlimited are the ways of preaching of the Torah, but they all have one goal to draw the beautiful [i.e., good] close, and to drive the ugly [evil] away. There is a sermon [whose purpose is] to cheer up the exhausted and the overburdened. We find an example of this in the second chapter of *Shabbat,* and the tenth chapter of *Pesaḥim:*[30] *When Rava arose to give his exposition of the Torah he began with something humorous.* In other words, when the sages were weary from their studies, they began exchanging humorous stories. And the exegesis of the Biblical verse that bids us spend a little time to refresh the weary can be found in the verse: *Seek Me* [interpret Me] *and live!*[31]

ר   5. Behold, I found this hyperbole in the Midrash *Song of Songs Rabbah,*[32] that when Rav Yoḥanan began his discourse, and saw that some were dozing off as he spoke, he said to them something impossible to believe [to wit]: *There was one woman in Egypt who bore six hundred thousand!* And they awoke with a start from their sleep laughing at what they heard. Whereupon he explained that it was Yokheved, who bore Moses our Teacher in Egypt, [and he became] the redeemer, who was equated to the whole people [that he led to freedom].[33] And this exposition [in the sermon] which is [intended] to wake up [the listener] who has fallen asleep and does not hear, can be derived from the text: *I will demand it* [i.e., attention] *from the watchman* [i.e., listener].[34]

---

[30] Talmud Bavli, *Shabbat* 30b and *Pesaḥim* 117a.

[31] Amos 5:4. The word דרשוני has the double meaning of "seek" and "interpret." David here takes the latter.

[32] Midrash, *Song of Songs Rabbah* 15:3.

[33] Cf. Exodus 32:10.

[34] Ezekiel 33:6. The word אדרוש can mean either "demand" or "preach." The

ש 6. Now hear this, ye princes of the land. There is an exposition [in a sermon] which the crowd cannot readily understand, because of its stupidity and limited understanding, and the preacher must bring the subject down to their level. For example, the marvels that are related in chapter two of *Shabbat*:[35] *The land of Israel will someday bring forth fine woolen garments and delicate white bread. [And he derived it from the verse:] "May he be as a rich cornfield in the land."*[36] Whereupon a [brazen] student scoffed at this like a troublesome dog, and therefore it was necessary to get rid of his objection.[37] *So he* [Rabban Gamliel] *showed him mushrooms and truffles, and as to [something corresponding] to wool garments,* the student scurried around wherever he could in the hills of palm trees until he showed him *the bark of a young palm.* What Rabban Gamliel was doing here was *to respond to the fool according to his folly.*[38] That was his superficial purpose. But his real intention was to impart understanding of the good things that were in store, as interpreted by the prophets, of the great plenty and tranquility when the Messiah will come at the time of redemption, with the absense of war, and God's right hand triumphant. For the nation and the kingdom which will not serve Israel will be destroyed, and then all will be converted to love God with all his heart, and with all his soul, and with all his might. The Jews will have light,[39] for they will constantly be occupied with the study of Torah. For then will be fulfilled [the scriptural promise]: *Aliens shall be your plowmen and your winedressers,*[40] [and] *comfort*

word הצופה can mean "watchman" (as it does in the text), or "onlooker," or "audience," as it does here.

[35] Talmud Bavli, *Shabbat* 30b, where the discussion is on the subject of speculations on the blessings of the Messianic Age, and how the doubts of a student are dealt with. For a similar theme, cf. Talmud Bavli, *Ketubot* 111b.

[36] Psalms 72:16. David omits the phrase "on the top of the mountains" from the quotation and introduces it here, where he has the student searching on mountaintops.

[37] The verb לפטרו, "to get rid of his objections," is a pun on פטריות, "truffles," in the talmudic text which he quotes.

[38] Proverbs 26:5.

[39] Talmud Bavli, *Sukkah* 8a.

[40] Isaiah 61:5.

ye, comfort ye My people, saith the Lord.[41] And when Rabban Gamliel realized that the crowd had inadequate intellectual capacity to grasp the hyperbolic [description] of the great good [of the messianic era], he described that great good to them in a simpler and less remote fashion. To extract the hidden meaning from it he said: Come and I will show you an example of this in this world [that is, in worldly terms]. Maimonides differs with this approach in his commentary to the Mishnah in the introduction to chapter ten of *Sanhedrin.*[42] And there is a precise verse that refers to the [technique] of interpretation directed to the limited understanding of the untutored, namely: *In the pride of his countenance [the wicked] does not seek Him.*[43]

7. Sometimes the exposition [in a sermon] illuminates a path for the preacher where he [finds it useful] to give it without precise reasons, because of the limited conceptual capacity [of the audience]. And in place [of the interpretation] which is its due, he explains it in simpler terms. For example when [in Talmud *Sukkah*][44] it is stated that *A figure of one square cubit had a diagonal line of one and two-fifths cubits [approximately].* Tossafot explains it [further, by saying]: *There is more to a portion when it is stretched out.* Or, we find [the following] in chapter six of *Genesis Rabbah*: *Rabbi Pinḥas stated in the name of Rav Abba: Where the hosts of the heavens situated? In the second firmament, which is above the heaven. From earth to firmament is a journey of five hundred years, and the depth of the firmament is a journey of five hundred [years]. And from firmament to firmament is a journey of five hundred [years],* and so he demonstrates how high it is. From

[41] Isaiah 40:1.

[42] Maimonides writes, in his commentary to the last chapter of the Mishnah, *Sanhedrin*; ". . . and for the most part, would that the *darshanim* who interpret such matters to the common folk that they themselves do not comprehend, refrain from doing so and keep silent . . . or to say that it is their own humble understanding and to interpret the meaning of the words literally."

[43] Psalms 10:4. We have here, in ידרש דרש, a pun on "seek and interpret." That is, the untutored should not try to understand the ineffable mysteries. It should be simplified and watered down for him.

[44] Talmud Bavli, *Sukkah* 8a, and Midrash, *Genesis Rabbah* 6:6.

this it is found that the distance to the apex of the circle
[orbit] of Saturn is seven thousand years. And he who has
studied the science of astronomy knows that all this is essentially true and correct. But the *agadic* passage just cited does
not go into the kind of precise details as you might find it in
the ספר המרחקים.[45] For the correct distance from the earth to
the apex of the orbit of Saturn is 7,024 years. The knowledge
of the distance of the earth from the planets has two useful
consequences. The first is to fill us with fear and trembling
when we become aware of our tininess, physical and spiritual,
as we compare our insignificance to the vastness of the planets
we behold, and especially the dimensions of the creations
who minister to our God. The second [useful consequence of
this knowledge] is to come to know and to recognize the
Creator's enormous power and perfection, Who moves all
those awesome planets by his power without hand or foot. He
is the Creator, He is the Fashioner,[46] He is the Judge who
causes to know and is known, as it is explained in the ספר
המדע.[47]

And the exposition [in a sermon] for him whose power of
understanding is limited, who, in his own mind is impover-
ished and weak, [is deduced from the text]: *In his disease he
sought not* [the Lord].[48]

מ 8. The experts in preaching made parables and spoke in riddles
when they dealt with homiletical material that was too deep in
concept. [This they did to prevent the crowd] from deducing
the opposite of what [the material] intended, and thereby,
heaven forbid, weakening their faith. But since *it is time to work*

---

[45] *Sefer haMerhakim* was a medieval book about astronomy. Cf. A. Neubauer,
Catalogue of the Hebrew Manuscripts in the Bodleian Library (Oxford, 1886), no. 1296.

[46] His use of the terms *beri'ah* and *yezirah,* technical terms in the kabbalistic creation theory, reflects his knowledge in this area.

[47] Moses ben Maimon, *Mishneh Torah* (Jerusalem, 1955), vol. 1, 2:10.

[48] 2 Chronicles 16:12. David omits the word "the Lord," for he is primarily interested in the words חליו and דרש.

for the Lord, they make void His laws,[49] they presented such ideas publicly in allegorical fashion. Even though these are profound matters, the righteous pursue them. This is illustrated in the first chapter of *Berakhot* in several passages, for example, the passage about Rabbi Ishmael's [experience] when he entered [the Temple] to burn incense,[50] when he said that he saw God[51] with his own eyes, and God said to him: *Ishmael my son, bless me.* Does God, heaven forbid, require [human] blessings? This is a serious problem for those who speculate. The earlier sages discussed this at length, and they explained the term "blessing" as an image wrapped in an image. The real meaning [of blessing] is found in the verse: *And you shall bless the Lord your God,*[52] which was spoken to Moses directly by God, and its purpose is to implant in our hearts the abiding faith that in very truth there is no other helper or supporter than He, and it is He who pours out in abundance, in His mercy, those many blessings upon us. Hence we must exclusively ascribe the power of blessing to our Creator. And the real meaning of the phrase *Ishmael my son, bless me* is: "Affirm that I am the only master and ruler of blessings." And the scriptural source for the exposition, which involves a profound idea, such as matters pertaining to God, *Whose head is a most fine gold,*[53] is found in Isaiah and Jeremiah,[54] and reads: *and they did not seek God.*[55]

[49] Psalms 119:26. Sometimes it is necessary to break the law to preserve it. For the interpretation of this verse in this sense, cf. Talmud Bavli, *Berakhot* 54a, 63a; *Gittin* 60a; and *Terumah* 14b.

[50] *Berakhot* 7a.

[51] This episode describes the highest form of mystical experience. The passage in Berakhot reads: ה' יה אכתריאל ראיתי. David paraphrases it as השם את וראיתי.

[52] Deuteronomy 8:10.

[53] Song of Songs 5:11.

[54] Isaiah 31:1 and Jeremiah 10:21.

[55] David reverses the idea for his purpose. The prophets bemoaned the fact that the people did not follow God, whereas he read it: "Don't seek God," that is, mystical interpretations that confront God's ultimate reality must be presented in veiled fashion.

ק 9. Yet another voice is heard in the exposition of the Torah in
our Talmud, in matters which the preacher sees in a dream,
and not in real life. For example, in chapter five of *Baba Batra*,
in the stories of Rabbi Bar Bar Hana,[56] concerning which the
sages wrote: *In such instances wherever one finds it stated "I saw it
myself"* [לדידי חזי לי], their teaching is concerned with a dream
[and not reality]. And these matters were written in concealed
fashion, because they contain many hidden ideas, which not
everybody merits knowing, because they are not sufficiently
purified in their deeds and in their speculation.[57] *A dream is
one-sixtieth of prophecy*[58] *[and may be properly used to bring good tidings to the weary people]* who are six hundred thousand in their
numbers and who in the future will rejoice and be happy in
all their affairs.[59] For their function as preachers is to do good
and not harm.[60] And you can derive this from Amos, who
wrote: *Seek good and not evil.*[61]

ר 10. Furthermore, our Master Moses [ben Maimon] was vouch-
safed a divine insight when he wrote in his introduction to the
Mishnah *Zeraim* that he considered the arranging of agadic
material in the Talmud by Rav Ashi as the height of wisdom;
and he wrote that one ought not think that the homiletical
material [in the Talmud] is of minor importance and of little
value, for it has a very important and rare meaning, containing many secrets and precious wonders. For when a rational
approach is taken to these expositions, it is possible to arrive
at an understanding of the general, abstract good. Now those
who practiced the homiletical art concealed such matters,
preferring not to expose them explicitly. For if you were to
look carefully at its plain meaning, you would find it difficult

---

[56] Talmud Bavli, *Baba Batra* 73 ff. Here we find a series of fanciful adventure
yarns.

[57] This refers to the special regimen for those who study Kabbalah.

[58] Talmud Bavli, *Berakhot* 57b.

[59] Note the pun, ששים/שמים, that is, "sixty" and "rejoice."

[60] Here there is a caution against the too widespread teaching of Kabbalah. See
Moses Isserles, *Torat haOlah* (Prague, 1567), pt. 3, chap. 4.

[61] Amos 5:14.

to understand; [hence] they set aside this matter [to be considered] with deeper matters [i.e., set aside for deeper philosophical and mystical considerations]. In the first place [they did this] to sharpen the thoughts of the students, that they might become selected initiates in the mysteries of the Divine; and secondly, to blind the eyes of fools that they apply their thoughts to revealed, and not to secret doctrine. For their intellect is not adequate [perfect] ever to face such [mystical] truths. And he gave further evidence [in support of] agadic expositions. And this is derived from the verse: *And Moses diligently inquired.*[62]

א 11. The Bedersi speaks the truth[63] in his *Ktav haHitnazzelut,*[64] when he divides [agadic] homilies into several categories. The first concerns a saying that relates some extraordinary matter that does not fly in the face of the natural order; however, it is probably unlikely that it would come about through an unusual cause.[65] In such a case we leave [the saying] at its plain meaning, for we may properly rely upon that complete [sage] who has made the statement, who bears witness to it in his time.

The second concerns sayings which relate some extraordinary matter that is outside the natural order [i.e., a miracle]. We leave them in their plain meaning as they are revealed,

---

[62] Leviticus 10:16. For the full text about Maimonides' statement on interpretation in preaching, see his introduction to his commentary on the Mishnah. Cf. Talmud Bavli, supplement to *Berakhot* in *M'Orot* edition, 50a. Basically this is a summary of that section, with many direct quotations.

[63] Proverbs 8:7.

[64] Cf. note 12.

[65] David excerpts the Bedersi argument and does it well. The latter's first category reads as follows: The first category—all [agadic] passages that report some extraordinary event which may be possible from the point of view of our own experience or the laws of nature, yet is unlikely in terms of remote possibilities whose existence is difficult to conceive, and which come into being with difficulty through strange causes and in a distant future; every matter of this kind that is related, from which neither strengthening of faith nor damaging it can be derived, we leave in its plain meaning, for we may properly rely upon that complete [sage], who has made the statement, who bears witness to it in his time.

like the other signs and miracles of the prophets and the
Torah, for there are elements in them that strengthen the
faith. For example, there are the miracles that were performed for the exalted saints, men of understanding, as
recorded in the third chapter of the [talmudic] Tractate
Ta'anit,[66] about Naḥum of Gamzu and Rabbi Ḥanina, and the
rest of the elect. And in this category there are also the signs
and the miracles that were performed in the Holy Temple, as
well as the resurrection of the dead, [a miracle] which God
will perform at some future time.

The third are sayings which run counter to the natural
order, which reason cannot accept and from which nothing
useful to the [strengthening of] faith can be deduced. But its
function is to give the students a respite from the intensity of
their studies, as, for example, the humorous stories of Rabbi
bar bar Ḥannah[67] and the like. These we must allegorize even
when the stories are seen within God's power to achieve
them,[68] for God does not lightly perform miracles, only for
saints in the time of their need, as it is explained at great
lengths [by the Bedersi].[69]

The fourth are statements which also record the transfor-
mation of the impossible [into the possible];[70] even though
they bolster faith like fortifications, we must strip them of
their surface meaning (i.e., allegorize them], for their judgments should not have greater weight than the literal
interpretation of the Torah and prophets.[71] And this is attested by the statements [of the sages] of blessed memory in the

[66] Talmud Bavli, *Ta'anit* 21a.

[67] Talmud Bavli, *Baba Batra* 73b.

[68] Even though it is possible for God to cause this, it is nonetheless pure fiction.

[69] The Bedersi lists many examples of how God is sparing in intervention by
miracles.

[70] That is, miracles.

[71] The sentence is not in order because of the rhyme. It should read: שלא יהיו יקר
משפטם מפשוטי התורה והנביאים. He forces the syntax considerably to achieve a rhyme.

chapters on the Chariot,[72] and I quote:[73] *Rabbi Ishmael said: "Whoever knows the dimensions of the Creator is assured of a place in the world to come."* It is also attested by [statements] in the first chapter of *Berakhot* [which quotes God as saying]: *Woe is me that I destroyed My Temple,*[74] or [the passage that states that] God wears phylacteries,[75] and many passages of this nature. We must examine such passages carefully by every method of philosophical approach in such a way as to prevent any possible anthropomorphic interpretation, as we do in the case of the interpretation of any scriptural passage that describes God in finite fashion. In those cases we must alter their surface meaning [by allegorical interpretation], to avoid the guilt [of such a sin], and explain them in such a way as to cause no harm, and to make it possible to be understood.[76] Or [in passages] that point to God's providence for Israel, as for example [in the statement] that wherever they were exiled, the *Shekhinah,* God's presence, went with them,[77] or the verse *that dwelleth with them in the midst of their uncleanness,*[78] which was interpreted to mean that even when they were in exile, He would fulfill their heart's desire (that is, cause the Messiah to come). And this idea is implicit in the verse *sought out of all them that have delight therein.*[79]

ק 12. Draw near to hear more. There are some conclusions in the Talmud that contradict one another. For example, in

---

[72] He is here referring to the mystical book שעור קומה, from which he proceeds to quote.

[73] שעור קומה is included in ספר רזיאל (Lemberg 1804), p. 35a, see also Eisenstein, אוצר מדרשים, vol. 2, p. 562.

[74] Talmud Bavli, *Berakhot* 3a.

[75] Ibid. 6a.

[76] See Rashi to Exodus 19:18, which reads, "to make clear to the ear in a manner that it can understand" [אנו מכנין אותו לבריאותו כדי לשבר את האוזן מה שהיא יכולה לשמע].

[77] Talmud Bavli, *Megillah* 29a.

[78] Leviticus 16:10.

[79] Psalms 111:16.

chapter three of *Moed Katan*[80] [we read]: *Length of life, children, and sustenance depend not on merit, but on the stars*; while in chapter twenty-four of *Shabbat*[81] we are informed: *The stars do not guide Israel*; and in chapter two of *Sukkah*[82] [we see that citing such contradictions] is [an integral part] of the talmudic discussion. And the specially elect [sages] all agreed that the maxim *everything depends on the stars* is held [only] by a few; for it contradicts the plain meaning of our perfect Torah, which is sealed with the concept of reward and punishment.[83] Hence the sages, in chapter twenty-four of *Shabbat,* interpreted the verse *and he brought him forth abroad*[84] as the source for their injunction: *give up thy astrological speculation* in a hurry. And evil (i.e, divine retribution) will overcome the wicked even if he always has a favorable horoscope. And the sign of this is the verse from Proverbs 11:26: *He that searcheth for evil, it shall come to him.*

א 13. Let me instruct further by referring to interpretations of the [sages] who preceded us, matters, occasionally found in the Talmud, that are a received tradition, of which there is no reference in the Torah, whereupon the sage must base it upon a scriptural verse by [a process of] deduction. This [process] has two advantages: to make these interpretations fluent in the mouths of the teacher and student alike, and secondly to enhance their importance with the crowd, for with their lim-

[80] Talmud Bavli, *Moed Katan* 28a. The quotation is garbled. The correct reading is חיי בני.

[81] Talmud Bavli, *Shabbat* 156a. The difference of opinion on the efficacy of astrology is here expressed, with Ḥanina for, and Joḥanan against it.

[82] Cf. Talmud Bavli, *Sukkah* 26b, where the *Gemara* notes that the law stated in the *Mishnah* that is being discussed is contradicted in the preceding *Mishnah*. See Rashi to this passage.

[83] And therefore you do not accept the idea of the guiding force of astrology.

[84] Genesis 5:15, where God takes Abraham out and shows him the stars of heaven, promising him that his seed would be as numerous. In addition to Talmud Bavli, *Shabbat* 156a, see also Talmud Bavli, *Nedarim* 32a and *Yoma* 28b. These passages reject astrology, but the *Targum* to Ecclesiastes 1:2, Rashi to Talmud Bavli, *Shabbat* 75a, and the *Zohar* to the sidra *Naso* in Numbers affirm it.

ited understanding they have not the remotest perception
whether that [Biblical] verse is to be taken at its plain meaning
or as a support for a rabbinical enactment. An example of
this is to be found in the first chapter of *Erubin*[85] [where it is
stated]: *[The laws pertaining to] standards, interpositions, and parti-
tions are [part of] the halakhah [that was given] to Moses at Sinai.*
The person raising the question maintains [that the *principle
of] limits derives from the Torah* and is based on the verse *a land of
wheat and barley,*[86] and Rabbi Isaac[87] says: *this entire verse applies
to standards.* To this the instructor can only reply that this is
not part of the *halakhah* that was given to Moses at Sinai, but
that the text is just used as a support for it [i.e., this rabbinical
enactment]. This is done so that the student might allow his
mind to forage about in the methods of acquiring fluency in
interpreting the perfect Torah. And the reference to this is
found in *Kohelet*:[88] *to seek and to search out by wisdom,*

14. Says the humble one, David [the] Preacher from Cracow, whose
name is inscribed [in acrostic as the first letter of each of the
preceding sections]: After [having completed] this introduction, with the help of the Most High who created heaven and
earth, *the right hand of the Lord exalts*[89] me, to thank Him with
praise and song, for having kept me in life and brought me
this far. For He has bestowed His wondrous mercy upon me
in miraculous fashion, rescuing me from so many terrors and
hardships as I wandered about and was buffeted from my ear-

[85] Talmud Bavli, *Erubin* 4a.

[86] Deuteronomy 8:8. The linking of the talmudic text to the Bible, using the
general principle of *gezerah shavah*—that is, similarity of words in differing con-
texts—is here made by a pun, שיעורין/שיעורין ("barley"/"limits").

[87] Talmud Bavli, loc. cit., reads: "Rabbi Ḥanan says, 'This entire verse applies to
limits.'" David's use here is puzzling, unless he is referring to Rashi's interpretation of this phrase, which suggested the use of the principle of a scriptural text supporting a rabbinic enactment.

[88] Ecclesiastes 1:13. In connection with the advice to explore wisdom, the words
לדרוש ולתור are used. Thus, says David, the preacher should always immerse himself
[שיתור לבו] in practicing his preaching [בחכמת הרגל דרושי התורה].

[89] Psalms 118:16.

liest years, with one setback after another, *for my comeliness was turned into corruption*.[90] The light of my intellect was progressively dimmed, for I was barred, against my will, from the academies of the Torah. There, many of the privileged [class] in learning and in wealth turned against me in several provinces, and prevented me from studying Torah in the proper time, because I was considered a pariah among them. It came to such a pass that my plight was reminiscent of scripture describing how David fled *to the fortress*[91] [from the Philistines]. For no [apparent] reason whatsoever they made me the center of controversy, and *David's place was empty*[92] in the academy. They also made it difficult for me to make a living by preventing students from studying with me and hearing Torah from me. They acted toward me as did King Ahaz [in his time],[93] until my heart within me pounded with fear that I might, God forbid, forget the Torah completely. So I said to myself: "Pay no attention *to that rebellious house*,"[94] and the spirit of God unfolded me like a garment, and I was sustained by a bounteous[95] spirit from the small amounts of water which I drew in joy[96] [from the wells of salvation] of many *yeshivah*-heads, namely the sages of Russia, Poland, Moravia, and Italy. They were the giants [of Torah] in Israel, always prepared [to help] any [student] with a problem.

15. Thus, in honor of the God of Israel, and of those who have taught me, I was persuaded to write several books to fulfill [the scriptural verse] *to bring forth the precious from the vile*[97] such

[90] Daniel 10:8.

[91] See Isaiah 23:16 and 25:5 ff.

[92] Isaiah 20:25.

[93] This is a very bitter comment, for Ahaz sacrificed his own son to Moloch! Cf. 2 Samuel 16:3.

[94] Ezekiel 27:3.

[95] See Psalms 68:10 for use of the term נדבות in this sense.

[96] See Isaiah 12:3. He alters the verse to apply it to himself by changing the verb from the second-person plural to the first-person singular.

[97] Judges 15:19. This *darshan* is drawn consistently to the image of Jeremiah's call to prophecy and to preaching. See the Introduction to *Shir haMa'alot l'David*.

as I. As [King] Solomon, of blessed memory wrote:[98] *Of the making of books there should be no end* to remove abomination and filth from the heart. For in writing reproofs and [giving guidance] in elevating oneself from baseness of spirit, [the preacher] is expressing his amazement, as is the case with leaven: *[when] he himself is seeking it in order to burn it, shall he then eat thereof!?*[99]

16. So I used to *give heed unto* a new *word* which I initiated, and which no one before me had used and I found something *good*[100] with which to begin in the matter of preaching [by interpreting the text] in three ways.[101] I am referring to the method used by our Master Baḥyah [ben Asher] in his Commentary to the Torah,[102] who interprets many scriptural verses in this manner. I have examined books by many outstanding writers, and have not found texts interpreted from the philosophical point of view except in the book דרך אמונה[103] and there some *agadot* and talmudic sayings are interpreted from the philosophical point of view but no other. The author of עקדת יצחק, Isaac Arama also uses only one method of interpretation. Thus the other homilists, as for example RaShbA[104] and the author of פרדס רמונים.[105] Hence it was my intention to explain some Talmudic sayings and passages from the Mishnah which were not dealt with by earlier [homi-

---

[98] Ecclesiastes 12:12.

[99] Talmud Bavli, *Pesaḥim* 11a.

[100] He refers again to Proverbs 16:20, with which he began. See paragraph 1.

[101] Bahya ben Asher introduced the fourfold interpretation of a text in preaching, borrowing from the method used by the Church Fathers: *p'shat*, the literal meaning; *d'rash*, the meaning in the light of rabbinic exegesis, i.e., the homiletical meaning; *sekhel*, the meaning from the allegorical point of view; and finally, *sod*, the mystical interpretation. For the masses, our author omits the fourth, because this was discouraged at the time. Cf. M. Isserles, *Torah haOlah* (Prague, 1569), chap. 4.

[102] *Biur Torah*, first printed in Pesaro in 1507.

[103] Abraham ben Shem Tov Bibago, *Derekh Emunah* (Constantinople, 1521).

[104] Solomon ben Adret.

[105] This was a systematic philosophic treatment of Kabbalah by Moses Cordovero (1522–1570).

lists], so as not to transgress the dictum: *Thou shalt not remove the landmark of the first pilgrims*[106] (i.e., do not plagiarize those who said it first!). I have prepared four different (interpretations for each Torah portion, and the intimation of this is in the [passage]: *Four cries did the Temple Court utter.*[107] With this resource the preacher will be able to preach in the *Temple Court* every Sabbath for four consecutive years something new interpreted in several ways without being upbraided [for repeating himself]. I shall carefully explain to us all, and bring support from earlier sages the sense of these [three] ways and the validity of this method in interpretation. This we shall do so that it not be said of me that I am *a citizen on earth and an alien in heaven!*[108]

17. First of all, let me explain that it is possible to take the name of a reprehensible man and to say that it is an allusion to the unalterable God. For example we find that the *Recanati,*[109] in his commentary [to the Torah], writes that Laban is a symbolic reference to the Holy One Praised be He, and he does the same with [the name] Ahasuerus, using a homily about the Ineffable Name,[110] a reference from *Genesis Rabbah, Vayeze,* as a basis for this. And should you argue: granted that we can say that [the name] Laban is [an allegory for] the [Ineffable] Name, for the entire Torah contains [in all its letters] the Names of the Holy One Praised be He;[111] but the Mishnah and the Talmud are not in that category, hence this approach is not here possible. [To this I counter] with my humble judg-

---

[106] Talmud Bavli, *Peah* 5b, and Deuteronomy 19:14. The author uses the quotation from *Peah,* where it cautions against interference with the rights of the poor. The word עולים is there interpreted to mean, "the poor." The author adds the word ראשונים and turns the phrase to mean "first pilgrims," that is, originators of an idea.

[107] Talmud Bavli, *Pesaḥim* 57a.

[108] Ibid., *Yoma* 47a.

[109] Menaḥem ben Benjamin Recanati (late 13th cent.) was an Italian kabbalist and halakhic authority, and author of a kabbalistic commentary to the Torah.

[110] For this usage see Midrash, *Tanḥuma,* to the pericope *Emor* (Leviticus 21 ff).

[111] Cf. Moses ben Naḥman's introduction to his commentary on Genesis (Charles B. Chavel, *Ramban: Commentary on the Torah* [New York, 1971], vol. 1).

ment that it is permissible, and the evidence for it is there. For we find that our Master Baḥya and the מדרש הנעלם from the *Zohar*[112] frequently derive the [idea of] the Evil Inclination from many words and names, and in the whole Torah there are sacred words which, by interpretation, are diminished for a lesser meaning. All the more so when we move up to holiness and declare that the names of the *Tannaim* and the *Amoraim* are used to suggest the First Cause. And similarly we may say that the names of the *Tannaim* and the *Amoraim* are sometimes used to suggest the Evil Inclination, that the names of the students not be honored, while the names of the masters are being degraded. We can even say that they are used to suggest one righteous Messiah, as for instance, *Rav Ḥanina says Ḥanina is his name, for it is written: "gathereth it for him that is gracious to the poor."*[113] Also, *Rav Yanai says his name is Yinun,* as it is stated in chapter eleven of *Sanhedrin*[114] and in [the *Midrash*] *Lamentations Rabbah.*[115] You will find the interpretation of names in many places in the Talmud and *Midrashim.* For example, in the first chapter of *Megillah*[116] [you find]: *Ben Yair, a son who illuminated the eyes of Israel in prayer; ben Shim'i, for God hears the prayers of the innocent; ben Kish, who pressed the Gates of Forgiveness.* And there they also draw a message from the names of Moses our Teacher. We find such examples in thousands of places.

18. The upshot of the matter is that we do not try to refute a *midrash* [i.e., an interpretation from the text] which can be interpreted in many ways. In the first place, because at times the *darshan* himself knows that there is a contradiction in it, but he avoids pointing it out because he wants to sustain his argument against the opinion [that it expresses]. The Talmud abounds in such examples, wherein the expounder refutes the

---

[112] An appendix to the *Zohar*.
[113] Proverbs 28:8.
[114] Talmud Bavli, *Sanhedrin* 98b.
[115] Midrash, *Lamentations Rabbah* 16:51.
[116] Talmud Bavli, *Megillah* 12a.

arguments of the objector, even when he knows in his heart that the other side is right. And sometimes he knows there is a contradiction and knows the resolution to it, but says nothing because it would be too long [to explain]. Now in order that we not be maligned for this statement, we can refer to chapter ten of *Yevamot*:[117] *Rav Papa desired to decide a case on the principle of "What could she have done"* [since it was an ex post facto situation]. *Rav Huna, son of Rav Josiah, said: "Shall we then rely on explanations?!" So Rav Papa desisted* [then and for all time]. Furthermore most textual interpretation are made with special corroboration and scriptural verses and simply additional support for them.

19. But they agree that a Bible verse cannot lose its literal sense. Not, however, in the way that RaSHbA[118] wrote in paragraph 416 concerning the Sages of Provence [whom he attacked for] preaching tainted sermons,[119] replacing the literal sense with the allegorical interpretation as the true meaning. However, he wrote this before the appearance of the כתב ההתנצלות [of the Bedersi]. Of course we should never tamper with the literal sense of a Bible verse, for that literal sense is certainly primary. However, there are some cases [in the Talmud] where an analogy completely alters the plain meaning [of a Bible verse], as, for example, in chapter two of *Yevamot* [in the matter of]: *he shall succeed in the name of his father's [brother].*[120] And

---

[117] Talmud Bavli, *Yevamot* 91b. A series of decisions, previously cited, indicated that "what could she have done?" suggested that the person involved might have been more careful. Rav Papa was aware of this but felt a need to be more liberal and humane in giving relief to the *agunah* (a woman whose husband had disappeared but could not remarry because his death had not been established).

[118] This reflects the struggle against the Provence mystics in the thirteenth century. They were influenced by Neoplatonism and radically allegorized scriptures. Cf. note 12.

[119] For the phrase, דרשות של דופי, see Talmud Bavli, *Sanhedrin* 99b: מנשה בן חזקיה שהיה יושב ודורש בהגדות של דופי.

[120] Talmud Bavli, *Yevamot* 24a, where, despite the plain meaning of the text, Deuteronomy 25:6, the child born from the levirate union need not be named after the deceased.

perhaps it is the truth that this method [of not expanding the literal meaning of a scriptural text by interpretation] was a problem for some sages, as we find it stated in chapter six of *Shabbat: Rav Kahana said: "By the time I was eighteen years old, I had already studied the entire Talmud, yet I was not aware [of the principle] that a [Bible] cannot depart from its plain meaning until today."*[121] However, observe the great wisdom of the sages in the phrasing [of the principle] that a Bible verse does not lose its literal sense, instead of saying that the Bible verse is *only* to be taken literally. [Had they done this] they would have shown that they intended [to prohibit extension of meaning by interpretation]. For interpretation and literal meaning do not need to be in conflict. The text [is strong enough] to support all [interpretation], and both [interpretation and literal meaning] can be true. The great Rabbi, Moses ben Naḥman (Naḥmanides), went into this at great length in his commentary to Maimonides' ספר המצות on the six hundred and thirteen commandments. And I myself have done that with sayings [from the Talmud] and some passages from the Mishnah, [demonstrating] the relationship of the literal meaning to the homiletical meaning, [complete] with reasons and evidence. All this, in order to preach and receive the rewards [for righteous deeds] and not to behold the Abyss as in the case of the rebellious son[122] and the proscribed city,[123] both of which never happened and never will, but are cited to be interpreted [by preachers] for the purpose of gaining the rewards [of avoiding such sins]. In the same manner there are some *halakhot* in the Talmud which mention things that never happen, whose purpose it is to instruct us in the Law and to interpret [their meaning] so that we might receive the reward [of doing the righteous deeds]. This is elucidated at length in *Tossafot* at the end of chapter twenty-three of *Shabbat*.

---

[121] Talmud Bavli, *Shabbat* 63a.

[122] Deuteronomy 21:18.

[123] Deuteronomy 13:13 ff.

20. Indeed, our human limitations and our ignorance are precisely what comes to our rescue.[124] For, were it in our power to understand the secret meaning of the *agadot* without difficulty, we should have been forbidden to interpret them altogether, as we find it stated by Rabbi Solomon ben Adret (RaSHbA) in his apologia which he wrote to explain why, after committing himself to write a commentary on the *agadot,* he decided not to do so, for were he to interpret them fully, he would be in the position of revealing mystical insights,[125] thereby subverting the intention of those who concealed them, guided by the purest of motives.[126] And were he to write it in clandestine and secret fashion, his original intention would not be realized.[127] Therefore, it is better that they remain as they are (i.e., uninterpreted), so that they are kept in the category of mysteries of the Torah, whose interpretation is forbidden, and they are left for the experts and sages in the field alone to explore. It is thus clearly established that sermons in public interpreting any *agadot* which are expressed in allegorical fashion [to conceal mystical meaning] are prohibited. Those who deal publicly with mystical themes bear the gravest responsibility[128] that their interpretation not lead to any manner of denial or heresy. He further stated, in his apologia, the central point that if it does not damage [the listener's] faith, philosophy may be included as we find it in the Ecclesiastes, whose words are words of Torah from beginning to end, receiving the truth from Him who uttered it [i.e., God].[129] The author of the *Guide* [Mai-

---

[124] Literally, "are in truth our remedy."

[125] Literally, "secret things."

[126] Literally, "who walked in the way of righteousness and innocence" (in contrast to the heretical uses to which mystical knowledge might be put, and its destructive consequences).

[127] That is, to instruct the people.

[128] He uses the term אשם ודאי (which he reverses). Cf. Mishnah, *Keritut* 3:1. The literal meaning of the term is: "definite guilt."

[129] Literally, "he received the truth from whomever said it."

monides] does the same thing in his eight chapters,[130] and we find a similar idea in the Introduction to *Menorat haMaor* of Rav Sherira Gaon.

21. It is written that most *agadot* contain heavenly mysteries and wisdom, [as well as guidance] in good manners, righteous conduct, ethical instruction, and the renewal of body and soul in the good qualities of the righteous.

22. Should you say, who authorized us to interpret a saying in more than one way, perhaps it has only one meaning? Or, how can we say that this is the proper meaning, perhaps, heaven forbid, [the preacher] distorts the meaning? Granted [in the case of] that which God spoke through the mouth of the prophet, we can maintain that its intended meaning corresponds to the *darshan*'s interpretation. But can we, with regard to what the sage has said on the basis of his own conclusions, say that what he intended conforms to our own interpretation of it? We shall see that these objections are not valid from the outset. We can cite as evidence [for our position] the passage from the tractate *Megillah*,[131] where, in a *Baraitha*[132] the question is posed as to her real intentions, when Esther invited Haman to the banquet.[133] One offers one theory,[134] one offers another, and what they end up with is an inference. *Rav encountered Elijah and asked him: Which of these reasons prompted Esther to act as she did? He replied: [All] the reasons given by all the Tannaim and all the Amoraim.* And should you say, perhaps there was divine inspiration in her words, as has been deduced from the verse *Esther put on her royal apparel,*[135] it is

---

[130] See Moses ben Maimon, *Guide of the Perplexed* (Pines translation), at the beginning of chap. 28.

[131] Talmud Bavli, *Megillah,* 15b.

[132] These are traditions and opinions of the *Tannaim* that are not embodied in the Mishnah.

[133] Esther 5:4, Talmud Bavli, *Megillah* 15a.

[134] In the passage cited in Talmud Bavli, *Megillah* 15b, many sages give a variety of motives for Esther inviting Haman to the feast. The fact that *all* are justified is David's justification for varieties of interpretation.

[135] Esther 5:1.

proper to counter this with the quotation from the first chapter of *Baba Batra*: *A wise man is even superior to a prophet,*[136] as it says: *that we may get us a heart of wisdom.*[137] *Who is compared with whom? Is not the smaller compared with the greater?*[138] The reason for this is that the prophet has only the signal that he gets from heaven, while [what emerges from] the understanding heart has a double value! We have evidence for this from the first chapter of *Arakhin* with respect to the prophet Joshua and the sage Othniel ben Kenaz,[139] for the sage Othniel revealed what Joshua the prophet concealed. And it is further stated in the first chapter of *Avodah Zarah:*[140] *Even the ordinary talk of scholars needs study*—to understand them. And as Solomon says [in Proverbs]:[141] *To understand a proverb and a figure, the words of the wise and their sayings.*

23. As evidence that most of the sayings of the sages are arranged [in the Talmud] as parables we can cite the passage in chapter six of *Erubin*[142] which states: *Rav Eliezer had a disciple who once gave a legal opinion in his presence.*[143] *"I wonder,"* he remarked to his wife, *"whether this man will live out the year."* And it came to pass as he predicted. *Rabbi bar Bar Hana related in the name of Rav Yohanan: That disciple's name was Judah ben Guria, and he was three parasangs distant from him. He was in his presence [when he taught the halakhah]* explained the instructor. *But was it not stated that he was three parasangs away?* countered the questioner. The explainer [in his retort] brought this as evi-

---

[136] Talmud Bavli, *Baba Batra* 12a.

[137] Psalms 90:12. "To get us a heart of wisdom." By means of a pun, the verb is taken to mean "prophet" and not "get"!

[138] For purposes of rhyme, David substitutes השפל בגבוה רמה for the talmudic קטן נטלה בגדול.

[139] The reference to Othniel is to be found in Talmud Bavli, *Temurah* 16a, and not in Talmud Bavli, *Arakhin.*

[140] Talmud Bavli, *Avodah Zarah* 19b.

[141] Proverbs 1:6.

[142] Talmud Bavli, *Erubin* 63a.

[143] This is categorically forbidden. See Talmud Bavli, *Berakhot* 31b, where it is stated that a student who does this is worthy of death!

dence: *According to your conception, what need was there for the mention of the disciple's name and the name of his father? The fact is that all the details were given in order that it not be said that the whole story was a fable.* This episode clearly proves [by the denial] that most of the words of the sages was based on riddles and fables. And just as it is permissible to deduce unlimited interpretations[144] from *halakhot,* we can do the same with the stories of the sages.*

25. To begin with, I elucidate the passage briefly through its PLAIN MEANING, to set at ease any problems the reader might have with an apparent contradiction [in meaning]. Then I go in greater detail [to interpret] the passage through its ALLEGORI-CAL MEANING,[145] because man is drawn after the Evil Inclination and earthly things, and there is neither escape nor succor from them, as we read in the Book of Ecclesiastes. *For there is not a righteous man upon earth that doeth good and sinneth not.*[146] So I present some examples, [hinted at in Scripture], to demonstrate how the Evil Inclination brazenly tries to gain mastery over us, and how the mind can overcome it with [allegorical] arguments that support the need to afflict [oneself] and suppress physical drives[147] in times of temptation,[148] and this is made clear in the Tractate *Tamid,* where the sages of Palestine[149] [stated]:[150] *He who wishes to live must slay himself.* By this they meant that he who wishes to be resurrected into the world to come, and to enjoy the things hidden away [for that purpose], should slay his desires and refrain from enjoying the pleasures of this world. We find an example of this in

---

* For 24. see page 170.

[144] Literally, "to teach mound of rules on every tip" (of letters in the Torah). See Talmud Bavli, *Erubin* 21b.

[145] The use of *sekhel* as the equivalent of *remez* in the fourfold interpretation of Torah texts (*PaRDeS*) is found in Baḥya ben Asher. Cf. note 101.

[146] Ecclesiastes 7:20.

[147] Literally, "affairs of the flesh."

[148] Literally, "in stressful times."

[149] He writes חכמי הנגב. The Babylonian Talmud uses the term מערבא.

[150] Talmud Bavli, *Tamid* 32a.

Rashi's interpretation of the verse[151] in Psalm 16, when David our King, reflecting deeply within himself, says: *I have said unto the Lord, Thou art my God*; and in Psalm 27: *In thy behalf my heart hath said, "See ye my face."*[152] And this, in itself, prompted me to interpret it in ALLEGORICAL FASHION, in order that the plowman shall not plow to fulfill his lusts,[153] and thus gain the rewards of hoped-for goods [namely]: resurrection, the world to come, and the time of the Messiah, which are interpreted from the prophets and the Talmud [from texts] which are not revealed to the crowd, and which are sometimes concealed even from some students.

Therefore I have chosen the three methods of interpretation, with the help of Him who dwells on high, corresponding to the three ways in which I interpreted the verse *He that giveth heed to the word shall find good* at the beginning of the introduction. Corresponding to the Creator, who is the flawless Absolute Intellect,[154] I again interpret by way of PLAIN MEANING [פשט]. And corresponding to the Torah and the Commandments, concerning which it is written: *A good understanding* [שכל] *have they that do thereafter,*[155] I interpret in the ALLEGORICAL MANNER for them. And corresponding to the reproofs and the moral suasion which are appropriate for all, for it is written of them: *to receive the discipline of wisdom,*[156] and it is by virtue of this moral discipline that we merit the [coming of] the Redeemer, of whom it is written: *and he shall reign as king and prosper*[157] [והשכיל] and be successful. I interpret in the HOMILETICAL MANNER, whose central theme is redemption, for the word *haMaskil* [means] Messiah. Now, since all these [three] ways are implied by the word שכל, I have

---

[151] Psalms 16:3. See Rashi to this passage and Talmud Bavli, *Menaḥot* 53a.

[152] Psalms 27:8.

[153] That is, restraint and an ascetic way help achieve the goals of the righteous.

[154] David uses the term *sekhel pashut* in this sense with a pun on pashut to refer to interpretation by plain meaning (*pshat*).

[155] Psalms 111:10.

[156] Proverbs 1:3.

[157] Jeremiah 23:5.

named this book *Maskil l'David* (David's Guide) and this [hint] is sufficient unto those who know and understand [esoteric meanings].

Now, in order that the verse *And David had great success [maskil] in all his ways and God was with him*[158] apply to me, as does the verse *A [Psalm] of David when he changed his demeanor*[159] for good, in joy and song, I have composed this introduction during the three days[160] before the Feast of Weeks in the year *she is more precious* [1571],[161] and it is in truth an Essay in Defense of Preachers.

26. At the end of the first chapter of *Yevamot* we read:[162]

Rav Hamnuna sat before Ulla, and was engaged in discussing a traditional law, when the latter remarked, "What a man! And how much more important would he have been had not Harpania[163] been his native town." As the other was embarrassed, he said to him, "Where do you pay poll tax?"—"To Pum Nahara," the other said. "If so," Ulla said, "you belong to Pum Nahara."

Rashi's comment [to the above text]: *And was arguing against it. Rav Ulla says of Rav Hamnuna: "What a man and what strength!" That is to say, what a great man he is! "Had not Harpania been his native town"* [meaning] *their heredity is tainted, and it is a place whither those of tainted heredity who cannot therefore find a wife go [for that purpose].*

There are [many] problems here that we must raise:

What was Rav Ulla's purpose in embarrassing Rav Ham-

---

[158] 1 Samuel 18:14.

[159] Psalms 54:1. King David changes his demeanor to feign madness; David Darshan turns the meaning in the opposite direction.

[160] That is, the שלשה ימי הגבלה, the three days of preparation for revelation at Mount Sinai, when the people were forbidden to approach the mount. Cf. Exodus 19:10–13.

[161] The numerical value of [[מפנינים] יקרה היא] is 331, i.e., (5)331 or 1571.

[162] Talmud Bavli, *Yevamot* 17a.

[163] Hipparenum, which was a wealthy industrial town in the Mesene district, an island territory lying between the Tigris and Euphrates, inhabited by a Jewish community of tainted ancestry, descendants of the Ten Tribes exiled by the Assyrians.

nuna inasmuch as he was bright and raising problems [about the matter under discussion]?

Was this a fitting thing for a man as eminent as he to do? Indeed, he should have praised him, as we find it [done] in many places in the Talmud, as, for example, in chapter four of the tractate *Me'ilah*[164] [where Rav Ḥanina raised an objection to] a tradition taught by Rab, *whereupon Rav Yoḥanan praised him, etc.*

And even in the case of someone not so bright, he ought not to have acted in this manner, because [of the principle]: *Open thy mouth for the dumb.*[165]

Furthermore, why should Rav Hamnuna have been embarrassed? He ought to have replied at once: "I am from Pum Nahara."

Now you might argue that Rav Hamnuna lived in Harpania because he had married a woman from there, but had paid his head tax to the town where he was born; and because of this fact was embarrassed, because he was under the impression that Ulla believed that genealogical status is determined by place of residence. This might explain why Ulla corrected him after this, as if to say that it was not so, and that genealogical status is determined by the town to which you pay [your] head tax, which is [incidentally] your birthplace.

But this [argument] is not so, for the real intent of the *halakhah* is that genealogical status is determined by the place of residence, as we may concluded there from the text: *What [is the meaning of] Harpania? A mountain whither everybody turns.*[166] To which Rashi adds the comment: *All those of flawed genealogical background, who could not find a wife, would go there [for that purpose].* To which Rashi adds the comment: *All who could not find a wife would go there [for that purpose].*

---

[164] Talmud Bavli, *Me'ilah* 160b. The author gives the quotation in a very clipped fashion, assuming the reader is familiar with the passage.

[165] Proverbs 31:8.

[166] Talmud Bavli, *Yevamot* 17a. A pun on "Harpania."

If this be the case, why would he have corrected him with [the question about] head tax? If you argue that Rav Hamnuna did not live in Harpania at all, he would have had no cause to be embarrassed. All he need have said was that he was not from Harpania.

And why did Rav Ulla find it necessary to ask him where he paid his head tax? Why did he not ask him who his father was and who were the members of his family, if it were his intention to find out about his lineage?

I have searched through the entire Talmud, and I have not found another place where it is even remotely hinted that it is permissible to denigrate the Torah learning of a scholar because of his lineage, except this passage. This is the opposite of the view of the Torah, as the interpretation in *Horayot*[167] of the verse *She is more precious than pearls*[168] suggests, that a bastard who is a Torah scholar takes precedence over a High Priest!

27. By way of brief introduction we deal with the first verse of our holy Torah, because it is the keystone:

In the beginning [בראשית] *God created the heaven and the earth.*

Most commentators have dealt at great length with this verse, and especially with the word בראשית. For example, Ibn Ezra, in the Introduction [to his commentary], and Baḥya and [his] choice morsels,[169] and it can be readily seen that the real meaning of the the opening verse of the Torah is the same as that which the sages derive by interpretation from the verse *She is more precious than pearls,* namely, that Torah is the source of genealogical status. This is why the numerical value of the verse *she is more precious than pearls* is the same as the numerical value for [the word] Torah, and is also the same as *This is the heart of David Darshan!*[170]

---

[167] Talmud Bavli, *Horayot* 13a.

[168] Proverbs 3:15.

[169] For use in this sense, cf. Hayim Yiẓḥak David Azulai, *Kikar l'Adam,* 24a.

[170] The text reads: זה לב דוד דרש (this is the heart of what David interprets). There is a problem, since the numerical value of this phrase is 562, far short of the 611

We find it written of Abraham that *he kept My charge, My commandments, My statutes, and My laws,*[171] and even though his father was an idolater, he became the first of the [new] lineage, the founding father, because of the Torah, as it is written: *for the father of a multitude of nations have I made thee!*[172] And thus the word בראשית is used to designate Torah as the sages interpreted it, for it was called *the first of his way,*[173]to designate Israel, who were called *the first of His harvest,*[174] and to designate Moses, as it is written, *He chose the first part for himself.*[175] In every case [the word ראשית] has the same meaning [that is to say, Torah].

It is well known that [the word] Torah has a numerical value of 613 when you add 2 for the first two commandments, *I am the Lord thy God* and *Thou shalt have [no other gods],* as it is stated at the end of the tractate *Makkot.*[176] *Moshe Rabbenu* (משה רבינו) has a numerical value of 613, as does *Adonay Elohei Yisrael* (ה' אלהי ישראל).[177] And the word בראשית has the same numerical value (613) as *baTorah* (בתורה), *with the Torah* He created. They are all encompassed in the word ראשית, to show that the Torah is the first in [our special] lineage. It is for this reason that we are called God's children, and thus [the sages]

required. If, however, we read דרשן instead of דרש, we get a numerical value of 612, which is close enough. There is enough space in the prescribed text to allow for the possibility of a letter being dropped. Note the conclusion of the Introduction to *Shir haMa'alot l'David,* where he notes that *David Darshan of Cracow* equals *Bet Ha-Midrash* in numerical value, minus one!

[171] Genesis 26:5.

[172] Genesis 17:5.

[173] Proverbs 8:22.

[174] Jeremiah 2:3.

[175] Deuteronomy 33:21. The latter part of the verse points to Moses: "He executed the righteousness of the Lord and His ordinances with Israel.

[176] Talmud Bavli, *Makkot* 24a, which points out that the word תורה has the numerical value of 611 and becomes 613 with the addition of the first two of the Ten Commandments.

[177] David uses אלקי, following the accepted practice of refraining from using the ה in *Elohim.*

interpreted [the verse] *these are the generations of the heaven and the earth when they were created* (בהבראם);[178] saying: *do not read it as:* בהבראם *but as* באברהם.[179] That is to say, just as the words *in the beginning [God] created* teaches that the Torah is the first in lineage, and there are therefore seven words in the first verse, as it is written, *she hath hewn out her seven pillars,*[180] so Abraham is the first in lineage because of the Torah. The patriarchs and matriarchs total seven—Abraham, Isaac, Jacob, Sarah, Rebecca, Rachel, Leah.

28. And after this introduction let us examine the meaning of this verse IN THE MODE OF PLAIN MEANING:

It is my humble opinion[181] that this passage has been placed in the Talmud to show that recognized status in this holy Torah does not depend upon the quality of lineage. This is demonstrated by the passage in the Tractate *Horayot:*[182] *A bastard who is a scholar takes precedence over a High Priest who is an ignoramus, for it is written, "She is more precious than pearls," i.e., [knowledge of Torah] is more precious than the High Priest who enters the Holy of Holies.*[183] However, the essence of [noble] lineage through Torah depends on the heart's intention, as we find it stated in chapter two of *Berakhot:*[184] *Whoever studies Torah not for its own sake, it were better had he not been born.* This [statement] is disputed by *Tossafot,* [as follows]: Is it not stated in chapter four of *Pesaḥim:*[185] *A man should always occupy himself with Torah . . . though it is not for its own sake, for out of [its study] with an ul-*

---

[178] Genesis 2:4.

[179] Midrash, *Genesis Rabbah* 12:8. The word הבראם reads אברהם when the letters are rearranged.

[180] Proverbs 9:2, which speaks of Wisdom as the first (ראשית) to be created by God.

[181] Literally, "feeble opinion."

[182] Talmud Bavli, *Horayot* 13a.

[183] The text in *Horayot* quotes Proverbs 3:15, and makes a pun on the *k'tiv* of the word פניים, whose *k'ri* is, פנינים that is, לפני ולפנים the Holy of Holies.

[184] Talmud Bavli, *Berakhot* 17a.

[185] Ibid., *Pesaḥim* 50b.

terior motive, there comes [study] for its own sake. The [passage in Tossafot][186] answers as follows: *It were better that he who [studies Torah] to show himself argumentative and boastful had never been born*; but in the case of a man who just studies Torah for its own sake, but is not boastful or argumentative about it [this is not the case]. I derive this meaning from a *Mishnah* in the first chapter of the Tractate *Avodah Zarah*[187] in the interpretation of the portion *Beḥukotai*. In the *Midrash Rabbah* [comment to the passage in Leviticus], we read:[188]

"If ye walk in my statutes": viz., those statutes [חוקים] by the help of which I marked out heaven and earth, etc., . . . they are called חוקים *because they are engraved [as a safeguard] against the Evil Inclination, thus it is written: "Woe unto them that decree [החוקקים] unrighteous decrees [חקקי און]."*[189] *Rav Levi expounded: It is like the case of a lonely settlement which was kept in disorder by invading bands. So the king appointed a commander to protect it. In the same way the Holy One Praised Be He said: "The Torah is called a stone and the Evil Inclination is called a stone." That the Torah is called a stone is proved by the text "the tables of stone [and the law and the commandments]";*[190] *that the Evil Inclination is called a stone is proved by the text: "I will take away the heart of stone out of your flesh."*[191] *The stone shall watch the stone!*[192] And it is known that there were two tablets of stone with five commandments on each tablet.

Now this is how the divinely inspired *Mishnah* reads:[193] *Rav*

---

[186] Cf. *Tossafot* to Talmud Bavli, *Taanit* 7b and *Berakhot* 17a.

[187] Talmud Bavli, *Avodah Zarah* 49b.

[188] Midrash, *Leviticus Rabbah* 35:1. Here we find word-play on בחקתי, the dual meanings being "command"/"carve."

[189] Isaiah 10:1.

[190] Exodus 24:12.

[191] Ezekiel 11:19.

[192] David quotes the passage from Midrash, *Leviticus Rabbah,* but omits phrases here and there without losing the sense.

[193] Cf. Mishnah, *Avodah Zarah,* at the beginning of chap. 4. Cf. also Talmud Bavli, *Avodah Zarah* 49b ff.

Ishmael says: If three stones are found side by side next to a [statue of] Mercurius, they are forbidden, but two are permitted. And the sages say: If they are seen near it, they are forbidden, but if they are not near it they are permitted. The *Gemara* [continues the exposition to state that] the essence of the idolatrous worship of Mercurius was that there were two stones below and one above.[194] Now [the phrase] *Rav Ishmael says: if three stones* really points to the Evil Inclination, who is called a stone in relation to the two tablets of stone. *Side by side*—that is to say, the one opposed to the other. Just as the Mercurius [idol] was one stone upon two, so it is that the Evil Inclination can gain dominance over the Torah, which is [made up of] two tablets of stone, in which case the Tablets of the Torah are captive and imprisoned,[195] and it is impossible to fulfill any commandments from it properly. *And two [are permitted],* that is to say, when two [stones] are on top, they are the Tablets [of the Torah]; whether one studies it for its own sake or to boast of his dialectical ability, the Tablets of the Torah are free [to be studied], for there is the possibility that it will ultimately be studied for its own sake and its commandments be fulfilled properly.

But the sages differ and say: *If [the stones] are seen to be connected with it* [they are prohibited], that is to say, if the purpose of a man's study of Torah is to boast of his dialectical ability, so that the tablets of the Torah make him appear eminent and important, the tablets of the Torah are imprisoned, and its commandments cannot be fulfilled properly. And concerning the individual who studies [Torah] to boast of his dialectical ability, it is written: *One sinner destroyeth much good.*[196] That is, many people will be influenced by and learn from the vile

---

[194] Actually this precise point is made by Rashi.

[195] His argument turns on a pun on מותר/אסור, which in the text means "permitted"/"prohibited," and in connection with Torah, he takes to mean "imprisoned"/"free."

[196] Ecclesiastes 9:18.

deeds of that scholar who studied [Torah] to boast of this dialectical ability, and they will say: *"Scholar So-and-So is permissive with regard to gambling and lust and such matters."* In that case, such a person, wise in his own eyes, squanders much good in people, and it is rightly said of him: *Better had he not been created,* etc.

And when they are not seen with him [as permitted]—that is to say, when he studies while occupied or at leisure, but the tablets of the Torah are *not seen with him* as [evidence] of boasting of his dialectical ability, the tablets of the Torah will be fulfilled properly.

Rav Hamnuna sat before Ulla and was engaged in discussing a traditional law when the latter remarked, "What a man! And how much more important would he have been had not Harpania been his native town"—for they [in Harpania] do not have the noble ancestry of Torah tradition. That is to say, Ulla believed that since Hamnuna was raising such problems and displaying such brilliance,[197] it might well have been that he was not studying Torah for its own sake, but rather to brag of his powers in it. That is why he said: *had not Harpania been his town,* as they say [further in text], *What is Harpania, a hill to which all turn*[198] *who are of blemished lineage,* that is, in Torah, and *cannot find a wife* who fears God, that is to say, Torah for the sake of heaven. They go there and study to boast of their dialectical powers.

It was this [dig] that caused Rav Hamnuna to appear embarrassed, in order that Ulla would realize that he was studying for the sake of heaven. For the word כסופה [used to describe how he reacted] is a good word used to describe a Jew who is not like the uncircumcised [Gentile], as it is stated in chapter eight of *Yevamot*:[199] *compassionate, modest, and charitable*—are qualities that identify the seed of Abraham.

---

[197] Lit. "sharpness and keenness."
[198] A pun on Harpania—a hill (הר) to which all turn (פונים).
[199] Talmud Bavli, *Yevamot* 79a.

And as though to interpret Ulla's surprise and his exclamation *What a man!* (מה גברא),[200] Rav Hamnuna replied that the letters of the word גברא represented the words *merciful* (גומל), *modest* (ביישן), *compassionate* (רחמן), *am I* (אנא), and that was really the reason for his embarrassment. And when Ulla discerned this fine quality in Rav Hamnuna, he wished to make it clear, and have him articulate it, and not just hint at it. Hence he said to him: *Where did you pay your head tax?*—that is to say, for what purpose did you study the Torah, concerning which it is written, *For its merchandise is better than the merchandise of silver,*[201] with the brain in your skull[202]—for the sake of heaven or to boast of your powers in it? So he replied: *To Pum Nahara.* Now Rav Hamnuna, because of his enormous brilliance, wished to respond [in kind] to the words of Ulla, who said, *What a man,* as though he knew what was in his mind, for he wished to test his perceptiveness in the discussions of scholars, who should be like a surging river.[203] For this reason he replied *Pum Nahara.* That is to say, my study of Torah is directed toward the Holy One above, who causes His wisdom to flow out to the sages, who are like a surging river.[204] That is to say, his study was for the sake of heaven and not for self-aggrandizement.

When Ulla heard this, he said to him, *You are from Pum Nahara*—[you are] to be considered among those saints whose intention is toward heaven. By using the word את (you), he refers to the את of the verse *Thou shalt fear the Lord thy God*[205] (את ה' אלהיך תירא) which suggests the sages who emerge in great numbers [from the observance of this commandment]. And it

---

[200] The letters of the word גברא become the initials for the words representing the four good qualities which he proceeds to mention.

[201] Proverbs 3:14.

[202] So the talmudic phrase comes out: "For what purpose did you use (היכא ויבת) the Torah (כסף), which you studied with the brain in your head (גלגלתא)?"

[203] There is a double pun in כנהר המתגבר, viz. מתגבר/גברא and פום נהרא/נהר.

[204] The influence of the Kabbalah is seen here.

[205] Deuteronomy 6:13.

is fitting to say of you: *Blessed be He who imparted His wisdom to those who fear him.* And praised be the Lord who chose the sages and their Torah, and who saw in this saying which I have interpreted that there is no lineage like the lineage of the Torah when it is studied for the sake of heaven. And for this reason it is written in the Torah: *You are children of the Lord your God,*[206] for we trace our noble lineage from our Father in Heaven, for *students are called sons.*[207] And this too is the plain meaning of the saying, that he who marries a blemished woman is also blemished, as we learn from the explanation of the words *from Harpania,* a hill to which all the blemished turn, etc., as they are wont to say, *Not without cause does the starling follow the raven,*[208] but because it is of its species.

AND IN THE ALLEGORICAL MODE

29. *In the beginning* [בראשית] *God created*: He wishes to state [that you are to read it] as though it were written: *God created with Reshit* [בראשית]. This is an allusion to the Evil Inclination, which enters the body in the beginning, as we find it stated in chapter eleven of *Sanhedrin,*[209] in reference to the verse:[210] *Sin coucheth at the gate.* That is why it is hinted that when God created the cosmos, He first used the attribute of justice, etc., and it is known that man is a miniature cosmos.

The heaven and the earth—that is to say, the Evil Inclination, which enters the body in the beginning, causes the soul, which comes from heaven, and the body, which comes from earth, to stand in judgment, as we find it also [in the interpretation of the] verse *He summons the heaven above and the earth below to judgment with him,*[211] in chapter eleven of *Sanhedrin,* in

---

[206] Deuteronomy 14:1.

[207] Midrash *Sifrei,* commenting on Deuteronomy 14:1.

[208] Talmud Bavli, *Baba Kama* 92b, that is, birds of a feather flock together.

[209] Talmud Bavli, *Sanhedrin* 91b.

[210] Genesis 4:7. What a twist to the interpretation of this verse in Midrash, *Genesis Rabbah,* which equates ראשית with חכמה ("Wisdom," "Sophia")!

[211] Psalms 50:4.

connection with the statement *He made the lame to ride with the blind.*[212] Hence, [because of the link of the Evil Inclination with the word בראשית], there are seven words in the [first] verse [of Genesis], corresponding to the seven names of the Evil Inclination, as it is stated in chapter five of *Sukkah.*[213] And at the final stage [of the process of creation God] joined the attribute of Mercy to the attribute of Justice, so that the mind might be strengthened. This is the reason for His placing [the attribute of Mercy] first, as it is written:[214] *On that day the Lord God made, etc.* And this too is a meaning that [can be derived from] this verse.

IN THE ALLEGORICAL MODE

30. *Rav Hamnuna sat before Ulla and was engaged,* etc. Rashi's commentary adds, *And was arguing against it.* The meaning [of this is] that Ulla was aware of Rav Hamnuna's wish to defend the Evil Inclination, as it is written: *He who hardens* [מקשה] *his heart falls into evil.*[215] We can further say that the word *traditional law* [שמעתא] in the text implies the Evil Inclination, for all the limbs of the body listen [נשמעים] to it.[216] Then Ulla remarked, *What a man!* [גברא] i.e., the [Evil] Inclination on the earthly side who desires mastery for he precedes the Good Inclination, which is the mind. *And what strength* [גוברי] suggests the mind, on the heavenly side, which the Evil Inclina-

[212] Talmud Bavli, *Sanhedrin* 91b. To the argument of Antoninus, that the body and soul can escape judgment by shifting blame from one to the other, the sages reply with a parable of the blind and the lame combining forces to rob an orchard and hence being jointly culpable.

[213] Talmud Bavli, *Sukkah* 52a. The seven words are: "evil," "uncircumcised," "unclean," "enemy," "stumbling-block," "stone," "hidden one."

[214] Genesis 2:4. In the term for God here used, ה' אלקים, the element representing the Attribute of Mercy (ה') precedes the element representing the Attribute of Justice (אלהים).

[215] Proverbs 28:14. The relation of hardening the heart (מקשה) to evil makes possible the link to the Evil Inclination, and so Rashi's מקשה is thus interpreted.

[216] This is a play on the two meanings that can be derived from the word שמע, "listen" and "traditional teaching."

tion permitted to gain mastery over it, and is therefore called the strong one [גוברי]. Both will have to give account of themselves in judgment, as we have already indicated by the quotation: *Let him call the heaven above, etc.*

Had you not—you are defending [the Evil Inclination]. *Harpania been your town*—the whole body, which is called a little city, turns to the Evil Inclination, which is called a hill, as we find it stated in chapter five of *Sukkah*.[217]

Rav Hamnuna was embarrassed—because of his desire to defend the Evil Inclination. *He [Ulla] said to him, "Where do you pay your poll tax?"*—That is to say, what is your wish for the mind, which is in the skull (גלגלתא), to master the Evil Inclination or to be mastered by it? *Said Rav Hamnuna to Ulla, "To Pum Nahara"*—that is to say, it is my desire that the mind gain mastery, and all will be drawn after it like a river, as it is written in the second chapter of Isaiah: *And nations shall flow after it* (נהרו). Just as all the nations will be drawn after the Messiah, so shall the evils of the body be drawn after the mind. So he said to him, in that case we do not need body and mind to give an account [of themselves] in judgment. Which is why he said: *You belong to Pum Nahara*—and the soul will return to the place of its origin.

MORE IN THE ALLEGORICAL MODE

31. *In the beginning God created the heaven*—the seven planets which are part of the configuration of stars in the heavens. *And the earth*—that the inhabitants of the earth be guided by them (i.e., the planets). Thus the seven words of the verse correspond to the seven planets. Now, toward the end of chapter twenty-four of [the tractate] *Shabbat*[218] there is a difference of opinion as to whether Israel is under the influence of astrology or not, and this text teaches us that the ordering of the constellations is in the hands of God because [the word]

217 Talmud Bavli, *Sukkah,* 52a.
218 Talmud Bavli, *Shabbat* 156a.

God stands next to [the word] *heaven* in the verse. [In the same way] the inhabitants of the earth are under [the influence] of the heavenly constellations, because [the word] *heaven* stands next to the word *earth* in the same verse. Yet despite the fact that everything is in the hands of God, as it is written, *The earth is the Lord's and the fullness thereof,*[219] nevertheless we learn from this that it is in the hands of God whether, heaven forbid, some evil results from the influence of the stars. And when a righteous man prays to God concerning that evil, God transforms it into good, as in the case of Isaac, as cited in chapter six of *Yevamot,*[220] *God answered his prayer,*[221] and as in the case of Abraham, at the end of the tractate *Shabbat,* where it is stated: *Lay aside your astrology.*[222] Similarly, when God punishes man through another wicked man, even though the wicked person who is the punishing agent is himself ill-starred, God exalts him nonetheless to use him as His instrument of punishment, as He always does with Israel by using the nations [for this purpose]. For because of their sins they compel the Holy One Praised Be He to exalt that nation, and you will find this interpretation of the verse *you have wearied me with your sins*[223] in chapter eleven of *Sanhedrin.*[224] We find the same thing in chapter five of *Gittin*[225] in the statement *All who oppress Israel become exalted.* Generally speaking, when God punishes an individual, prayer and repentance are helpful. However, if some evil that befalls a man is caused by a wicked person who is under a favorable star at that particular time, his prayers to the stars that the wicked man's horoscope be changed are ineffectual, because the latter is an agent [of God's will] and can only act as he is directed, just as that

---

[219] Psalms 24:1.

[220] Talmud Bavli, *Yevamot* 64a.

[221] Genesis 25:21.

[222] Talmud Bavli, *Shabbat* 156a.

[223] Isaiah 43:24.

[224] I have not been able to find reference to this verse in Talmud Bavli, *Sanhedrin,* chap. 9. There is a reference in *Sanhedrin* 104b similar to the one in *Gittin* 56b, with respect to the exalted position of those who oppress Israel. The Biblical quotation is from Isaiah 8:23.

[225] Talmud Bavli, *Gittin* 56b.

verse in Exodus [and the comment by Rashi] suggest:[226] *Be not rebellious against him; for he will not pardon your transgressions, for My name is in him,* to which Rashi adds the comment: *For he is an agent and must perform his mission.* Thus, when he prays to God he receives no answer, for the agent has already performed his mission. He must therefore hope that God will put an end to the power of the stars quickly, and he [the wicked one] will fall because of his own [sins]. This can come about only if he overpowers the wicked one through his intensification of his study of Torah. If this is not the case, it is possible that God might make it possible for the wicked man to succeed even after the influence of the stars has waned, in order to punish him through this evil.

We find evidence for this in talmudic passages which appear to contradict each other, [but do not,] for the contradiction is resolved above by a passage in the first chapter of *Gittin:*[227] *Mar 'Ukba sent for advice to Rav Eliezer saying: Certain men are annoying me and I am able to get them into trouble with the government, shall I do so? He traced lines on which he wrote [quoting]: "I will keep a curb upon my mouth while the wicked is before me"*[228] *[that is,] he added, although the wicked is before me I will keep a curb on my mouth. Mar 'Ukba again sent to him saying: They are worrying me very much and I cannot stand them. He replied [with the quotation]:*[229] *"Resign thyself unto the Lord, and wait patiently (התחולל) for him" [that is to say,] he added, wait for the Lord and He will cast them down prostrate (חללים) before thee; go to the Bet haMidrash early morning and evening and there will be an end of them.* Then there is this passage toward the end of chapter six in [the tractate] *Shabbat:*[230] *In accordance with whom do we suspend a cluster of grapes on a [sterile] date tree? In accordance with this Tanna. And [this passage is preceded] by And he the leper] shall cry "unclean, unclean," he must make his grief publicly known, so that the public may pray for him.*[231] Based on this passage, we might ask

---

[226] Exodus 23:21.

[227] Talmud Bavli, *Gittin* 7a.

[228] Psalms 39:2.

[229] Psalms 37:7.

[230] Talmud Bavli, *Shabbat* 67a.

[231] Leviticus 13:45. In the Talmud, this portion of the passage comes first. David reverses it to underscore the point he is making.

why Rabbi Eliezer did not send word to Mar 'Ukba that he make his grief publicly known so that the public might pray for him. But I have already indicated the reason [he did not do so], namely, that Mar 'Ukba's grief was not visited upon him from heaven as punishment, so he did not need to have others pray for him; but in the case of the palm tree and the leper, whose grief is from heaven, he needs such prayers even from others. He that understands will find this pleasing.

Now the hidden meaning of this matter appears to be that those men of Israel who oppress their fellows are treated like other nations, and are placed under the control of the stars, and they have no portion in the God of Israel with regard to His Providence because of the magnitude of their sins. For the moment fate smiles on them,[232] and they are successful in accordance with their favorable horoscope, but when the influence of their stars wanes, their destruction comes from themselves, as Rabbi Eliezer discussed [them when he said] that they have no merit after that, and they will stand [in judgment] for the enormity of their sins. And we have seen how many individuals and families who rule and oppress their fellows have been destroyed, they, their power, and their wealth. Perhaps this is the meaning of the saying: *Power buries those who wield it,*[233] and along these lines we read in chapter six of [the tractate] *Sotah,*[234] *And some say it was Rav Simeon b. Pazzi who declared that it is permitted to flatter the wicked as it is written: "The vile person shall no more be called liberal, nor the knave said to be noble,"*[235] *on the general principle that in this world it is permitted.* And in the first chapter of [the tractate] *Megillah,* we find it stated: *It is permitted to contend with the wicked*[236] only when they are not favored by fortune, but when they are favored by fortune and their hand is powerful, it is permitted to flat-

---

[232] Literally, "the hour smiles upon them." This attack on the leaders of the community, who represent the secular authority and abuse their powers, is significant indeed.

[233] Talmud Bavli, *Pesaḥim* 87b, where the phrase is רבנות מקברת בעלה David uses a synonym, שררה.

[234] Talmud Bavli, *Sotah* 41b.

[235] Isaiah 32:5.

[236] Talmud Bavli, *Megillah* 6b.

ter them to stay alive. You may act thus in order to fulfill what is written: *and live by them*[237] and not that he die by them. And this is the meaning of the saying.

MORE IN THE ALLEGORICAL MODE

32. *Rav Hamnuna sat before Ulla and was engaged*[238] *in discussing tradition-al law*—this means that Ulla was being oppressed by some other persons and was having a bad time of it![239]

In discussing a traditional law—even though he prayed morning and evening concerning them, as is done in the reading of the *Shema* [prayer],[240] wherein it is written: "[you shall say it] when you lie down and when you rise up."[241]

Said Ulla to Rav Hamnuna: *What*[242] *a man, etc.* We read in chapter seven of the tractate *Menahot*,[243] where with reference to the quota-tion *What does the Lord require of you*, it is suggested that the word מה [what] be read as מאה [a hundred], which are the hundred blessings of prayer. That is to say, through prayer, which is denoted by the word מה. *And what an eminent man*, that is to say, through prayer, which is denoted by the word מה, a man can be saved from the others who gain mastery over him. And when you remain in your troubles and have not been rescued from your adversaries,[244] [then

---

[237] Leviticus 18:5.

[238] There is a pun here to make his interpretation: "was engaged in" (קָא הֲוֵי), and "woe" (הֹוי).

[239] Literally: "he had oy and vey!" (והיה לו הוי ואבוי).

[240] Another pun: שמעתא, "traditional law," and שמע, "hear," the first word of the "Hear, O Israel," as found in Deuteronomy 6:4.

[241] Deuteronomy 6:7.

[242] There is a pun here: גוברי/גברא, "man"/"mastery."

[243] Talmud Bavli, *Menahot* 43b.

[244] A portion of the page has been torn and blurred, and I have attempted a restoration of the text on the basis of context as follows:

[מ] אה ברכות התפילה . . .
[אחר] ים ומה גוברי כלומר
[שנתח]ברו עליו. ומאחר שאתה . . .
[מצר]יף. אי לאו דהרפניא . . .
[ש]אי אתה נענה וכמוזכר . . .

the talmudic passage applies to you], that is, *Had not Harpania been his town*—[Harpania] a hill to which all rejected prayers go, as we find it stated in שערי אורה, that there is a place called *Pesilim* (פסילים) where all rejected prayers go, which is why a specific place is mentioned.[245]

Rav Hamnuna was embarrassed[246]—that he [Ulla] suspected him of having offered a rejected prayer, and thought that perhaps fate was smiling upon the wicked man who oppressed Rav Hamnuna, because the stars favored him, and hence prayers against him were not quickly answered. Only when the favorable influence of the stars would come to an end would the wicked man be destroyed because of his own [sin]. And it is known that the courses of the planets have influence for good or ill. He . . . [247] was embarrassed, because he was desirous that the influence of the stars be to his benefit.

Now the sentence *where did you pay your head tax* can be taken to mean: with respect to the favorable influence of the planets, were you thinking that fate was favoring the wicked man who was harming you, or not, [and if not] was nevertheless doing you harm?

Whereupon Rav Hamnuna said to Ulla, *to Pum Nahara*,[248] that is to say: "I was thinking that the stars were shining upon him, and the hour was favorable to him," and that is why he used the word *nahara*, which means "shining upon." Ulla then said to Rav Hamnuna, "In that case *you are from Pum Nahara*—the evil you are suffering comes from a wicked man whose stars are favorable to him. For this reason your prayers will not be received so quickly, even though they are proper prayers and not blemished. And were not the astrological hour favorable to that wicked man, your proper prayer would undoubtedly have been answered quickly, and you would have been promptly saved.

[245] See שערי אורה by Joseph Gikatila, author of a classic kabbalistic work in the twelfth century, vol. 1, p. 140 (Jerusalem, Mosad Bialik, 1970)—פסולות ("rejected") and פסילים. Exegesis by pun.

[246] The talmudic אכסיף ("embarrassed") is interpreted by pun as כסוף ("desire," "favor"). גלגלתא ("skull") becomes "where did you direct your mind?" (דעתך), i.e., "What was the direction of your thinking?"

[247] Several words of the text at this point are blurred.

[248] Pun נהרא/מנהיר, "river"/"shine."

AND IN THE HOMILETICAL MODE

33. *In the beginning God created*—this verse is an allusion to the fact that with the primary purpose[249] of the creative process has to do with heaven and earth, which represent the macrocosm, [having been brought into being] for the sake of man, who is the microcosm, so that he might be like the angels, who are called the sons of God, as it is written,[250] *I said: ye are godlike beings and all of you sons of the Most High, etc.* Now since this was the primary purpose of the creative process, it can never be abrogated, even though the first man [Adam] brought upon himself the contamination of the Evil Inclination from the primal serpent. However, with the advent of the Messiah, the contamination of the Evil Inclination will be removed, as it is written:[251] *and I shall remove the heart of stone from your flesh, etc.* As it is written in the mystical interpretations of the Torah, [the initials of the word ADaM][252] stand for Adam, David, Messiah. Furthermore, there are seven words in the verse corresponding to the seven shepherds[253] who will lead us when the Messiah comes, namely, David in the center; Adam, Seth and Methuselah to his right; Abraham, Jacob, and Moses to his left, as we find it stated in chapter five of *Sukkah*. And this too is a meaning of the verse.

IN THE HOMILETICAL MODE

Rav Hamnuna sat before Ulla and was engaged in discussing a traditional law—that is to say, it was Rav Hamnuna's purpose to suggest that even when the Messiah comes with the fulfillment of the verse:[254] *How beautiful upon the mountains are the feet of the messenger of good tidings*

---

[249] ראשית כוונת. Here the word ראשית in the text is interpreted to mean "primary purpose."

[250] Psalms 82:6.

[251] Ezekiel 11:19.

[252] This *gematria* is first mentioned by Moses de Leon. Cf. Gershom Scholem, *The Kabbalah* (New York, 1974), p. 348.

[253] Talmud Bavli, *Sukkah* 52b. Cf. also, Micah 5:4.

[254] Isaiah 52:7.

that announceth peace,[255] *the harbinger of good tidings that announceth salvation*—even then the power of the Evil Inclination will prevail. And that is why it [the talmudic text] says, *and was [engaged],*[256] i.e., the travail of the Evil Inclination would [still] be [there].

[In discussing] a traditional law—even in the time of the fulfillment suggested by the verse [cited above] *that announceth salvation.* As Samuel said in chapter eleven of *Sanhedrin:*[257] *The only difference between this world and the Messianic Age is the subjugation [of Israel] by the nations.*

Ulla then said of Rav Hamnuna:[258] *What a man!*—i.e., what a great man he is. That is to say, Rav Hamnuna believed that just as there is a distinction now between one who overcomes the Evil Inclination and one who is overcome by it, it will be the same in the Messianic Age. This does not accord with the significance of the first phase of the creation process,[259] and it contradicts the verse *I said, ye are godlike beings, and all of you sons of the Most High, etc.* The interpretation that there will not be a difference is also derived from what is written . . .[260] above. The other verse, too, supports this

[255] By means of a pun, he relates בשמעתא ("with a traditional law") to משמיע ("that announceth") and interprets the former as meaning "Messiah."

[256] קא הוי—and was engaged in raising difficulties about a traditional law. Hence the קא suggests the Evil Impulse, and the interpretation becomes "the Evil Impulse will still be [there.]"

[257] Talmud Bavli, *Sanhedrin* 99a.

[258] The edge of the left side of the page is torn, making it necessary to reconstruct several words on the basis of context, as follows:

אמר עולא עליה דר(ב)

המנונא מה גברא ומה גוברי כמה הוא גדול. כלומר שרב המנונא חושב כמו שי(ש)
היפרש עכשיו בין מי שמתגבר על היצר הרע ובין שנתגבר מהיצר הרע. (אז)
יהיה לזמן המשיח ולא יהיה אז כמו כוונת תחילת הבריאה והוא נגד הפסוק (אשר)
אמרתי אלקי' אתם ובני עליון כולכם. משמע שאז לא יהיה היפרש מדכתיב . . .
וגם הפסוק מעיד כך כדכתיב והסירותי לב האבן מבשרכם.

[259] See the first part of par. 33, where the creation of heaven and earth as macrocosm is interpreted to mean that man as microcosm is like the angels.

[260] One word is blurred here. It is, however, clear that David is referring to Biblical references he has already used, so whatever the word may be, it refers to the verse just quoted.

view, as it is written: *I shall remove the heart of stone from your flesh, and I shall move far from you the "serpent."*[261] Nor is there a problem with the statement of Samuel that *the only difference between this world and the next is subjugation [of Israel] by the nations,* but *subjugation by the nations* can also be taken to mean that the Evil Inclination will be subjugated, for it is referred to as *an old king and a fool* in the verse *better is a poor and wise child, etc.*[262]

Had not Harpania been his native town—that is to say, even though you are not among those who come from Harpania who will go there in the future [in the end of days] to seek true perfection, even those who are not elect, like the nations of the world; and of course Israel, who are elect. The heart of stone will be removed from both of these, as it is written:[263] *And it shall come to pass in the end of days, the mountain of the Lord's house shall be established as the top of the mountains . . . and they shall say, come and let us go to the house of the Lord, etc.* Now the Talmud passage [we are considering], and Rashi's comment to it, [states]: *What is Harpania? A hill to which all who are rejected*[264] *[go]*— they reject and nullify their idolatry by giving up the foreign women, turn [in repentance] and go there.

Rav Hamnuna was embarrassed. After this Ulla wished to probe Rav Hamnuna's opinion on resurrection, and that is why he said: *Where did you pay your head tax?* That is to say, [the word כסף] implies the spinal cord, which is the silver thread[265] that runs from the skull [גלגלתא] of the head and all life depends on it—do you believe that it will be restored after death?

To which Rav Hamnuna replied to Ulla: *To Pum Nahara*—for the verse of Isaiah 42, *I will make the river islands, etc.,*[266] will be fulfilled,

---

[261] Joel 2:20. Here there is an interesting pun on צפוני. In Joel, it means: "from the north." David thinks of צפעוני ("serpent"), which makes it the Evil Inclination!

[262] Ecclesiastes 4:13. Thus שעבוד מלכיות becomes: "subjugation of kingship" and not, "subjugation by the kingship."

[263] Isaiah 2:2.

[264] Rashi's comment describes Harpania as a hill (הר) to which the ineligible for marriage (פסולים) go. He has it mean the hill to which, in the end of days, the nations will turn after repudiating their idolatry.

[265] Ecclesiastes 12:6.

[266] Isaiah 42:15.

and that chapter deals with the theme of resurrection, as we read: *let the inhabitants of Sela exult, let them shout from the top of the mountains.*[267]

Thereupon Ulla said to Rav Hamnuna: "In that case *you are from Pum Nahara*, for you have succeeded in explaining that true perfection comes with the resurrection that follows the coming of the Messiah and then *He will swallow up death*[268] so that the Evil Inclination will have no power. Now the sages are evasive on the theme of resurrection and the world to come in chapter eleven of *Sanhedrin*,[269] as are many of the later sages, such as the Ramban in his *Gate of Reward and Punishment*[270] as well as his comments on Maimonides [Code] in his section on the Laws of Repentance. Blessed and exalted be God, awesome in his deeds, who made me worthy of completing this too on the Three Bounding Days.[271]

[267] Ibid. 42:11.

[268] Ibid. 25:8.

[269] Talmud Bavli, *Sanhedrin* 90a ff.

[270] Rabbi Moses ben Naḥman, also known as Naḥmanides. His *Sha'ar haGmul* was first published in Naples in 1490.

[271] The שלשת ימי הגבלה are the three days that the Children of Israel prepared themselves for the Revelation of the Torah, that is, three days before the Festival of Shavuot.

24. We may further state that on occasion in Mishnah and *Gemara*, the sages use a surplus letter or word here and there, to make possible, perhaps, to deduce more than one meaning from it, or some rule of conduct or ethics, to express the faith authentically and unbreached. This is especially the case when the preacher uses a text from the Bible, or from the Talmud or Midrash, or from works of philosophers or commentators, and *winnows the words with shovel and fan*[a] to connect one text to another. Sometimes he will do it with *gematriot* which are the hors d'oeuvres of wisdom. In chapter two of *Zevahim*[b] the sages *subtract, and and interpret* [as follows]: *"From the blood of the bullock"* [means] *he is to receive blood [direct] from the bullock.*[c] The same thing occurs in chapter five of *Zevahim*: *[The text says] "And he shall take,"* [which intimates] *he shall [be]take himself,* to which Rashi comments: *Reverse it in order to explain it.*[d] In short, there is no limit to this sort of thing in Midrash and Talmud, and in all [sacred] books. The real goal is to justify and strengthen the true faith, that the sermon not be tainted, heaven forbid [and lead the people astray]. Therefore I come trembling before the King of Kings with my prayer that my words be acceptable.

---

a Isaiah 30:24.

b Talmud Bavli, *Zevahim*, 25a.

c You may subtract a letter from one word and add it to another where the context warrants it, and then interpret the text with this alteration. The the partitive מ is removed from מדם [blood] and added to הפר [the bullock], so that it reads: and he shall take the (not, of the) blood from the bullock.

d Talmud Bavli, *Zevahim*, 48a.

CATHOLIC THEOLOGICAL UNION 5401 SOUTH CORNELL AVE., CHICAGO, ILLINOIS 60615 TELEPHONE (312) 324-8000

JUL 1 8 1984

Department of Biblical Literature and Languages

July 20/84

Dear Frank:

Here is the book at long
last. It was finished in
Berkeley & that's thanks to you.
I shall never forget.

With affection.

[signature]

JUL 18 1988

BIBLIOGRAPHY

Abarbanel, Isaac. *Naḥlat Avot*. Venice, 1566.

———. *Zevaḥ Pesaḥ*. Modena, 1557.

Aboab, Isaac. *Menorat haMaor*. Mantua, 1563.

Abraham b. Eliezer Halevi. *Mashrei Qatrin*. Constantinople, 1510.

Adret, Solomon. *She'elot u'Tshuvot*. Vol. 1. Bnai Brak, 1958.

Amram, David W. *Makers of Hebrew Books in Italy*. Philadelphia, 1901.

Arama, Isaac. *Akedat Yizḥak*. Venice, 1554.

Azkiri, Eliezer. *Sefer Ḥaredim*. Venice, 1601.

Baer, Solomon. *Avodat Yisrael*. Jerusalem, 1937.

Baḥyah ben Asher. *Bi'ur Torah*. Pesaro, 1507.

Balaban, Majer. *Italienische und spanische Aerzte und Apotheker im XVI. und XVII. Jahrhundert in Krakau*. In *Heimkehr*. Berlin, 1912.

———. *Die Judenstadt Lublin*. Berlin, 1919.

———. *Yiden in Polen*. Vilna, 1930.

Balletti, Andrea. *Gli Ebrei e gli Estensi*. Reggio-Emilia, 1930.

Baron, Salo. *A Social and Religious History of the Jews*. Vols. XIV and XVI. New York, 1969, 1976.

Baruch ben Isaac of Worms. *Sefer haTerumah*. Venice, 1521.

Bass, Shabbetai. *Siftei Yesheinim*. Amsterdam, 1676.

Ben-Jacob, Isaac. *Oẓar haSfarim*. Vilna, 1880.

Benjamin Ze'ev Wolf of Szebrezcyn. *Et Raẓon*. Zólkiew, 1777.

Ben-Sasson, Hayim Hillel. *Hagut v'Hanhagah*. Jerusalem, 1959.

———. *Perakim b'Toldot haYehudim biY'mei ha-Beinayim*. Tel Aviv: Am Oved, 1969.

———. *Toldot Am Yisrael*. Vol. 2. Jerusalem, 1969.

Ben-Yehuda, Eliezer. *Complete Dictionary*. New York, 1958.

Berekhia Berekh b. Yitzḥak Isaac. *Zera Berakh I*. Cracow, 1646.

———. *Zera Berekh II*. Amsterdam, 1662.

Bernstein, Simon. *Diwan l'Rabbi Yehuda Arie miModena*. Philadelphia, 1932.

———. *Luḥot Zikaron*. Cincinnati, 1935.

Bettan, Israel. *Studies in Jewish Preaching*. Cincinnati, 1939.

Beẓalel of Slutsk. *Sefer Amudeha Shiv'ah.* Dyhernfurth, 1693.

Béziers, Yedaiah Penini (HaBedersi). *Iggeret HaBedersi.* Warsaw, 1881.

Bibago, Abraham b. Shem Tov. *Derekh Emunah.* Constantinople, 1521.

Bonfil, Robert. "HaRabbanut haItalkit biTkufat haRenaissance." Doctoral diss., Hebrew University, 1977.

Braudel, Fernand. *The Mediterranean and the Mediterranean World in the Reign of Philip II.* New York, 1972.

Breuer, Mordecai. "HaYeshivah haAshkenazit b'Shilhei Y'mei ha-Beinayim." Doctoral diss., Hebrew University, 1962.

Brisk, Asher Leib. *Sefer Divrei Kohelet.* Jerusalem, 1905.

Buber, Solomon. *Kiryah Nisgavah.* Cracow, 1903.

Chavel, Charles B. *Ramban, Commentary on the Torah.* New York, 1971.

Cowley, A. E. *A Concise Catalogue of Hebrew Printed Books in the Bodleian Library.* Oxford, 1971.

Coucy, Moses. *Sefer Mitzvot Gadol.* Rome, 1470.

Danby, Herbert. *Mishnah.* Oxford, 1933.

Darshan, David b. Manasseh. *Shir haMa'alot l'David.* Cracow, 1571.

———. *Ktav Hitnaẓẓelut l'Darshanim.* Lublin, 1574.

———. (Copyist of) *Perush haYeri'ah haG'dolah,* by Reuven haẒarfati. Modena, 1556 (MS. British Museum).

Davidson, Israel. *Thesaurus of Medieval Hebrew Poetry.* New York, 1924–33.

Delacrut, Mattityahu. *Commentary to Shaarei Orah.* Cracow, 1600.

———. *Sefer Ẓurat ha-Areẓ.* Offenbach, 1640.

———. *Sefer Ẓel Olam.* Munkács, 1887.

Dembitzer, Hayim Nathan. *Klilat Yofi.* Cracow, 1888.

———. *Mikht'vei Bikoret.* Cracow, 1882.

Dinur, Ben-Zion. *B'Mifnei HaDorot.* Jerusalem, 1955.

Dubnow, Simon. *A History of the Jews in Russia and Poland.* Vol. 1. Philadelphia, 1916.

———. *Pinkas haMedina.* Berlin, 1925.

Duran, Isaac. *Shaarei Dura.* Lublin, 1574.

Eisenstein, J. D. *Oẓar Yisrael.* New York, 1907.

Eliezer b. Samuel of Metz. *Sefer Yereiim.* Venice, 1566.

Elton, G. R. *The New Cambridge History: Reformation.* Cambridge, 1965.

Enelow, Hyman. *Menorat haMaor.* New York, 1929–32.

Friedberg, Hayim D. *Bet Eked Sefarim.* Antwerp, 1928–32.

———. *Toldot haDfus haIvri b'Poloniah.* Antwerp, 1932.

Fuenn, Samuel Joseph. *Kiryah Ne'emanah.* Vilna, 1880.

———. *Knesset Yisrael.* Warsaw, 1886.

Fuerst, Julius. *Bibliographisches Handbuch der gesammten juedischen Literatur.* Leipzig, 1849.

Fuks, L. *Das Schemuelbuch des Esrim Wearba.* Vols. I & II. Assen, 1961.

———. *Das altjuedische Epos Melokim-Buk.* Assen, 1965.

Garrison, F. H. *History of Medicine.* Philadelphia, 1929.

Gerondi, Pereẓ b. Isaac Kohen. *Sefer Ma'arekhet HaElohut.* Ferrara, 1557.

Gershom ben Shlomo of Arles. *Shaarei Shamayim.* Venice, 1547.

Gevirtz, Stanley. "Of Patriarchs and Puns." *Hebrew Union College Annual,* Vol. XLVI (1975).

Gikatilla, Joseph. *Shaarei Ora.* Jerusalem, 1970.

Glicksberg, Shlomo. *HaDerashah b'Yisrael.* Jerusalem, 1940.

Goldenthal, J. *Der Commentar des Rabbi Moses Narbonensis.* Vienna, 1852.

Gottlieb, Yedidiah. *Sefer Ahavat Shem.* Lublin, 1648.

———. *Sefer Shir Yedidiah.* Cracow, 1649.

Graetz, Heinrich. *Geschichte der Juden.* Vol. 9. Leipzig, 1877.

Haberman, A. H. *Gezerot Ashkenaz v'Ẓarefat.* Jerusalem, 1945.

Hayim bar Yosef Michael. *Or haḤayim.* Frankfurt a/M, 1891.

Ḥayyat, Judah. *Commentary to Ma'arekhet haElohut.* Ferrara, 1557.

Heilperin, Israel. *Bet Yisrael b'Polin.* Jerusalem, 1948.

———. *Pinkas Va'ad Arba Araẓot.* Jerusalem, 1945.

Heineman, Joseph. *Derashot b'Ẓibbur biTkufat haTalmud.* Jerusalem, 1970.

Herẓ, Naphtali. *Perush al haMidrash Rabbah meḤamesh haMegillot.* Cracow, 1569.

Heyman, Aaron b. Mordecai. *Torah haKetuvah v'Hamesorah.* Tel Aviv, 1967.

Horodetzky, S. A. *Encyclopedia Judaica.* Vol. 9. Berlin, 1930.

Isaac ben Joseph of Corbeil. *Sefer Mitzvot Ḳaẓer.* Cracow 1596.

Isserles, Moses. *Torat haOlaḥ.* Prague, 1569.

———. *Mekhir Yayin.* Cremona, 1559.

———. *She'elot u'Tshuvot.* Cracow, 1640.

———. *She'elot u'Tshuvot haReMa.* Jerusalem, 1970.

Kaidanover, Avi Hirsch. *Kav haYashar.* Frankfurt a/M, 1705.

Lattes, Isaac di. *She'elot u'Tshuvot.* Vienna, 1860.

Lewin, Louis. *Die Landessynode der grosspolnischen Judenschaft.* Frankfurt a/M, 1926.

Lieberman, Saul. *HaYerushalmi kiPshuto.* Jerusalem, 1935.

Mahler, Raphael. *Toledot haYehudim b'Polin.* Merḥavia, 1946.

Malter, Meir Yeḥiel. *Ir Tehillah.* Warsaw, 1896.

Margoliouth, G. *Catalogue of Hebrew and Samaritan Manuscripts in the British Museum.* Vol. III. London, 1909.

Meir of Tarnopol. *Maor haKatan*. Furth, 1697.

Midrash Ḥamesh Megillot. Cracow, 1587.

Midrash Rabbah. Warsaw, 1921.

Midrash Tanḥumah. Mantua, 1533.

Minz. Judah. *Sefer She'elot u'Tshuvot*. Munkács, 1898.

Mishnah. Warsaw, 1884–89.

Mordecai *Commentary*. In *M'Orot* edition of Babylonian Talmud. New York, 1929.

Moses haDarshan. *Midrash Bereshit Rabati*. Jerusalem, 1940.

Naphtali, Hirsch b. Jonathan. *Ntiv haYashar*. Dyhernfurth, 1712.

Neubauer, Adolph. *Catalogue of the Hebrew Manuscripts in the Bodleian Library*. Oxford, 1886.

Pirkei Avot. Yiddish Translation. Cracow, 1601.

Puchowitzer, Judah Leib b. Joseph. *Derekh Ḥokhma*. Frankfurt a/o, 1684.

Rabinowitz, H. R. *Diuknaot Shel Darshanim*. Jerusalem, 1967.

Recanati, Menaḥem. *Biur haTorah*. Venice, 1545.

Roth, Cecil. *A History of the Jews of Italy*. Philadelphia, 1949.

———. *Jews of the Renaissance*. Philadelphia,, 1959.

Schipper, Yiẓḥak. *Kulturgeschichte fun di Yiden in Polin b'ays'n Mittelalter*. Warsaw, 1926.

Schirmann, Ḥayyim. *HaShirah haIvrit b'Sfarad uProvence*. Berlin, 1934.

———. *Mivḥar haShirah haIvrit b'Italiah*. Berlin, 1934.

Scholem, Gershom. "Meḥukar l'Mekubalim (Agadat haMekubalim al haRambam)." *Tarbiẓ*. 1935.

———. *Major Trends in Jewish Mysticism*. Jerusalem, 1941.

———. *The Kabbalah*. New York, 1974.

Sefer Daniel. Yiddish Translation. Cracow, 1588.

Sefer Rabbot. Cracow, 1588.

Sefer Raziel. Rosanes ed., 1804.

Sefer Yeẓira. Horadno ed., 1806.

———. L. H. Frank ed., trans. by Isidor Kalisch. New York, 1977.

Sela, Avraham. *Ẓror Hamor*. Cracow, 1605.

Shemtov b. Shemtov. *Hasagot Moshe Askar*. Ferrara, 1556.

———. *Migdal Oz*. Venice, 1524.

Shulvass, M. *The Jews in the World of the Renaissance*. Leyden, 1973.

Simonsohn, Shelomo. *Toldot haYehudim b'Dukasut Mantova*. Jerusalem, 1962.

———. *History of the Jews in the Duchy of Mantua*. Jerusalem, 1977.

———. "Sefarim v'Sifriot shel Yehudei Mantua 1595." *Kiryat Sefer* 37, no. 1 (1961–62).

Solomon b. Moses. *Merkevet haMishna*. Salonica, 1782.

Steinschneider, Moritz. *Catalogus Librorum Hebraeorum in Bibliotheca Bodleiana*. Berlin, 1852–60.

van Straalen, S. *Catalogue of Hebrew Books in the British Museum*. London, 1894.

Talmud Bavli. *M'Orot*. New York, 1962. Soncino Translation, 35 vols. London: Soncino Press, 1945 et seq.

Talmud Yerushalmi. Cracow, 1609; Krotoschin, 1866; Jerusalem, 1968.

Tishbi, I. "HaPulmus al Sefer haZohar b'Me'ah ha Shesh-esrei b'Italiah." In *75th Anniversary Festschrift for Gershom Scholem*. Jerusalem, 1968.

Wachstein, Bernhard. *Katalog der Salo Cohn'schen Schenkungen*. Vienna, 1911.

Waxman, Meyer. *A History of Jewish Literature*. New York, 1938.

Werblowski, R. J. Zwi. *Joseph Karo: Lawyer and Mystic*. Oxford, 1962.

Wettstein, P. H. "Darshan." *Ozar Yisrael*. Vol. 4. New York, 1910.

———. *Kadmoniot MiPinkesaot Yeshanim*. Cracow, 1913.

———. *L'Toldot Yisrael v'Hakhamov b'Polin*. Cracow, 1913.

Wiener, Samuel. *Psak haHerem*. St. Petersburg, 1897.

Wolff, Johannus Christophorus. *Bibliotheca Hebraea*. Leipzig, 1715.

Yehiel ben Shelomo of Minsk. *Seder haDorot*. Warsaw, 1869.

haZarfati, Reuven. *Perush haYeri'ah haG'dolah*. MS., Modena, 1556.

Zinberg, W. S. *Geschichte fun der Literatur bei Yiden*. Vol. 5. Vilna, 1935.

Ziv, Asher. *She'elot u'Tshuvot haReMa*. Jerusalem, 1970.

Zohar Hadash. Cracow, 1613.

Zohar. Sulam ed., Jerusalem, 1954/55.

Zunz, L. *Gottesdienstliche Vorträge*. Berlin, 1882.

INDEX

מהמלאכים מנקרא' בני אלקי' . כדכתי' אני אמרתי אלקי' אתם ובני עליון כולכם
וג'ו' . ומאחר שראשית הבריאה היתה לזאת הכוונה לא יהיה לבטלה אע"פי שאדם
הר אשון המשיך עליו זוהמת היצר הרע מכחא הקדמוני' עתיד שיתבטל זוהמת היצר
הרע לזמן המשיח כדכתיב והסירותי את לב האבן מבשרכם וג'ו' . ואמרו בסתרי תורה
אדם ר"ת אדם דוד משיח . וז' תיבות בפסוק כנגד ז' רועים לימות המשיח דוד
באמצע אדם שת מתועלא לימינו · אברהם ויעקב ומשה מסמאלו כדאיתא
פ' החלול : והיינו נמי כוונת המאמר

על דרך המדרש

ותיב רב המנונא קמיה דעולא וקא הוי בשמעתתא : ר"ל שכוונת רב המנונא
היתה שגם לזמן המשיח שיקויים מה כחוו על ההדרים רגלי מבשר מסמיע
שלום מבשר טוב מסמיע ישועה וג' . שגם אז יסלוט היצר הרע . וזה וקא הוי ר"ל
קיסוי היצר הרע יהיה : כשמעתתא נם בזמן שיקויים מסמיע ישועה . כמאמר שמואל
בכלחק אין כין העולם הזה לימות המשיח שלא שעבוד מלכיות . אמר עולא עליה דר'
המנונא מה נברא ומה גוברי כמה הוא גדול . כלומר שרב המנונא חושב כמו מי
שיפרט עכשיו כין מי שמתגבר על היצר הרע ובין מי שתגבר מהיצר הרע ·
יהיה לזמן המשיח ולא יהיה אז כמו כוונת תחילת הבריאה והוא כנד הפסוק אך
אמרתי אלקי' אתם ובני עליון כולכם · מסמע שאז לא יהיה היצר הרע מדכתיב
ונם הפסוק מעיד כך כדכתי' והסירותי לב האבן מבשרכם . או וזאת הנבופי אריחיק
מעליכם . ולא יקשה על שמואל שא" אין כין העולם הזה לימות המשיח אלא שעבוד
מלכיות היינו נמי שיסתעבד היצר הרע שנקר' מלך זקן וכסיל כפסוק טוב ילד מסכן.
כי לאו דהרפכי"א מאתיב · כלומר אי לאו אתה מאותן דהרפכיא שיעלו עתיד לסס
אפי' אותן שאינן מיוחסין כגון האומות לבקש השלמות האמתי ולא ישראל המיוחסין
שלכולם יסתלק לב האבן מהם · כדכתיב והיה באחרית הימים נכון יהיה הר בית ה' ·
ברואש ההרים וג' · ואמרו לכו ונעלה אל בית ה' וג' · וכדפי' הנמרא וכשי אקב · מאי
הרפכיא הר שהכל פונין סם כל כסולין ספוסלין ומכטלין עז שלחן עד · שאין מונאין
ושה זרה תחת ידיהם פונין והולכין סם : איכסיף רב המנונא : אחכ' כא עולא
לחקור מרב המנונא איך שהוא סובר בעכין תחיית המתים וזם כסף גלגלתא להיכא
יסכת כלומר מום הסדרה חבל כסף סכמסך מהגלגולת סל ראש שכל החיות תלוי כו·
להיכא נתת דעתך אם יחזור אחר המיתה או לא . אל רב המנונא לעולא לפוס נהרא
דהיינו שיקויים בפסוק בפסעיה כיסעיה מ"ב ושמתי כהרות לאיים ואותה פרסה מעבין התקתי'
כדכתיב לפניו ירוכו יוטכי סלע מראש הרים ינחו : אל עולא לרב המנונא לב מפום
נהרא את שתובל לתרן שהשלמות האמתי יהיה הכל לזמן תחיית המתים אחר ביאת
משיח ואז כלע המות סלא יסלוט היצר הרע וכבר הפלוגו כזה הענין מהתחייה ומעולם
הכא חכמי התלמוד כפ' חלק וכמה וכמה גאוני עולם כמו שמוזכר בשער הגמול
להרמב"ן וקנת ממכו כהגהות מיימוני בהלכו' תשובה · יתברך ויתרוםם של נורא
עלילה · מזיכנו להסעלים גם את זה כשלמת ימי הגבלה :

סליק סליק סליק

פסאס . וכמה וכמה דאינו כזמנינו זה בני אדם ומשפחות פמושלים   ומצדים
לחכיריהם וכאבדו מן העול'הם וממשלתם ועושרם : ולאפשר סזה טעס מדרה נ.קברת
בעליה וכהאי גוונא איתא כמוטה פ' ואלו כאמרין ח"ר שמעון בן פזי מותר   להחניף
לרשעים בעולם הזה סב' לא יאמר עוד כדיב ולכילי לא יאמר סוע   מב:כ
דכעולם הזה סוה סרי · וכפ'ק דמגילה אית' מותר להתגרות כרשעים היינו כסאין
הסעה מחקקת להם · אבל כזמן סהסעה מסחקת להם וילד תקיף' מותר להחניף נהם
כדי סלא יהרגנוהו . לקיים מה סב' . וחי כהם גלא סימות כהם : והיינו כוונת   המאמר
עוד על דרך השכל
לב יתיב רב המנוכא קמיה דעולא וקא הוי כמסעתא דל' סעולתא היה מוק פ'ה מאחרי
והיה לו ה"יו ואכוי · כמסעתא · אעפי'סהיה מסכים ומעריב עליהם כתפילה
כמו סעוסין כקריאת סע'מ סכתוב בן כסככך ובקומך · א' סעלא לרב המנוכא מה   ג
נכרא וכו' ואיתא פ'. התככת מה ה' אלהיך סואל מעומך אל תקרי מה אלא מאה סהם
אה כרכות התפילה . כלומר התפילה סנקראת מה . כה יכול אדם להתנבר על
יס.   ומה נוכרי ·   כלומר והתפילה סנקראת מה יכול אדם להכנל מאחרים
כרו עלין ·   ומה כך סאה.כ.סאר כנרותיך מאחרים   ולא כונלת
נך · אי לאו דהרפכיא מאתיה הך סכל הפסונין כתפלתן פוכין סם וכסכיל
חי אתה כעבה וכמוזכר כסערי אורה סמקום אסד יס סנקראת פסיניס נב: התפב.ות
 פסולות ככמסות סם . והוא סנקט מנע' איכם'פ רב המנוכא סחטדו סעמה תפלה
פסולה · ולסוף חסב עולא דילחא רסע המינר לרב המנוכא הסעה   מסחקת
מנד מערכת הנלנלים ואין התפלה כסמעת כל כך מהרה לא עד סימהר ויכלה בח
הסמערכ'ואז הרסע כלה מאלין · וידע סמערב' הנלנלים לטוב ולרע . ומה סל.....ו'וף
וכוסף הוא סיהיה מערכת הנלנל'לטוכה עלין · וזה סרמו כסף נכלנתא דל' הכיסוף
והחמלה מהנלנלים סהוא לטובה . להיכא יהכת כדעתך על רסע סטרע לך אם היתה
הסעה והסמזל מסחקת לו · אן לא היתה מסחקת לו ובכ'א הרע לך ·
אל' רב המנוכא סעולא נעולה לפוס כהרא ·   כלומר דעתי כוטה סהמזל היה מכ'יר וחורח
עלין וסעה היתה מסחקת לו וזה סנקט כהרא · לסאן כהורא · אל' עולא לרב המנוכא
· ל'כ חפוס כהרא את · כלומר מרסע סהמזל מכהיר וחסחק לו אתה מקבל רעה · סב'
תפלתך איכה מקובלת כל כך מהרה אעפי' סהיא הנוגה ואיכה מהתפלות הפסולות ·
נאם לא היתה הסעה מסחקת לאוחו רסע כלי ספק היתה תפלתך ההנונה כסמע ז
תכף וסיית כינול :
ועל דרך המדרש
לג בראשית כרא סקי' כא' לרמז סהיתה ראסית כוונת הכריאה מסחיים וארץ
פרס העולם הגדול כסכיל האדם סהוא עו'.סקטן סיהיה כחמד
מהמנהכים

בראשית ברא אלקים את השמים · מערכת השמים ז כוכבי לכת · ואת לא
הארץ שכהם יונהגו יושבי הארץ · וכ' ז תיבות בפסוק כנגד ז
כוכבי לכת . וכשלהי שבת וכפ' אלו מנלחין יש פלונתא אי יש מזל לישראל או לא.
וכא להורות כאן שהמערכת ביד אלקיס דסמיך ליה אלקים את השמים · ויושבי
הארץ תחת מערכת השמים דסמיך ליה את השמים ואת הארץ · ואעפ' שהכל ביד
הק' כה כדכתיב לה הארץ ומלואה עכ' כלמוד מזה שהמערכת ביד הק' כה אם יגיע
או חיזה רעה מנד המערכת · והאדם הנדיק מתפלל להס' על אותו הרעה · הפ'
מהככו לטובה · כענין ינחק ויעתר לו ה' . בפ' הכא על יבחתו . וכענין אברהס
גא מאהטגביניכות שלך שלהי שבת · וכן כשהס' מעבים את האדם ע' אדם אחר רשע
ואעפ' שאותו רשע שמעבים בו את האדם אין לו הנלמה אפי' מנד המערכת עכ'
הקב'כה מגביהו כדי להעניש בו להעניש שהס' עושה תמיד עם ישראל ע' האומות
שהם מטריחין בעינותיהס להקב'כה להגביה לאותה אומה כומה כיו ס׳דרסו על פמוק
הוגעתני כחמאתיך בפ' חלק . והל כמינר לישראל כעשה ראש בפ' הכזוק ·וגן
כשמעגים את היחיד אז תועיל התפלה והתשובה · אבל אם יגיע לאדם חיזה רעה
מנד רשע שהטבעה משחחת לו מנד המערכת . לא יכול האדם להתפלל אל המערכת
שיהפוך לאותו רשע המערכת לרעה · כי הוא שליח ואין בידו כ'כ תמר בו פי
לא ישא לפשעיכם כפ' משפטים ופי' רש' כי הוא שליח ולא עשה אלא שליחותו : ונס
כשיתפלל להס' אינו כעבה שהשליח כבר עשה שליחותו · אלא נריך להמתין ולבמת
שינמר הס' כח המערכת מהרה והוא יפול אחכ מאלין · אך כתכאי שיתגבר הוא על
הרשע כעקידת התורה . דאם לא כן דילמא הקב'כה יבליח לאותו רשע אפ' אחר כלות
המערכת כדי להעבישו בו . ורחייה נרחה לזה ממאמרי התלמוד שנרחות סותרות
להדדי ונעם זה יתורנו דאיתא פק דגיטין שלח ליה מך עוקבא לר' אלעזר בני אדם
העומדין עלי וביד' למוסרם למנכות מהו שרטט וכתב ליה אמרתי אשמרה דרכי
מחטוא בלשוני אשמרה לפי מחסום כעוד רשע לכגדי אעפ' שהרשע לכגדי אשמרה
לפי מחסום - שלח ליה קא מנערגי לי טובא ולא מניכא דאיקום כבו שלח ליה דנם לה'
והתחולל לו דום לו לה' והגא יפילם לך חל ליס תללים הסכס והערב · עליהם לבית
המדרש והם כגון מאלין : ואיתא שלהי במה אשה כמאן תלין כבשא בדיקלא כהאי
תכא וטמא טמא יקרא מב'אן סנריך להודיע נערכ לרכים ורכיס יבקשו עלין רחמים ·
ולפי זה יקסה לר' אלעזר אמאי לא שלח למר עוקבא דמר עוקבא לאו מסמיא כפק
עלין רחמים · אלא שעמא דמלתא כדכתיבכא דנערתא דמר עוקבא לאו מסמיא כפק
דרך טובא לא שיך ביה רחמיס מחסריכי שיבקשו עלין · אבל הכא נכי ריקלא ומנורע
דנערתא דידהו מן שמיא שיך ביה רחמיס אפי'מאחסריכי : יונעם למבין : והסוד מזה
הענין נרחה שהגא שאלו מסוס סאלו נכי אדם מישראל בנוק חלק כענין הסהנחה בגודל
כשאר השמים תחת המערכת ואין להם חלק בנוק ישראל כענין הסהנחה בגודל
מס אם והשעה משחקת להם ויבא תקיפם כפי' הורחנ' מערכתם וכאנמר ה'מערכת
הם כלין מאיבין כמו שאלין ' שעור כי חין להם זכות אחכ' ש'עימדו בטוכתם כגודל

ובגין דא אותיב ליה לפום כהרא' כלומ' דכוונת אולפני הוא לפומא קדישא דלעילא
דמשפיע מחכמתיה לחכימין דאיכון כבהר המתנבר · דהיינו נשם ולא לקכתר · וכד
שמע עולא מלתא דא · הל מפום כהרא את · מאיכון קדישין דכוונתיהון לשמייא
וכמלת את רמז ליה דאת מאיכון חכימין דאתרבו מאת ה' אלוקך תירא · וייהות
למימר עלך כרוך שחלק מחכמתו לירא'ו : וברך רחמנא דכבר בחכמין ובאוריית'א
דלהון דאהזו במאמר דא דפרישנא דלית ייחוסא כייחוסא דאורייתא דאיהי לשום
שמים · ובגין דא אכתיב עלן באוריית'א בכים אתם לה' אלקיכם דאכן מתייחסין כתר
אכונה דכטמיה דתלמידים קרויין בנים : ונ'אהכי כמי פטטיא דמאמר דמאן דנכב
אתר פנומיה איהו ודאי פנים כדמשמע מהרפכיח הר שכל הפסולין פוכן שם וכנ'
וכדאמרי'כעלמא לא נחמנא הולך הזרזיר אנל העורב אנל מפני שהוא מינו :

ועל דרך השכל

כ ט **בראשית**   כרא שקים רל כאלו כתוב כרא שקים ראשית רמז על היגר הרע שכה
כראשית אל הגוף כדאיתא בחלק מפסוק לפתח חטאת רובן ·   והוא
ש רמזו שמתחילה כרא הקב'ה את העולם כמדת הדין וכנ' · וידוע שהאדם עולם קטן :
את השמים ואת הארן כלומר היגר הרע שכא בראשית אל הגוף גורם שיעמדו לדין   אל
הנשמה שכא מן השמים והגוף שכא מן הארן כדאיתא כמי בחלק מפסוק יקרא   אל
השמים מעל ואל הארן לדין עמו נבי מרכיב חינר על סומא ·   ועל כן ז תיבות כפסוק
כנ'בד היגר הרע סים לו ז שמות כפ' החליל ·   וכמסוך סתף עמו מדת רחמים סיתנבר
השכל והוא שהקדימו כדכתיב ביום עשות ה' שקים ונו' ·   והיינו כמי כוונת המאמר

על דרך השכל

ל **יתיב**   רב המכוכא קמיה דעולא וקא הוי פי' רש'י מקשה ·   והכווכה שעולא הכין איך
שרב המכוכא רנא להלין בעד היגר הרע כדכתיב ומקשה לכו יפול ברעה ·
וזה שאמר כמ'שעתא שהוא רמז על־יגר הרע שכל איברי הגוף כמש'מים לו · והשיב לנ
עולא מה נברא שהוא היגר הינר מנד הארן שרונה להתנבר מפני שהוא קודם ליגר טוב
שהוא השכל ·   ומה נוכרי רמז על השכל מנד השמים שהניח היגר הרע להתנבר עלוי
ועב נקרא נוכרי ·   סביהס עתידין ליתן את הדין כמו שהקדמכו יקרא אל השמי'מעל
וכנ' ·   אי לאו אתה מלין ·   דהרפביח מאתיה שכל הגוף שנקבא עיר קטנה פוכן ליגר
הרע שנקרא הר כדאיתא הר המכוכא כעבור שרנה להלין בעד
היגר הרע ·   אל עולא לרב המכוכא כסם גלנותא להיכא יהבת ·   כלומ' השכל הכלבכף
שבלגלולת להיכא יהבת ליה סיהוא הוא מתנבר על היגר הרע ·   או יהא נגבר סיתנבר
היגר הרע עלין ·   אמר ליה רב המכוכא לעולא · לפום כהרא' כלומר כווכתי שהשכל
יתנבר וכולם ימסכו אחריו כבהר ·   כדכתיב ביטעיה מי' ב' וכהרו אליו כל הגוים כמם
סימסכו אחר מסיח של הגוים כן ימסכו כן האיברי'אחר השכל :   אל אב אין נדיכין
נוף וסכל ליתן את הדין וזה שאמר אם כן מפום כהרא אם כן מפום את ותחזור הכשמה למקום
                      מונכה ·   **שעו**

וידוע שלוחות אבנים היו שנים על כל לוח ה' דברות · והיינו שנקט הכתב האבן

ר' ישמעאל או שלא אבנים זו כנגד זו כנגד מרקולים אסורות · ושתים מותרות · וחכמים

חומרים שכראות עמו אסורות · ושאין כראות עמו מותרות : גמרא · ועקר עד של

המרקולים היתה שתים אבנים למטה ואבן אחת למעלה · והכוונה ר' ישמעאל

אומר שלא אבנים דהיינו היצר הרע שנקרא אבן ושתי לוחות לוחות · זו כנגד זו

כלומר זו כנגד זו : כנגד מרקולים שהיתה אבן אחת על גבי שתים דהיינו היצר הרע

שהוא אבן אחת מתנבר על התורה שהיא שתי לוחות אבנים · אז אסורות וחבושות

לוחות התורה ולא יכול לקיים שום מנוה ממנה כראוי · ושתים כלומר בזמן שהשתים

למעלה שהן הלוחות בין שלומד בין שלומד שלא לשמה ובין שלומד לקנטר ולהתייהר · מותרות

לוחות התורה שאיפשר שילמוד אחכ לשמה ויקיים מנות התורה כראוי · וחכמים

חולקים על זה ואומרים שכראות עמו · כלומר שלומד לקנטר ולהתייהר שהוא כראה

עם לוחות התורה בגול וחשוב · אסורות לוחות התורה ולא יקיים מנות התורה כראוי ·

ועל אותג אדם שלומד לקנטר ולהתייהר כאמר וחושא אחד יאבד טובה הרבה · ר'ל

מפני שכמה וכמה בכי אדם נגררין ולומדין ממעשים מכוערים של אותג הכם שלומד

לקנטר ולהתייהר ואומרים הלא אפילו פל' ת'ח מיקל בדבר זה כגון כשחוק וכתאנות

וכדומה · ואכ זה הכם כעינו סולל ומאבד טובה הרב מבכי אדם ונדקו מה שאחרו

מוטב שלא כברא וכו' · ושאין כראות עמו · כלומר שלומד כמתפסק ודרך טיול

ולא שיהא כראות עמו לוחות התורה לקנטר ולהתייהר · מותרות · לוחות התורה

וכוודאי יקיים אחכ מנות התורה כראוי : והיינו כוונת המאמר :

רב המנונא   יתיב קמיה דעולא וקא הוי כמתעתא אמר מה כברא ומה נובדי לאו

מהרפניא מאתיה שאינן מיוחסין כיחום התורה · כלומר עולם הוה

סביר הואיל ורב המכוכא מקשה כל כך ומראה חריפות וחידוד דלמא אין כוונתו

לשמים דלא למד אלא לקנטר ולהתייהר · וזה שאמר לאו מהרפכיא מאתיה

וכדאמרינן מאי הרפכיא הר שהכל פונים בו דכל הפסולין כייחוסא דאורייתא שאין

מוכחין אסם יראת ה' שהיא התורו'לסם שמים פוכין והולכין סם ולומדין כדי להתייהר

ולהכסא כהר · ומלתא דא גרס לרב המכוכא דאכסיף כדי סירנים עולם דכוונתו

לשמים מסום דכסיפא איהי מלתא טבא טבא כבר ישראל דליתא

ב

כערל כדאיתא פרק הערל רחמנים כיישכים גומלי חסדים כידוע שהוא מזרעו של

אברהם אבינו · וכלו רב המכוכא הוה מפרם ליה לעולא דהוה תמה ואמר מה כברא ·

והשיב כראשי תיבין גומל כ'מן ר'חמן א'כי · וזה הראה כמאי דאכסיף · וכד חזל

עולא סימן יפה כרב המכוכא הוה כעי למיקם על כרור העכין ולשמוע מפין כוונתו

ולא כרמז · ואל כסף גולגלתא להיכא יהבת · כלומר אורייתא דכתיב בה כי טוב

סחרה מסחר כסף · דאת מעיין כמות סבגלגלת להיכא יהבת כוונתך לסם שמים · או

לקנטר ולהתייהר ל'ל לפום כהרכא · והכא רב המכוכא מגו חריפותיה דסני לאהדא הוה

ימוטיב ליה פוד · על כדוריה דעולא דאמר מה כברא כאלו הכין מכוונתו · דבעא

לקנטר ליה כמילי דת'ח דכריך למיהוי כנהר המתנבר ·   וכנין

מח

כסף גלגלתא דאיתי דוכתא דאגיילוד : סא ודאי ליהא : דסא קושטא דסלכתא דאולין בייתוסא בתר
דוכתא דדר ביה כדמפסקין סם ספי הרפבזא כך שכבל בוקין כב : וכדפ׳ רעא כל פסולין שלא עובסין
אסס פוגין והולכין לסס • וה״כ ספי היקן ליה בכבסף גלגלתא : ונתי תיקא רב סאמכא
לא הוה דר בהרפבזא כלל : מכל שכן דלא הוה ליה לסכסיף דלועא ליה לאו מהרפבזא אבא : ועוד
ספי בעסא עולא דא״ל להייבא יהבת כסף גלגלתא : פסא״י לא סאל ליה מזן אבנך נעסן איבון כגי
מספחתך אי הוה כוונתן לידע יחוסיס : ועוד פספסי כבולא תלמודא ולא אסכחסא דוכתא דלחא כה
אפי׳ רעיא דיכילין לגלול כאוריתא דכר אוריין בגין יחוסא אלא על ור דא : וסוא סף רעת סתוריס
כמו סדרסו בסוריות אפי׳ סמוד ע״ח קולא לכ״ג עס האדן מפסוק יקדס סיא עבנבים :
וכקדיס קנת פסוק ראסון מתוריתי׳ כו הקדוסה • מפני סהיא אבן הראסה :

בראשית ברא אלקים את השמים ואת הארץ :

הנה כבר האריכו רוב המפרסים כזה הפסוק וכברט כמלת בראסית • כמו האבן
עזרא בהקדמה • כחי ופרפראות וכראה בקינור סבם כוונת הפסו׳ מהתחלת התורה
הוא כמו כוונת רז״ל מה סדרסו רבל מה כוונתו סעתק הימס היא התורה

ועב יקרה היא מפביכים כתסכון **תורה** וכם כחסבכן **זה לב דוד**
דרש • ומעינו כאברהס סכתוב בו וסמור מסמרתי מטותי הקותי ותורתי ואעפ
סהיה אביו עובד על כעסה הוא ראס היחם כסביל התורה כדכתב כי אב המון גוים
כתתיך • והוא סאמר **בראסית** כמו סדרסו רזל כסביל התורה סנקראת ראסית
דרכו וכסביל ישראל סנקראו ראסית תבואתו • ובסביל מסה וירא ראסית לו והכל
כוונה אחת • כי ידוע תורה כגימטרי׳ תר״ן עס אככי ולא יהיה לך כדלית׳סוף מכות
מסה רכיבנו כני׳ תרי״ג • ה׳ אלקי ישראל כני׳ תרי״ג וכן כראסי׳ת כבי׳ כתורה זכר
בתורה תרי״ן • וככללים כול׳ כמלת ראס׳ת לומר סזאת התור׳ היא ראס היחם • וטעם
זה אבן מקראיס בכים לה • והייכו סדרסו אלה תולדות סמים והארן בהברא׳ס אל
תקרי בהברא׳ס אלא באברהס בראברהס • כלומר כסם סבראסית ברא מורה סהתורה ראס
היחס • ולכך ז׳ תיבות בפסוק כדכתיב חנבה עמודיה סבעה • כך אברהס ראס היחם
כסביל התורה ; והאבות עם האמהות ז׳ אברהס יחק יעקב סרה רבקה רחל לאת :

על דרך הפשט

ועל זאת ההקדמה סקדמכו כראה גס כוונת המאמר
מאי דחזי לן בדעתא דקלישא דלא הוקבע מאמר דא בתלמודא אלא כגן לברר כיה
כמי דהאי אוריתא קדיסא לא תליא בייחוסא כדאיתא בסוריות ממזר ת״ח קודס לגב
על סכאמר יקרם היא מפכיכים מכהן גדל הכככם לפכי ולפכיס • אלא עקר יימוסא
דאוריתא בכווכא דליכא כדאיתא פ׳ היה העוסק בתורה סלא לסמה מוטב לו
סלא כברא ונהסקו הכו׳ ונהא אמרינן פ׳ מקוס סבהבו לעולם יעסוק אדם כתורה אפילו
סלא לסמה סמתוך סלא לסמה בא לסמה • ותרנו הא דעביד לקכתר ולהתייהר מכטב
לו סלא כברא והא דעביד כמתעסק בעלמ׳ולא לקכתר ולהתייהר • ופוכה דא עבידכא
סמך על מסכה חדא דמסכת עז לר פ ׳יסמעאל בדרסת פ׳ כתקותי • דאית במדרט כעם
אם כחקותי תלכו חוקים כחוקקתי בהס סמיס וארן וכו׳ • חוקים סהס חקוקים על יער
הרע הזד הוי כחוקקים תקוקי הון • אר לו מסל למקום אירמון סהוא מסאבע בגיוסת
הוסיב בן המלך קוסטיכוס לסמרין כך אמר הקבה התור אבן • ויבר הרע אבן • התורה
אבן דכתיב לוחות אבן • ויבר הרע אבן דכתיב והסרותי לב האבן מבסרכס • האבן
גירוע תסמור את האבן : :

והנה כתחילה כדרכי על דרך **הפשט** בקצרה · להשקיט לפעמים מה מאטב **בה**
המטיח כתחילת עינינו נסתירה · וחא"כ על' דרך **השבל** האריכתי קצת
המאמר · מפני שהאדם כמשך אחר קינר הרע והחומר : ואין לאדם מהם המלטה
נמכלת · כדכתיב כי אין אדם נדיק באדן אשר יעשה טוב ולא יחטא בספר קהלת :
והכלותי קצת רמי זוע אוך סיני שרע רונה להתגבר בתוזת · ואיך סינביד עלין
השכל בטעבות כודקו' · סנריך לסנף ולהמית עכיויני החומר בטעות דחוקות : כמכואר
במסכת תמיד טעמו · שאמרו חכמי הנגב הרונה לחיות ימית את עכמו : סהכוונה
הרונה להחיות לעולם הכא ולניהמת מהכעלם · ימית את תאוותיו ולא יהכה מזה
העולם : ודונמתו כתפסוק מכינו · סדבר עם לבו וכפסו ד"ד מלכינו : כמו ספי' רא"ל
מומור יו כתפוק אמרת נח' אדני · וכמזמור כו כתפסוק לך אמר לבי בקשו פני : וזה
בענמו הכריאסכי לבאר חא"כ על דרך **המדרש** · כדי שאחר התלאות תמיד לא
יקרום החורם · וכזה מוכות המקוות לעתיד ירוניי · לתקיית המתים ולעולם הכא
ולזמן המסיח : המפורסים בכביאים וכתלמוד שאיהס גלויים להמין · וגם לקנת
התלמידים הוא לפעמים כדבר סמן :
ועל בן כררתי גל הראב נ' דרכים כעארת סוכן רומה · כגד ג' דרכיס ספרסעי על
פסוק מסכיל על דבר ימנא עוב כרים היסקדימה · כגד הכורא סה וא
שבל משה כלי חימרין · כררתי על' דרך **הפשט** כהדרון · וכמד התורה
והמנות סכתוב עליהם **שבל** · סוב לכל עומיהס · כררתי על דרך **השבל**
לעיניס : וכנגד התנוכחות והמוסרים הראויים לכל · סכתוב עניהס לקחת מוסר
השבל · סכזכות הימוסר כזכה לגוחל סכתוב עליו נח"ך מיך **והשביל** וינלח ·
כררתי על דרך **המדרש** סעתקרו מעכן הגאוחה **והמשביל** מיים · ומטעם
זה שאלו הדרכים כמלת **שבל** כללים · קראתי זה הספר **משביל לדוד** די
למכינים ולמסכילים · וכבי סיקניים כי ויסי **דוד** בכל **דרכיו משביל** וס' עמו ·
לדוד כמסתן לטוב טעמו : כעמחס וכנבלס · סידסקי ואת הסקל"ים תוך נ' יני סנבלת : כשכת
יהרה היא מפניכיס · וסיא בלאט כעב סטעכלות לדרסמים : סלק

התכללות העקר · שאם לא יזיק בדת יכולין לעמוד על חכמת המחקר : **כמו שעשה**
קהלת שהתחילתי וסופו דברי תורה · וקבל האמת ממי שאמרו כמו שכתב כח' פרקין
בעל המורה : וכן בסס רב שרירא גאון במזמרת האמור בהקדמה : **כתוב רוב**

כא האגדות הם סודות עליונות וחכמה · ומדות טובות והנהגות ישרות ומוסרים · **יתיקון**
הגוף והנפש ויכפם כמעלת ישרים · ואם תאמר מי התיר לנו לפרש מאמר יותר מדרך
כב אחד · דילמא לכוונה אחת הוא מיוחד : או איך נוכל לומר זאת היא כוונה הגונה ·
שמא יחטיא ח'ו הכוונה : כשלומא מה מדבר הסו' על פי כביא · נוכל לומ'שהיא מכוון
גם לזאת הכוונה שמפרש המכיח · אבל מה שדבר חכם מענמו ומסברתו · מי יאמר
שפירון לזאת הכוונה שאנו מפרשים אותו : ונראה שזאת איכנה טענה כתחילה ·
ראיה מהא דאמרינן במסכת מגילה : שמקשה שם בגרייתא כשזימנה אסתר את
המן מה היתה הכוונה · זה אומר בכה וזה אומר בכה ואומר לסוף במסקה ·
אשכחיה רבה לאליהו אל כמאן חזיא אסתר רוח הקדש ועבדת האי · אל ככולהו תכחי · וכולהו
אמוראי : ואל'ת דילמא אסתר כמי דברי דברי רוח הקדש בדעתה היו ערוכות · כמו שדרסו
סס מן · ותלבש אסתר מלכות · מאמר מפ'ק דכתברא חכם
עדיף מכביח : סכ'וכביא לבב חכמה · מי כתלה כמי הוי אומר השפל בגבות ורמה :
והטעם לפי שהכביח אין לו אלא הסיגנון שמרדין לו מן השמים · אבל לב צבון אין
חקר כפלי כפלים · ורא'יה מפ'ק דערכין מהכביח יהושע וחכם עתכיאל בן קכז ·
שהחזיר החכם עתכיאל מה שדעת יהושע הכביח גם · **ואמרו עוד בפק דע†**
אפי' סיחת חולין של חכמים נריכה תלמוד על הבכה · **וכמאמר שלמה להבין מ†ל**

כג ומליכה דברי חכמים וחידותם : ורא'יה שרוב דברי חכמים על דרך משל ומסודר ·
ממאמר במסכת ערוכין פ'הדר : תלמיד אחד הורה לפכי ר' אליעזר : ואמר לאשתו
תמה אם יוניא זה שבתו וכעשה מה שגזר : וארכבכ'ל א'ר יוחכן אותו תלמיד שמו
יודא כן גוריא . ורחוק ממכו שלא פרסאות היה : כפכיו היה תירן המתרן · **ויה†**
רחוק ממכו ג' פרסאות קאמר הטיב המקשה | במרן · והביא המתרן ראייה ·
ולוטעמיך שמו וסם אביו אבו למה שלא תאמר מאל היה · מזה ראייה מכוררת שרוב
דבריהם כבנויים על חידות ומשלים · וכמו שהותר כמי לדרוס על כל קוֹן · ויקון הלכות

כד תילי תיליס : כן נוכל לומר שדברו חכמים לפעמים · במטכה או בנמראו מלות
יתרות כדי להוניא ממכו כמה טעמים : או לדרוס ממכו איזה מוסר והנכגה · ודרך
ארן · להעמיד דת האמת בלי פרן : וכל שכן כשמכיח הדורש ראיה · **מפסוק או**
תלמוד או מדרשים · או מספרי חכמות או מהמפרשים : ומכפה הדברים כבמוזרה
ורקת . כדי לחבר אחת אל אחת · ולפעמים כס כן דרך גימטריאות · **שהס לחכמה**
פרפראות · ובפ'ב דזבחים מוסיפין וגורעין ודורסין ממכו , ולקח מדס הקר דס מהפר
יקטלכו· וכפ' איזהו מקומן עוד תראהו · ולקח לו יקח פ' רע' סרסיהו למפרע
ודרסהו : סוף דבר אלו הדברים אין להם שיעורים , **במדרסות ובתלמוד ובכל**
הספרים : אך הכל הולך אחר החותמת , להיטיר ולהחזיק דת הקאמת ; **שלא יקין חו**
דרסות סל דופי . ובכן אבא כאיל לפכי מלך המלכים סיחיו לרבנן אמרי פי :

וכן רבי ינאי אומר סמו יכון · כמו סמכנואר בתלק ובמדרש איכה כמינן : · ודרישת
השמות · בתלמוד ובמדרשים בכמה מקומות · כגון פ'ק דמגילה · בן יאיר בן שהאיר
עיניהם של ישראל בתפלה : · בן שמעי שמ'ע ה' תפלת תמים · בן קום שהקים על
שערי רחמים · וכן דורש שם משמות של מ'מ רביכו · ודונגמתן כ'אלף מקומות מכינו :
ותכלית הדבר אין חשובין על המדרש · לכ'ה טע'מים חו' מכורש ·   חה' לפי יח
שלפעפי' הדורש בעצמו יודע על דכריו סתירה · וש'תק ממכ' כדי להעמיד מה שהקשה
כנד המקרא · וא'יתא בתלמוד בכמה מקומות דונגמתו · שהמתרץ סותר דברי המקשה
אע'פ שהוא בעצמו יודע שאין האמת אתו :   · גם לפעמים יודע סתירה ויודע כמי
להשיב תשובה עליה · ולא חס לברט מפני אריכות דבריה · וכדי שלא תוניא דיכה ·
ראייה קנת מיכמות פרק האשה רבה : רב פפא סבר למעבד עובדא כמאי הוה לה
למיעבד · כין דהוה כדיעבד · וא'ל רב הונא בריה דרב יושע · ואמינוייא כינום
וכסמוך כתמיה · ופסק רב פפא מלהורות · מיד ולדורות :   · ועוד רוב המדרשות
עניים כחיזוקים ·   · והיו להם רק סמך הפסוקים :   · אבל הם מודים שהמקרא מידי
פשוטו אינו יונא · לא כמו שכתב הרסב'א סימן תי'ו על חכמי פרוב'י ננא :   מדרשו   יט
דרטות של דופי שהוניאו הפשוט וסמו הבמשל לאמת · וזה כתב הרסב'א קונדס שראה
כתב ההתכנכלות כחתמת ·   · ולהוניא הכתוב מפשוטו חס וחלילה ·   · כי הפשוט ודאי
תחילה :   · זולת כשיש כגזירה שוה ומפיק מפשוטו לגמרי כמעט מקומות · · כמו יקום על
שם אביו כף' כ' דיכמות · ואם האמת שזה הדרך כתחילה לקנת החכמים היה קשה ·
כדראיתא כמסכת שבת פ' כמה אשה :   · אמר רב כהנא כד הוינא כר תמני טרי הוה
גמירנא כולה תלמודא ושמעתא ·   · ולא ידענא דאין מקרא יונא מידי פשוטו עד
השתא :   · וממה שאמרו אין המקרא יונא מידי פשוטו תראה נודל חכמתם · ולא
אמרו אין המקרא אלא כפשוטו אלא זאת היתה כוונתם ·   · שיש לכו המדרש עם הפשוט
ואיכו יונא מידי כל אחד מהם · ויסכול הכתוב הכל ויהיו אמת שכיהם · וכמה האריך
הרב הנדול רמ'כן כזה העכין · כהשנגתיו על ספר המנו מהרד'מבם בתרי'ג מכין · וזה
הדרך עטינו במאמרים וכקנת מסניות · פשט ומדרש בטעמים ורל'אות :   · הכל כדי
לדרוש ולקבל שכר ולא לראות שאת · כדראמדינן בכן סורר ועיר הנידחת · שלא היו
ולא עתידין להיות · אלא דרוש וקבל שכר הס לראיות · ומסעם זה כמה הלכתות
כתלמוד רוחי' · שהוזכר כהו דברים דלא שכיחי : להראות לכו הדין ודרוש וקבל שכר
בחיבת · כמו שהאריכו התוספת ס'פ שואל כמסכת שבת :

אמבם

ב   קלקלתיכו וחסרון ידיעתינו היא היא כאמת תקנתיכו :   · דהייכו אם
היינו מביכים כסודות ההגדות בקלות ·   · היתה לכו הדרישה אסורה
כהם כמו שכתב בכתב ההתכנכלות : שהתכנגל הרס'כא אחרי שייעד לחבר חבור כפי'
האנדות ·   · וכמנע מחיבורו כי אמר שאם יכתר פירושם תכלית הבאור יהיה כמגלה
סודות · ומחטיא כווכת המעליומים · שהלכו דרך ישר ופתים · ואם יחברהו כהסתר
וכהעלמה · לא הוסיף על הכווכה הראשוכה האחוזה :   · על כן ראוי שיוכחו כמו שהם
והיו מכלל סתרי התורה שכלאסרו דרישתם :   והם

מונחים לחכמים המביכים מדעתם : הנה התלאמת שהדרישה כרבי' אסורה · כפילרוס
אחת מן ההגדו' שהיא דרך מ'של לאמורה · ודאי אם כזה אל הסגלים הסתר עכייכי' ·
לא סיהיה כפרדוכסם כפיגלה כד כפירה ומיכות כשו' פכי' : וטו' כתב כ'כת ההתכנכלות

מד

ובללו ממני ‏ ‏ ‏ ‏ ‏ ‏ וקפקד מקום דוד כ'ישיבה : ועוד גרמו לחסר סיפוקי ופרנסתי ‏
שלא ‏ ‏ ‏ ‏ ‏ ‏ ‏ ‏ התלמידים לשמוע תורתי : ועשו כי מעשה אתז . עד סלכי בקרבי פתז ‏
כי כבר סובטת ‏ ‏ ‏ ‏ ‏ ‏ אסכח חנו התורה לנמרי ‏ ‏ ‏ ואמר לי לבי אל תפנה אל בית הסרי ‏
על כן כתעוררתי ‏ ‏ ‏ ‏ ‏ אפי' בסעת הסתר פנים ‏ ‏ ‏ שלא תסכח התורה מפי אחרוכים : ‏
מוציר מי הסערה ‏ ‏ ‏ ‏ ‏ מסכת העגלה , ורוח ה' לבסתי כסמלה : וסמכתבי רוח כדבות , ‏
ותי'סל'יח ‏ ‏ ‏ ‏ ‏ ‏ ‏ ‏ ‏ ‏ ‏ ‏ סאחבתי בטאון מקנת רבאסר יסיבות : והם חכמי רופ'יח ופולן ומערסרן ‏
גאוני ישראל ‏ ‏ ‏ ‏ ‏ ‏ ‏ ‏ ‏ ‏ ‏ ‏ סהיו מובכים תמיד לכל סואל : והכה לכבוד סקי ישראל ולכבוד מורד' ‏
כמאמר : ‏ ‏ ‏ ‏ ‏ ‏ ‏ ‏ ‏ ‏ ‏ ‏ סהורוכי הסמבמתי לחבר קנת ספרים . לקיים להוכיח מזולל כמוכי יקרים : ‏

טז ‏ ‏ סלמה סה עבות ספרים הרכה אין קז . ‏ כדי להסיר מהלב התעיוב ויסקז : כי כעוד ‏
‏ ‏ ‏ ‏ ‏ ‏ ‏ ‏ ‏ ‏ ‏ ‏ ‏ ‏ סכותב ‏ ‏ תעכחות וסעלות רוח איך יגביה . כגון גבי חמן אדמהדר עליה לסורפו חיהו ‏
והייתי ‏ אכול ליה כתמיה : ‏

ו ‏ ‏ **מושכיל על דבר** ‏ ‏ ‏ חדם סאתחיל סלאקלמדכי כו אדם · ומצאתי ‏
‏ ‏ ‏ ‏ ‏ ‏ ‏ ‏ ‏ ‏ ‏ **טוב** ‏ ‏ ‏ ‏ בעכין הדרסות על ג' דרכים לקים ‏ : ‏

על דרך חיבור רבינו בחיי כפירוס ‏ ‏ ‏ ‏ ‏ ‏ ‏ ‏ התורה . סהוטיח כמה פסוקים על דרך זס ‏
לאורה . וכדקתי בספרי אכסי תבוכה · ‏ ‏ ‏ ‏ ‏ ‏ ‏ ‏ ולא מנאתי על דרך הסכל מאמרים אלא ‏
בספר דרך אמוכה · וחוא על קנת אגדות ומאמרים · על דרך הסכל לבד ולא דרכים ‏
אחרים · גם כעל עקדת ינחק . על דרך אחד מיתן חוק : וכן יתר הדרסנים · ‏ ‏ ‏ כמו ‏
הל'סבח ופרדם רמוכים · והיתה מוכתי לכאר קנת מאמרים נמסכיות סלא ‏ ד כרו כן ‏
הקדמונים · ‏ ‏ ‏ ‏ ‏ מסום אל תסב נבול עולים ראסונים : ‏ ‏ וקבעתי לכל פרסה ד' מאמרים ‏
לפחות · ‏ ‏ ‏ והרמז כנעתה עזרה ארבע כוותות : דהייכו ‏ ‏ סיוכל הדורס לדרום ‏ ‏ בעזרה ‏
בכל סבת ד' סנים רכופים · ‏ ‏ מאמר חדם על כמה דרכים כלי גידועים : ‏ ‏ וטעם אלו ‏
הדרכים והיתרס לידרס · ‏ ‏ עוד לסביין אותם כפרט · וכביח ראיות מהקולמדים · ‏ ‏ סלא ‏
יאמר עליכו יצירא כארעא ונינורא כסמי מרומים : כראם וראסון ככאר סכוכל ליקח ‏
בם מאדם מנוכה · וכאמר סהוא רמז על צ א סל מוכה : כמו סכתב הרמק'מ כפירוס · על ‏
לכן זה הק'כה וכן לאמארוס : ‏ ‏ וסביח ראיה מכראסית רבה ומאגדה כם נקוב · ‏
כפרסת וינא יעקב : ‏ ‏ וכם תאמר כאלומא סבוכל לומר לכן זה הסם · מכבי סהסתורם ‏
כולם בסמותין סל הקבה כתרסם : אבל המסבע והתלמוד סאינס כן · דילמא זה הדרך ‏
לא יתכן : ‏ ‏ וכראס לדעתיכו הסקרים · כי היא הכוותכת ונתמם ראיה וסכרא : ‏ ‏ כי ‏
מניכו רבינו בחיי כמדרם נמדרם הכעלם מסזוהר מפרסים הרכה מלות וסמות על יתר הרוע · ‏
והתורה כולה מלות קדוסות מורדין לגרוע : וב'ם וקן סבוכל בקדם להעלות ולומד ‏
כי סמות התכאחים והאחמורחים רומזים על עלת העלות · ומזה כמי כוכל לומר כי סמות ‏
התכאחים והאחמורחים לפעמי'על יעד הרע רמוזים : סלא יהיו סמות התכלמידי' מכוכדים ‏
וסמות הרכ מבוזים : וכן כוכל כמי לומר מרומזים על מסיח נדיקיכו · כגון ר' קנ'י.ח ‏
אומר חביכא סמו סב לחוכן דלים יתכבגו : ‏

‏ ‏

וזה כמאמרם ז"ל בפרקי המרכבה' א"ר ישמעאל כל היודע שעורו של יוצר כראשי'מוכתם
לו שהוא בן העולם הבא' וכן בפ"ק דברכות הוי מהחרבתי את ביתי ושהקבכס מניח
תפילין. והרבה כדומה לאלו המ"ן' נכפרכס על כדדי אחת מהחכמות' אלא
יורה ח"ו על הגשמות' כאשר' אכן עכסיכ בקנת כפוטי התורה המורים על
ההגשמה' שכוניהס מפשוטס כדי שלא יהיה עלינו אשמה' ונבארס על נד מאין
בו נוע' בכונן לשבר את האון מה שיכונה לשמוע' או מורה על השגחת הש" על
ישר אל כמו בכל מקום שגלו שכיכה עמהס' מפסוק השוכן אתם בכל טומאותיהס'
ספירו'וא חצפי שהס כגלות הוא ממלא חפ" רנוכיהס' והסימן דרושיס לכל
מפניהס' תליס קיא'

ק
רבו עוד לשמוע כמכ"ו בתלמוד קנת סברות' שהאחת לאחרת יב
סותרות' כבון כפ" ואלו מגלחין בכי מי זמוכזי לאו בזכותא
תליא מלתא אלא כמזלא תליא מלתא' וכפ" מי שהחשך אין מזל לישראל וכפ"הינן
בשמעתא' והסכימו עליהס ידידיס' כי מאמר הכל תלוי במזל סברת יחידיס'
מפכי שמותר פשט תוריתכו התמימה' שהיא בעוכס ושכר מתוימה' וכן דרשו פ'
מי שהחשך מפסוק ויוכא אותו החוכה. לא מאצטגניכות שלך כמרונה' ורעס
תבל לרעת אעפי' שמזלו מורה טובה בכל זמן' ודורס רעה תבואמו הוא כאמת
הסימן' משלי יא כז'

א
בינה עוד וחזכרה דרשות הקדמיס' דברים מקובלים הכמבאיס יג
בתלמוד לפעמים' ואין להס רמז בתורה' והוכרח החכם
לסמוכו על פסוק מדרך סכרא' וזה לשתי תועלות אמורות' הא' שיהיה כפי רב
נסתלמיד סגורות' והב' להחשיב בעטי ההמון אותה הדרשה' לפי קוצר דעתם
אס הפסוק אסמכתא או פסם אין להס הרגשה' ורונגמתו פ"ק דערובין שיעורין
מחינין חנינין מסיני הלכה למשה' ותכף שיעורין דאוריתא הקטפה המקפה'
מפסוק ארץ חטה ושערה' וא"ר ינקבו כל הפסוק הזה לשיעורין מורה' ולא היס
בפי המתרן מאומה' אלא אין הלכה למשה מסיכי וקרא אסמכתא בעלמא' כדי
שיתור לבו תמיד בקבלת הרגל דרשי התורה התמימה' והסימן לדר"גם ולתור
בחכמה' קהלת'

אמר הקטן הרשם דוד דרשן מקדאקא' בסייעתא דלעילא דעביד עד
סמיא ולרקא' אקר
זאת הסקדמה' ימין ה' על'ידומה' להודעת לו בכל מיכי הילול ורינה'
שהמויתי והבניבי עד סכה' מאקר שהפליח חסדו עלי כפלאי פלאות'
זהונ'יאכי מכמה כהלות ותלאות' שהייתי מטולטל ומכודכד מכטורי מדיחי אל דמי'
וכהפך עלי למשחית הודי וכחי' ואור שכלי הלך כגדלדל' כי מבית ישיכות התורה
הייתי כעל כרחי כבדל' כי קמו עלי בכמה מדינות'רביס נחמכה וכעושר' וכטלו
ממכי לעין בתורה שעת הכושר' מפני שהייתי ביניהס כזוכנדה' עד שמתקיים בי
צדוד כח מפכיהס אל המכונדה' ועשו עלי כפ"נס מריבה' ניתקד

והדרש מפני עומק המושג כגון דבר אלהי אשר כתם פז ראשו ‧ ס' ואת ה' לא
דרשו : ישעיה לא ‏ ירמיה י'

ט ק וכל דרשות התורה כשמע עוד כתלמודינו ‧ כדברים שראה החכם
בחלום ולא כמראית עינו : כגון כהמוכר את הספינה ‧ כספורי דרב'
בר בר חנה : שכתבו הגאונ' בקנתם ‧ כל היכא דאמרינן הכא חזי לי בחלום
הוראתם : ונכתבו אותן הדברים בסתימא ‧ מפני ס"ס כמה סודות בעלמא : שאין
הכל זוכים להבינם ‧ לפי שלא נטהרו כמעשיהם וכעיונס : והחלום כנבואה אחד
מששים ‧ לכבר כמורות טובות לעם חלושים : שהם ספים רבוח כמייכס ‧ ועתיד
יהיו שמים ושמחים בכל ענינכם : כי חכמים המה להטיב ולא להרע ‧ וסימנך
דרשו טוב ואל רע : עמוס ה' ‧

י ד וח ה' דבר עוד כרבינו משה כסדר זרעים כהקדמה ‧ סקכיעות
הדרשות כתלמוד חשב לרב אשי לגודל חכמה : וכתב אל תחשוב
שמעלת הדרש מעוטה ותועלתו חסרה ‧ אבל יש כו תבונה גדולה ויקרה : מפני שהוא
כולל כמה סידות ‧ וכפלאות חמודות : כי הדרשות ההם כשיסתכלנו בו הסתכלות
שכלי ‧ יובן כהם מהטוב ההוא הכללי : ומה שהיו אנשי החכמה מעלימין אותו ‧ ולא
רצו כבירור לגלותו : ואם כתים על פשטו תמצא דברים מן השכל רחוקים ‧ עשו
ענין זה לעניינ' עמוקי' ‧ האח ללטוש רעיוני התלמידים : כדי שיהיו כסודות שהיות
יחידים : והשכי לעודר עיני הכסילים ‧ שלא יזהירו לבותם כפכיימית רק כנגלים :
מפני שאין שכלם שלם ‧ לעמוד על האמתות לעולם : והאריך עוד כראיית הדרשה :
וסימנך דרום דרש משה ‧ ויקרא י'

יא א מת יכנה הכו של הכדרשי כבתב ההתנכלות ‧ שחלק הדרשות לכמה
מעלות ‧ הא' כמאמר שיסבר כח דוש ענין שאינו כבגד טבע הינירה ‧
אבל הוא הוא אפשר רחוק מיניאת הנגעתו כסכה זרה : כשאירהו על פשוטו כודאי ‧
לסמוך על כעל המאמר המעד בעיונתו הוא כדאי : והכ' המאמרים סיסברו
כחידוש שום דבר יונא ממוהג טבע הינירה ‧ כשאירס גלויים כפשוטם כשאר מופתי
הנכיאים ואותות התורה : מפני ס"ש כדברים ההם חיזוק כאמונה : כגון האותות
שנעשו לחסידים עליונים אכשי תבונה : הכזכרים כמסכת תעבית כפרק החסידים ‧
כמום איש נס זו ור' חכיכא ושאר ידידים : וככלל זה האותות והכסים ‧ שנעשו כבית
מקדש הקדם ‧ ותתיי המתי'שעתיד הקבה לאדם : והג' המאמרים היונאים מהמכהג
הטבעי שאין הדעת סובלת ‧ ולא ימשך ממנו כאמונה שום תועלת : אלא להרווחת
תלמידי' מכוכד עיוניהם ‧ כמילי כדיחותא דספורי דרבה כר כר חנה ודומים להם :
כל אלו כוניאם מג.וויים ‧ אעפ'י שהם כחק הס' ראויים : מפני שאין הס' מחדש
אותות כחינס אלא לחסידים כעת הנורך ‧ כאשר הוא מבואר סם כאורך : והכ'
המאמרים הזוכרים סיכוי מהכמנעות הקיימות ‧ אעפ'י שהשגיכו ההוא מוכיל
כאמונות כהומות : אז כודאי כוניאם מפשוטם ‧ שלא יהיו יקר מפשוטי התורה
והנכיאים מספטם :

כי הגוי והממלכה אשר לא ישרתו ישראל יאבדו . כי אז יתהפך כל אחד לאהוב השם
בכל לבבו ובכל נפשו ובכל מאודו : ליהודים יהיה אורה . שיהיו פניו' תמיד לעסוק
בתורה : כי אז יקניים . והיו בני נכר אכריכם וכורמיכ' . נחמו נחמו עמי יאמר
אלקיכם : וכאשר ראה ר"ג קונר דעות המון הכסילים להשיג . הפלגת רוב הטובה .
צייר להם הטוב ההוא בדרך נכל וקרוכה : ולהוניא להם המשפט הנפלס · אמר כל
וזרואך דוגמותנו כוס זעולם . ולונמת זה הלמבט מחלק · כפירו' משכיות בהקדמת
פרק חלק : והדרם מפני קונר סכבת כסיל סימן מפורם · כנוכה אתו
כל ידרוגו : תליס י'

ב תיכות הדרסו' יאירו לפעמי' . לומר אותם החכם כלי דקדוק הטעמים ז
מפני קונ' המשיג בעיניו · וכמקן הראוי לו מכאר אותנו על מכונו : כגון מה
שאמרו כל אמתא כרבועא אמת ותרי חומשי באלכסונ' · הוכיחו בתוספפו'כ'ק דסוכ'
דאיכ' טפי פורת' כבווכ' : וכן איתא כפרסה ו' דכראשית רבה · שאמר ר' פינחם
בסם ר'חכא : היכן כל נבח הסמי' · נתוני' . ברקיע הסני סהוא למעלה מהשמים הם
מוכנים : ומן הארן ועד הרקיע מהלך ת"ק סנה . ועוביו של רקיע מהלך ת"ק כבוכ' :
ומהרקיע עד הרקיע מהלך חמס מלה · כמה הוא גבוה ראה : כמנא מן הארן עד
גכנוכית גלגל סכתי ז אלפי'סכים · ומי סעיין בחכמ' התכוכה ידע סאלו הדברי'בכלל
אמתיי' ונכוני' · אכל דברי אגדה כפרט כאו בכלל דקדוקי' · כמו סהו'מכוא' כספר
כמרחקים : כי ממרחק הארן עד גכנוכית גלגל סכתי ז אלפים וכ"ד
סנה : וידיעת סעור המרחק אסר כין הארן והגלגלים : לסתי סיכות הם מועליס :
הא' להכהילנו ולהפחידנו . כהסיגנו קטנות עצמינו ובופינו : כסנערוך סכלו'כפסינו
לגופי הגלגלים הנראים לעיינו · כל סכן כערך הככדלים מסרתי אקינו : והכ'
לידע ולהכיר טוכם גכור' הכורא וסלימותו . המניע כל אלו הגלגלי'הנראיס כלא יד
וכלא רגל כגכורתו : הוא הכורא הוא היוגר הוא הדיין הוא להודיע ולידע · כמכואר
בספר החמד : והדרם מפני קונר המסיג סהוא כדעתנו חולי
ורם · ס' וגם כקלייו לא דרם : דכרי הימים כ' י'ן

מ סלו מסל עוד חכמי הדרסות ודכרו כחידות · מפני עומק · סמונב ח
כאותן האגדות : סלא יכינו אותו כהפך הכוונה · ויעסו חו' רוסם
מק כאמונה : אך עת לעסות לה' הפרו תורה . והוניאו אותם כרמו לאורה :
אעפי' סהם דכרים עמוקים · ילכו כס נדיקים : כמו סהו' כפ"ק דכרכות בכמה
מאמרים מכואדת · כמו המאמר דר' ישמעאל כסככם להקטיר קטורת : סאמר
ראיתי את הם) כעיני · ואמ' ישמעאל כני כרכני : וסגריך חו'הסי' אל הכרב'דכר קסה
על המסיינו' . כאסר האריכו לדכר כו חכמי'קדמוני'ס : ופסטו כמלת כרכה נורה
ולכסו נורה . והעתק כפסוק וכרכת את ה' הכאמר למסה מפי הגכורה : סהכווכ' כו
סנקכע כלכבינו אמונה קיימת : סאין עוזר וסומך סלא הוא כאמת : והוא המסכיע
ריכוי הכרכה כרחמיו עלינו · ועל כן אין לייחם כח הכרכה אלא ליונרינו : ויהיה
הכוונה כיסמעאל ככי כרכני . תן לי הודאה אסר ונוסל רכוי הכרכה לכד אני :

משכיל על דבר ימצא טוב

א **דך** תמים אמכילה · למשכיל אורח חיים למעלה · לתת ליוצר בראשית גדולה ·
אשר כחכמ' ברא כל הארץ על תילה · לא בעמל וביגיעה כי אם בתלה · כדכתיב
בדבר ה' נעבו בתחילה · ולבסוף כתיב גירא שקים את כל אשר עשה והנה טוב עלה ·
והכל כפסוק משכיל על דב'ר ימצא טוב ככללה :

ב **ני** המשכילים יזהירו כזוהר הרקיע בקדושה · וכפרט המשכילי' כתור' המחומשה ·
מנתנה על פי השם ביד משה · עם תורה שבעל פה סדירודה משה · ועשרת
הדברים אבן הראשה · שכל דכור ואמירה על לוח אבן חרושה · טוב לי תורת פיך
לקהילת יעקוב מורשה · גם זה מפסוק משכיל על דב'ר ימצא טוב כדרשה :

ג **רך** יעס והשבל לקחת מוסר · וכביסות יוסר · כיון לחוטאים מאת היוצר · להעבירם
בזה וכבא בעת מיטר · או להשבירם כטוב האוצר · כדכתיב אומרים ה' כונר ·
וידוע כי דיבור לשון תוכחה קשה נוסר · לזכותו לם'ור מאת השם שאין לו מעטר ·
גם זה יוכן כמשכיל על דב'ר ימצא טוב כפסוק קטר :

רמזנו לבאר תעלולת דרכי הדרשות · שעתקרס לסימן עם תוכחות קטות :

ד **רכי** דרשות העגרה יתחלקו לאין שיעור · כולם לקרב היתה ולהדקין הכיעור :
ים דרא לשמח נפשות חלושים ונאכחים · כמכואר כפ'כמה מדליקין ובערבי
פסחים : כי הא דרבה מקמי דפתח להו באורייתא · אמר מלתא דבדיחותא · או
כד הוו חלשי רבנן מגירסייהו · במלתא דבדיחותא פתחי פומייהו · והדרום להחזיק
ולהחיות כפם חלושה קנת זמן · דרטוכ'י וסי'ן הוא הסימן · גמום ה' :

ה **רך** אנו עוד מנאתי במדרש שיר השירים רכא נגמחל · שפתם ר'יוחנן בתוך הדרשה
פומא · כד חזא דהוו מתנמנמין כדרשא · התחיל לומר להם דבר בעיניהם
קטה : ם'רבוא כמנרים ילדה אשה אחת · והוו מתערי מסכתייהו ומתעמירין בכחת :
והוו כעיניהון כדבר האכד · עד ספירם להו א' יוכבד : מילדה כמנרים למסה רביע
הגואל · מהיה סקול ככנגד כל ישראל : והדרם להקיץ המתנמנמם והחרש · סימן
מיד הנוטה אדרם : יחזקאל ל'ב

ו **שט** מטו עוד רוזי ארן · ים דרש שלא יוכלו ההמון להבינו במרן · מפני
סכלות קונר בזבתם · והוצרך החכם לסכינס בעניין קל הראוי לדעתם · בגון
מה שאמרו כפרק כמה מדליקין כפלאות · עתידיה ארן ישראל שתוניא כלי מילת
וגלוסקאות · וסמכום על פסוק יסי פיסת בר בארן · עד שלגלג עליו ההוא תלמיד
וכלסונו ככלב מרן : וכטבור זה הוגרך לפטרו כראוית · ואפקיה והראה לו כזהין
וסטריות : ואכלו מינת רדף התלמיד באשר ירדוף בהרים הקורא · עד שהראהו
ככרא בר קולא : ורבן נמלל'ל ענה כפיל כאולתו · היתה כוונתו : אבל עקר הכוונה
כאשר הפין רבן גמליאל כזבות התכוכה : כטובות הכלאות · המפורסים כדברי
הנבואות : משוכע נדולה : ונשלוה לזמן המשיח כעת הגאולה : מנד העדר המלחמה
גימין ה' רומחה ·
בי הגוי

רמזי קידוסי המאמר

התנצלות לדרשנים

נסיא סקלוּת ספר **משכיל לדוד** וכבר ראו אותו נאותו עוֹלם וקלוסוּ כנן עורין עסר"ר
יצחק כלאל זל ותסר"ר שלוס לוריא זל ותסר"ר עמא איטריל זל שהכניסו חיים לכל ישראל גם
יקר נדולי הדור סט" ישעֶרס כולס הפליגו הרבא כשבחו · עבֶר אותו הסכס סכולל
עוסר"ר דוד דרסן כן סנלון אקדרום אסר"ר עמשש זל כ"ד אקראקא · דורא
טוב לעתו לעת סזאת בקהילא מעולרס לובלין :

הביאו להדפיסם אחרי שלא זכה להעמיד מדרש כאלו הגלילות · כמוזכר כהקדמת
ספר עיר המעלות :: קנא רונא לשלס כדרו לסוס פעמיו לארץ הקדוסא ב" ישם רונא
א"ה לסדר הסיבורים השלשא · והם ספר מסכיל לדוד וספר מגדל דוד סכבר חיבר ·
וספר תהלה לדוד סעדיין לא כתבתים כו הדיבר :: וכעבור שראה קנת מלעתים על
קדרסות · סוניא לאחר חדמות : הקדמת ספר מסכיל לדוד מכחר מפכיכיס · וסל
כאלמת כתב התכבטלות לדרסנים : יחסום פי הלנס · אסר לכאר סתת רנס :: וסל
ראויה מכל התלמו ומכל המדרסים · סאדרסות כאלקו לכמא ראסים :: וכלם כרזרים
כנהרייס · כטיכוט לבו לאכת סכטמים · והראה אהכ לתלמידיס עקר וטורם ·
איך סיובֵל לחבר הפרסא עם המאמר והמדרם : ולקח טאוק חסוק ראשון
מהתורא · והוניא ממכו בקטור כמס תידוּסן לאורא : וכולם
מקוברין על מאמר כופא הדרום · כדמין כיאור ופירוס :
ויוכעס למכן כיאן הרקק · ויסאוֹת חכם וחופן לקח ·
ובעבֶר הסני רסמכו בקטור הירדוסים · לבל
מי סיחפון יחין
דרוסים :

נדפס סמוך אחר שבועות · בשנת קרוב
ב" להחיש ישועות : פה לובלין הבידה

שבחינא כתבי להדורי ליה ומכין סניאין · כנין דך יהיככא רשותא לפתוט חכום
אורי כן שלמה כהן דאתׁשיס כריום שירתא דתכוכה ליׁמון מרכורי דיכיל לרכחא
כניניה וכנין כל מאן דכתׁי ליכול כארא · כתבאי דכעי לאהדורי להלכתיה
דרבחתא ויומא חדא בכל יומא ורחׁ קׁמחא · ׁונדען תׁיונבא וזמנא חדא בכל
שבתא · ואחרלׁכך · ואמנא חדא לׁבית ורחׁיא כג ימי חוׁיהׁי הכין נגיד יג זׁא
וׁעירא דוד דרׁסן מקׁרלׁקׁא · כיׁחא רׁכיׁעׁאׁה דׁאׁדׁר תׁיׁונבא ׁשׁיׁם לׁבׁק פׁס
מרׁס דׁמׁׁין לׁרׁונׁכׁרׁי :

אתן שכח ומעלה ליוׁלת העׁלׁות · לׁסׁוׁף סׁׁר שׁיׁר הׁמׁיׁעׁלׁות · וׁלׁקׁׁילׁת
קׁרׁאׁקׁׁא הׁמׁפׁוׁארׁה · אׁׁר הׁׁא בׁחׁכׁמׁה וׁכׁׁׁיׁס מׁהׁוׁדׁרׁה · וׁלׁׁׁר
מׁׁׁׁׁׁׁׁ מׁי יׁוׁכׁל · כׁי הׁׁה רׁׁׁׁה נׁׁׁׁ בׁׁׁׁ מׁׁׁׁ כׁׁ וׁהׁׁה כׁׁׁׁ

אׁכׁן הׁרׁׁׁׁׁ : וׁׁה יׁׁכׁר כׁׁׁׁׁׁ ׁׁׁׁׁׁ ׁׁׁׁׁׁ לׁׁׁׁׁ הׁׁׁׁׁ הׁׁׁׁׁׁ
אׁׁ ׁׁ ׁׁ ׁׁׁׁ אׁׁׁׁ מׁׁׁׁׁ ׁׁׁׁׁׁ · וׁׁׁ ׁׁׁ ׁׁׁ וׁׁׁ הׁׁׁׁׁׁ ׁׁׁׁׁ
מׁׁׁׁׁׁ וׁׁׁׁׁׁ : ׁׁׁ וׁׁׁׁ ׁׁׁׁ הׁׁׁׁׁ · ׁׁ ׁׁ ׁׁׁ
ׁׁׁׁ ׁׁׁׁ · ׁׁׁ ׁׁ וׁׁׁ ׁׁׁ · ׁׁ ׁׁׁ ׁׁ ׁׁׁׁ וׁׁׁ ׁׁׁׁׁ :
וׁׁ ׁׁ ׁׁ ׁׁ ׁׁׁׁ וׁׁׁׁׁ · ׁׁׁ ׁׁׁׁׁׁׁ וׁׁׁׁׁ ׁׁ ׁׁׁ :
ׁׁ ׁׁׁׁ ׁׁׁ ׁׁׁׁׁ ׁׁׁ ׁׁ ׁׁׁ · ׁׁׁׁ ׁׁׁ ׁׁׁׁׁ · ׁׁ
ׁׁׁׁ ׁׁׁ ׁׁׁׁ ׁׁׁׁ ׁׁׁׁ · ׁׁ ׁׁׁׁ ׁׁ ׁׁ ׁׁׁ ׁׁׁ · ׁׁ ׁׁ ׁׁׁׁ
ׁׁׁׁ ׁׁׁ ׁׁ ׁׁ ׁׁׁׁ · ׁׁׁ ׁׁׁׁׁ ׁׁׁׁ : ׁׁׁ ׁׁׁׁׁ ׁׁ ׁׁ ׁׁ ׁׁׁׁ
ׁׁׁׁׁ · ׁׁ ׁׁׁ ׁׁׁׁ ׁׁׁׁ ׁׁׁׁ : ׁׁׁ ׁׁׁׁ ׁׁ ׁׁׁ ׁׁ ׁׁׁ ׁׁׁׁׁ · ׁׁׁׁ
ׁׁׁ ׁׁׁׁׁ ׁׁׁ : ׁׁׁ ׁׁׁׁ ׁׁׁ ׁׁׁ ׁׁׁׁ ׁׁׁׁׁ · ׁׁ ׁׁׁ ׁׁׁׁ
ׁׁׁׁׁ ׁׁׁׁ ׁׁ ׁׁׁ ׁׁׁׁ · ׁׁ ׁׁׁ ׁׁׁׁׁ ׁׁׁ · ׁׁׁׁׁׁ ׁׁ ׁׁׁׁ :
ׁׁׁׁׁ ׁׁׁׁׁ ׁׁׁ ׁׁׁׁ ׁׁ ׁׁ ׁׁׁ · ׁׁ ׁׁ ׁׁ ׁׁׁ ׁׁׁ ׁׁׁ ׁׁׁ ׁׁׁ ·
ׁׁ ׁׁׁׁׁ ׁׁׁ ׁׁׁׁׁ · ׁׁׁ ׁׁׁׁ ׁׁ ׁׁׁ ׁׁ · ׁׁ ׁׁ ׁׁׁׁ ׁׁׁׁ ·
ׁׁׁׁ ׁׁׁ ׁׁׁ ׁׁׁ · ׁׁׁ ׁׁׁׁ ׁׁׁ ׁׁׁׁ : ׁׁׁ ׁׁ ׁׁׁׁ ׁׁׁׁׁ ·
ׁׁׁ ׁׁׁׁׁ ׁׁׁ ׁׁׁ : ׁׁׁ ׁׁ ׁׁׁ ׁׁׁׁ · ׁׁ ׁׁ ׁׁׁׁ ׁׁׁׁׁ ·
ׁׁׁ ׁׁ ׁׁׁ ׁׁׁׁ ׁׁׁׁׁ : ׁׁׁׁ ׁׁׁׁ ׁׁׁׁ ׁׁׁ ׁׁׁׁ ׁׁׁ ·
ׁׁׁ ׁׁׁׁ ׁׁׁ ׁׁׁׁ : ׁׁׁ ׁׁׁ ׁׁׁׁׁ ׁׁׁ ׁׁׁ : ׁׁׁ ׁׁ ׁׁׁׁ ׁׁׁׁׁ ·
ׁׁ ׁׁ ׁׁׁׁ ׁׁׁׁ : ׁׁ ׁׁ ׁׁׁׁ ׁׁׁ ׁׁׁׁ ׁׁׁ ׁׁׁׁ ·
ׁׁׁ ׁׁׁ ׁׁׁ ׁׁ ׁׁׁׁׁ · ׁׁׁׁׁ ׁׁׁ ׁׁׁ ׁׁׁ : ׁׁׁׁ ׁׁׁ ·
ׁׁ ׁׁׁׁ ׁׁׁׁ ׁׁׁ · ׁׁׁׁ ׁׁ ׁׁ ׁׁׁׁׁ ׁׁׁ ׁׁׁׁׁ · ׁׁ
ׁׁׁׁׁ ׁׁׁ ׁׁׁׁ ׁׁׁׁ ׁׁׁׁ ׁׁׁ ׁׁׁׁ ׁׁׁׁ ׁׁׁ :

אׁׁ ׁׁׁ ׁׁׁׁׁׁׁ ׁׁׁ ׁׁׁ ׁׁ ׁׁׁׁ ׁׁ ׁׁ ׁׁ ׁׁ ׁׁׁׁ · ׁׁׁ ׁׁׁׁׁ ׁׁ ׁׁׁ ׁׁׁׁׁׁׁ
ׁׁׁׁׁ ׁׁׁׁׁ ׁׁׁׁ ׁׁׁ ׁׁ · ׁׁׁ ׁׁ ׁׁ ׁׁ ׁׁ ׁׁׁׁׁ ׁׁׁׁׁ ׁׁׁׁ ׁׁׁ ׁׁׁ ׁׁׁ
ׁׁׁׁׁ ׁׁ ׁׁ ׁׁׁׁ ׁׁׁׁ ׁׁׁׁ ׁׁ ׁׁׁ ׁׁׁׁ :

להטעינו כמתן סתרים · לכפות אף נחרונים · ולזור כתוב אחרין ·
כסגנרס לכא סעריו · לנדא טול מכעגורו · ראו אור נדול · לאכיון חלא
דגדול · ולעבני מטוב כדול · רב ברכה ואורה · יבא קל ייזרה · לעזר
לדחוק כזרה: · היא הכהן התוור · מאיר בן אליתזר · מקייס מבות הגנור ·
כמה מעלות טובות · מזדו ומעד הזכות · בלו עירוב ותערובות:
הין ועשר מסר · וכתו לאירוסין מסר · והכלדונכייא הפה שאמר:
נדיכיס פתחו סער · ותביולוהו מוז הסער · כמיות זקן וכער:
ונכפרט לאים פיכה · ותהדרוהו כעין טובה · לזכות ולגא לתוכה:
סרכו עליג מתן: · ותקיימו כתון תתן · ותזכו לכמסוס מתן:
ישים עליכס אלקיכס · ויאר פכיו אליכס ויכנה המקדם כימיכס · ויוסיף
כח הכונל · כשרית כורא המוסל · סמוך לפרט אשל: · אמן הדוכר כאמת
וכבדקה · דוד דרסן מקריאקף · תלמיד הנאון ר'יבחק כנבלאל · הכוטח ככל אל ·
ותלמיד הנאון רבי שלמה אנסטרא · הטמרה מעות ואסמאלרא · נסלא להתגלם
מכסרו · אחי אמי המיאירי:

שיר קכלה על שמיטות יתד וארבע תנועות

א זמר כרננים · נלגא יגא פכים · ומוחל עלכונים · לסוני סי שנים ·
ו כתן התורה · כע נם כנכורה · והדריך כשירה · ככל עת ומכים ·
ר בולו הטוכס · כמסדן הרמכה · לזראות סחוכה: · אסר עיניו ווניס ·
י בוה עגינו · לאראף כפסיני · וירחאן ציניכו · כטוכות הבבונים ·
כ חמלת הכריות · עסית הבשמיטוות · כהמון נס חוות · וטופות הבשטיס:
כ דיגתע הטט · כהלביות הבשמיטה · לבל יחליף סטה · ככל הכסימוכ:
ט כמו אין חיקר · לכרהיוק העקר · להחויק סעתר · כמכחר מפנוניס ·
ל דוד סס חורה · כהזמין לו נורא · כחיר הסס חורי · ומנות כהניס:
מ כונס סס ליפמן · כביניה מתון מן · ככל עבן וומן · יכקט הנכונים:
ס לא הראה עיכו · כהסחיטות סיכו · וככנס אף לפכו · כעל פה נס כפנים:
כ כר סהט ופה · ונס לא כתצלפה · סלאם כתכיפה · ובדק הסכיניכ:
ה לא הרסיתיהו · סחיטה אל פיהו · ונס כל ירנהו · מזומן כל מוכיס:
ג תעוו לו כתנאו · לסכח ולא לנבאו · להמויא לו סעבאו · אכאר כלפניס:

כגין דלאו אייהו עגיר עכל מאן דדמו לכר אליקין מזן דכעי לידע כזומק חד
עבייכה

16

אגרות קלות

במספר הנכור · אך נסתכלתי על מאמר החכם אם אשכיל תשב הומי ואם אסכיל
תלמדוני · ועוד סיבת את מחסי פני · כי עד עתה אל המנוחה ואל הנחלה
לא באתי · אך כאשר אשמיע שלום אבשר טוב · אחי החשוב כמר יעקב עולה ונוסא
בנן רטוב · סימין לו הקבא כחלו נחלה חבורבת · ירחות ה'היה תתהלל ותרוחא
נכרת ממלכת · הלא היה כתב נדולים ומלכי ארץ · אכסו סם אחות מחיר כורדנאן
סנודר כפרן · אסרי וטוב נו · מי סיגבלה כך בנורלו · ועוד מורי הנאון מהדר
יוסף מינן יצא למצא תרף ומזור · ותקסע דירתו בקק קאוי מחוור · והוכרחתו
להחליף המטבות · שלא יחכב אותו מללמוד סוס מוכב: · ומצאתי אינו באמן לפני
בכל חכמה צמוקה · שמו כודב כשערים מוהדר דוד דראן מקרוחקא · סחרבין תגרם
בבית כני הכנרלנאתי הסריס הנכבדיס · הלא היא סולחם ערוך עצות כינס
במקוס רדיס · להכין חמרי דעת כומכי מדע ושכל · לספר סכחו כצבייני
סידיטה מי יוכל · אורו כתלמוד וכפוסקיס · לסורות התוכם מ תות ומקיס ·
עלי סור כינות בעדיי · כמדרסו ואנדתו על אר ן יסדיי · ונתחכס כחכמת
סמחקר · להכין כין טוב ורע לאמת ושקר · נס סם לו דרך ועיון · כמלאכת
סכנוח וסהנוין · ומכחין כין קל לכבד וכבל הכביניס אדוק · להכין מסורת
פסוק ודקדוק · וכפרט ספיר נורת סכלו כדרך הנככ ת · על דרך האמת
וסקבלה כנור כמסנתן · נס כמלאכת הכתיכה · נוהר ע זה לתיכה · ויהי
דוד בכל דרכיו מסכיל וס'עמו · כרוך סככה לו כטולמו' · אכן כמטותא מייך
לכל יהי למסא לאדוני · · סאילה אחת קטנה חכוני סכוני · · להראות אלי נליוע
ידיך הנקיה כאשר היא בכל הארן כודעת · לרסום על קלף אלף כ'ת כתיכה
מרוכעת · עם סיומנו וקכלותיו · עב כל חלוקי אותיותיו · להראות הטעמיס
וסארים אתניופי כתינכן התפארת · ולא יסור מבין עיני למטן תהיה לו לעדה
ולמשמרת · נס אחי הספל כלי סטן וכלי פגע · מוכן ומזומן לפרתך בכל עת
וכבל רגע · אף על פי סהנופות רמוקית · הלבכות קרובות ודמוקות ·
כאם הנעיר אשר על פי רבותיו וכהל · כן דודתך יהנעא כער לא ימוס מתוך
האהל:

קבין ושיר

מחיר לעולם וורק · יאור ויהל וישמח · למטו לדל הטורח · מאורות נדולים
ופרנסיס ראסיס ורככיס · האירו לעכי פכיס ·
אנך תתנו לעמל · ולטורח להיות תומל : ולכוס סיחכא נומל · אור זרח
לנדקס · לסענינו כדת וכחוקה : כלי סטייס ודקיקה: · יאירו פתח דכריס ·
לסטטינו

'וכאשר וקציביה · אנשי אמונים · על לום כונד נפן סוריה · סמו דן בר גוביה
ונקרא בכינויו דן רייזא · מלמד בעריב · לא אריכא ולא גוצא · והוא מן דל
בקראקא הבירה · והכיח אצלכו וותרו אלמוכה היה כרורה · ונכיח אותם
בגוכה יותר מי"ב שנה · ולא פקד א.תה לא בכתב ולא במימון · כי מכט
תעבכות בלבו טמון · כי כמה פעמים רתבכו עליו בכידו וחרמות · לאחוד
וכגוב נאשת צלמות · והוא החלק אמריב לאלוהים · ובקם היה אותם דוחיב ?
כדי שלא יראו החרמות לבכבדי ארן · לגדור גדר בפרן · על כן במטותא
מיכויכו בכל מקום כינית התימות ידינו · תחקרו אמריו כדי כד נא קטא לדייכא
ותאסרו לו מן גופא הן ממונא · עד דייקוס קמיכין לדיכא · ויהא אבגיכן
קשור וקטור · עד דיבכ ם לו ופטור · אשרי המוטא והגביא · פטורים לחרת
בינה בת דוד הלוי · נבועה וחסידה בכל מעטליה בכל שמחה ודבה · כל הראוי
לבכלה חין כבלה מעבכתבס · מיוחסת ומוורות כעכמה · ובכלל אין כידה רעם
מאומה · רק הצבוב בו והחמרון · והונך כחושך וכטירון: ונמכסה דמעה את
מוכח ה'ובב כחקה וכבי · על אשר כונד באשתכעתריו כאשר כתוב בספר מלאכי ·
לרן אכחנו התעוני מטם יחד · גורנו עליו בלי כאד · בחרם המיר וכאבכועה
דאוריייתא' · עד דיפיים להבד אתתא' · ויהא מכודה בכל האומות · אם
לא יגדור אלו ספרבות · לכבום או לפטור אשת העגונה והעגונמה · אשר
בגולכיה תעמה · וכל הרומאה התימתנו · יחרד אכוכו · לכבדילו מעבת
ומרחל הבנ:רים חקס · עד במייושר מב שטקס · ולא יזכו לכל הברכות
אשר נמבר סתנ:ים ערוכות · הדוכר באמת וכבדקה · דוד דרסן
מקראקא:

אגרת לבחור אכינדור שהלך ללמוד לקרימונא מן ויביביאם ·

מי הוא זה
ואיזה הוא אשר מלאו לבו לגשת אלו כבתב א' לשון · לא יהנו בנ-וכס ידיהם
לספ · ולא ימושין: כי הוא הגובר על כל בני גילו בלשון ודבור · כברמז כשמו אכינדור
במספר

קדישין דמתדבקין בסתר ימיכא דאיהו אתר דישראל קדישין מתדבקין ביה ותבלא
דילין דקשוט כנוכא דכותיכין קדישין טובייכין דחכוימין דמתנגטקין כא,רייהא
ועבדין עובדין דכשרין אינהו קהל קדישא דמן אוכן · ורוח דהנה ועץ חיים
נבאומבן קהל סאיובן לא תאותיולא יתיר · תחיה באם · נא סוא נעוולת דנח
לאתמשכא וויאות לסדר קדימהן בעתותא וכולהי ייתי בעתותא תחי דמתאהין חנן
אתוחין לאתא ויסתליס רעותו דילן על ידי דהנהו קדישין בסויעתא דקידשא בריך
נבות אמן · פמותא פייעכו ותרנו בטביכו איך כמסר בידי נוים ח מתאוינבו · וסמו
בוכר יבאק משה דלות · חו כתקיימו בן אחתהקנבות ואין קוטה ואין פודס ונגאל
ונתלינה סיסא כאבר חם וסנוק כפם אחת מישראל · וכבר סמתכו עגיכב · סיא
ממומוו כורינכם : וכבק זה ממעלתבס סלא תחומסו על ממוכו ומאורו · ותשתבלו
בכל מאותני כא בעמד · ואבעלו אם לא יסיא פרוטס מסלו · מכל מקיס אל
תתרמסלו · כי אחו ואבאתו בחמים וכוכיס עד למרומ · סרוביס להיות עריס
פתרוס · ולמכור כל מה סיס להם כנבלו וכטואון · ולא יכיאו אותו כסוס ממווק
וכפרט סנס אבחמו חתנומ מטה כתמוד לעבודי · אונלי ורחמ עניו הקבה ויחוור
פלא וכוח כבתר כמה בפעות ונוווות · וכפרט אסתו הבכוצה כאלמכות חיות ·
וכאמתויא לא תעיתלת ממוסכא · · כי חסר מכיתה הברכה · וולכן אל תתראלו
מאלאסתרא כמוניה רכא · בלי סמן ודיכה · רק כאהבכה וכמעגב · ותידרסא
אתמחקרו על מקיימו · וכוכות זה ינן עליבס הקבה ממרוומו · ונוויא אתכב עב כל
יסראל מהשכים והגלית · ויק,יס בכב סכרכות,תמיחת סאלית וכקלבות אמן ·
ברוכר כאמת וכבדקה · דוד דרסן מקרזקא

להנהיל אוהבי יס ואוחרותיהס אמלא · וכ.אין אוינון ככי עלמא דמסתדרא
כאוריית אתרחים לעבנ ואתרימי לגנת אוינסין בכל יומ ירוהד
דעלמא דאתי הה,ד לבהמיל אובכי אובכי יס מאויומ דא עלמא דאתי דנא פבק לעלמין
וכטיל אנר טב עילאה לנא וכי בס כר כא אמרא ומתו איהו כ כדלונקמיה חכריא
בפריק חלק כנוכא דאינון כורויכין כו יבין קדיסין חכמי איטליה דמסתתלו כאוריותא תדיר
ולא תחויקו ביבותא לבפסיהו ואינון רחמיין לעביא ולתתא ובעוכביהון דקשום
חסמיו ירותא דעלמא דאתי · ובקשוט אתמאמר עליהו להבתיל אובכי יס · ורוא
דמלה להנבתיל אוהבי · זה הוא חכמי איטלא · מוסבכניה דדין כמוסבכניה דרין ·
נא ף וקביה ורלאיס וכאין אוכון דקבה יהוב להון אוריית למבדא כל אורחין בתיחין
ונלאתעניח להו כמה רוין ולוארין עלאין וכמה פתאחן וכברכאן לעילא כניך
דיניהון דקשוט דעבדין כטלמא וכנין כך יתאלאון איהרותיהון דהסוא טבא
דאתענני לטלמא דאתי ועיויהו אתמאמר אוצרתיהס אסלא ורוח דמלה ואוצרותיהם
חוסבכניה סוד ראשיה חקניה · קפלכו אוינכב פרוסיס · נעיריס זיספסיב א ..
רסעים

ארעא וזרעות עליה ואיש ותרומות יהרסנה · ורוח דימלה ואיש תרומות יהרסנה
כח זכין מכוון טורינו הרב רבי כרדכי בעל מלאכת אלכמ"יא · כנין דא כאטונא
מחזירכו · דלא להוי כטובא עלייכו · למטכח כמלתא דא אורחא דקטוט ·
לאפיק מיכיה ככסין ופטוט · כפה ר"ך כרושא וכתר כפרך ודקוסין · ולא יגין עליה
סלצין וטרסין · ותסדרו הכא הממון כדי למנסכ כנפיה לגוכדרין · לכדוכיה
ולתכבשיטין ולמוהרין · ואכ לא כטוכין ליה אלא מחוניה כעכין טרטמו ולא ממסו ·
כנין דמתקרי הכא ר' מרדכי קכ רסו · ומארי רשוותא יעכדו עליה ווער · וכדין
הרכ רכי מרדכי מ"ו ואחיד לכ:לא כרכ"א רעד · ואיהו לא עסיק כזוכנה הלכבות ·
וכמלאכת האכזכמ"וא עכיד לככתיה ילגות ויכבות · ומטפט הככות כא כנין
עלרוקמיה · דכאתרא דכצא למטת'ל ללארם יהרם כמוחיה · וככר ידוע דחכרת
איקין כקרבכן · וטוכדין טבין ע כדיכן · ואתין ידעין לאמטיך כרכתא לאתר
דאיטטרין · עבדו כפוס מכ מתכון דתתקיפין להדא כעטתא דלא ארין · ותם יעו
לאים · ולפטור ארבע פטרי רחמיס · ותיכו לפטוק ואיטטיך לי כאמונה כזדק
גכמטפט ונ'חסכ ונברחמיס · אמן הזוכר כאמת וכנדקא · דוד דרמן מקירחקא :

תחלת ממושכה   מחלת לכ ועץ חיים תאוה כאה · דא הוא דתכן
דליתליה לכר כס לאסתכ'לא כרטותיה לנכי קכה אכ
אתין או לא אתי מ'ט כנין דאי איהו אסתכ'ל כה כמה מאריהון דדינא אתי לאסתכלא
כיה כעוכדנו · ורוח איהו דהא הטוא אסתכ'לות' דאיהו מסתכ'ל כהטוא כנינא
גריס ליה מחלת לכ · מאי מחלת לכ דא איהו מאן דקלים תדיר עליה כס
לאסטאה לניגלא ותת' · כדלאוקמוה חכרייא פרק קמא דרלם הטנה ג'דכרים
מוכירין תובנותיו טל אדם וחד מכהן עין תפלה כמו ספירם הרכ סכ ועץ חיים
תאוה כאה · תי'וכן מאן דכעא דקכה יקכל נלותיה יסתכ'ל כאוריית' דאיהו עץ חיים
וכדין תפוה כאה · מאן תפוה דא הוא דרנא דכל נלותין דעלמא כידיה ועתיל לין
קמי מלכא עלאה.וכאה קחי לאסלמא רטותא דהטוא כר כס · כגוונא דא
אית כעטלמא איכין ככי כסא מארין דוויכין כיטין דלא יתקכל כעותא דכר כס
קדמיהון כנין דאיכון אטימו לכא ואטימו כ:רחי דקיימין תדיר לאסטאה על ככי
כסא ווי להון ווי לחולקיהון · ואית כעטלמא איכון ככי כסא דיתקכל כעותא דכר
כס קדמיהון כנין דאיכון קדישין מארין דרחון דמסתכלי כאוריית'א תדיר דמלכין
וכו'על ככי כסא · טכ להו 'כעטלמא דין וכעטלמא דאתי · ורוח דימלה תוחלת
ממושכה כמושכן הלא זו הם ערלי לב וערלי בשר לא פתות ולא יתיר · ואיכהו
מחלי לכ דאיכהו הכריכו עטלמא ואתדין לנופא קדיטא דכר יטראל ככולרין וכטכ'וייא
וכנין דא לא ניחות לטדר כעטותא קדמיהון ·   כרס כהפוכא איכון ככי כסא
קדישין
7   כ   4   כ

שאלות ותשובות

כשכיל מלומד זכ...וכה • ויה מטען רתוכן שלא רכה לשתן שלא כפני הראש
כשכיל שהיאשה אינכ וכולה להשעיו פניכ כפכיו כית דין זה איוכ מעכרג דהא
אם מטברין לסן סופרי הדיינים ולמטעון לפכיהם אמחו אין תופסין להשעיו וכל שכן
בגדון זה כהוא חיוטי שאם יתוטו מהשעכמו מעריכם לכה לכ...ין ושלתו וקראיו •
ויכול לטטעון כעם אמר כבגדיכ ולא יכולה להשעיו ואין סכרא לחלק כאן כין קדימה
לאיחור הואיל ואינכ שעינה מטעכה כרא...ונה שלא היתה שם • והוא פטוט
ועל כל פנים ליכו מלכרא שלא יטעון רתוכן קודם שתכא מהא שתטון לפי דיקדוק
הטומקים שלא כא היא כרלא דכולא כיה ואשתכחו תמן אמלי רכרכי רחשי היטי...כל
ושעיכו עתיה מימו כד...כל דה • והא דהוי לי כתבתי כנחמה תמומ התלאות וכ...כב
מקרי הרדקי הקטן דוד דרמן מקריאק...א •

אגרות יקרות

מלך במשפט יעמיד ארץ • ואיש תרומות יהרסנה :

תא חזי כד כרא קכה עלמא עולאה אתקין כולא כדקא ...אות • וחפיק כהורין
עולאין מהדרן לכל סטרין וכולא איכו חד וכרא סמי דלעילא וארן דלעילא ...אתמנכ
כולהו כחדא לתועלתא דלתתא • ...אוכא תתתא מקיימו ...ארעא כדיכא דקטום
דעכדי כדא מלך כמשפט יעמיד ארן • דא דוד מלכא דכתב ויסי דוד עושק
משפט ...דקה ...נוח • ואיהו קיים ...ארעא וכוכותיה קיימא לכתר דכא • ...איש
תרומות יהרסנה • דא רחכעם • תא קכ...כ כניכיהון דכ...דיקי לא כ גכ דפורעכותא
אתגור על עלמא מתעככא כניהון ולא עלמא על עלמא • כל יהוי דדוד מלכא
אתקיימא ...ארעא כניכיה ואוו כתר דכא אתקיימא דכתי ...וכ...תי על השעיר
...ואת ל...ו...ענה לאכני דוד עכדי • כנווכא דא כל יהוי דיעקכ וכל יהוי
...יוסף לא עלמא פורעכותא כעלמא • ולית לן דרא דלא איתכיה כיעקב וכל דוד
...כ...וסף דידעי אורחוי דקכה למיול כהו כגין דאיכון מסתכלי כאורייתא ...מחא ולולד
וערכין דיכא דקטום • כנווכא דכ... קידטין עליוכין ...אוכו קהל ורתכ...כחורט דידע
לתקכ...א אורחוי דקכה ולא יעכדון מחו...י חוריתא וכאכ חולקיהון כעל...כ דין וכעלמ...
דא...תי דכ...ניכיהון איתק...יימ ...ארעא יתק...יימ כגין דימא דקטום דעכדין תדיר • ...וי...את ...כליהון
מלך כמשפט יעמיד ...רן .רכ מכ מלכי רבכן: ורוח דמלה • מלך כמשפט יעמיד ארן
כהשעכון מכוון אלו גאוכים מן קהל וראנקכאורט • כגין דא אתכ...כ אכן מתכומי דלהתכ...
למקכל על חד כ...רא רכה דאיהו קריב לפרווכתכין ...שמיה ירוט מהדר מרדכי כעל
מלאכת אלכ...מיאל • וע...כ...ין דיליה דאיהו עכיד עכ כני כ...ייתיה ...ל...ו עוכ...דין
דקטוט דאיתלויה ...רכ כ...תין רברכין דלא כסיכן • ...זעירתא דכולהון כתכ...ת סכין
ואית ח ...בין דפריום מהונון ...סכן להו תרסל...ין כלו פרוטה • ...אוף לא סדר ל...כ
תרומה ...עטיל להן ולט...יפוליי...הו על קהל קדוסיכו קרא...קא ...כגדל כ...כין ה ...ו ...הרכב
...ר...א

פתתבוה אשתו בבית דין הבני עומד כמקומה כי כל מה שנושאת וכותית תוך הבית
הוה משלי כי אין לה נכסים מיוחדים כגון נכסי מלוג וכדומה ועל כן אם היה
מתסדת בדין צריכה לשלם ממוני' · ועוד תזהט טענת ראובן התינע ותביינ
שאין לה עסק צמו כתביעה זו ואם תכינו מטעבתו שוולתה לא ינמר הדין אכוא
אותה לבית דין · וקם דיין אחד והשי"ב לשמטן אין לראובן ס'ס דבר על
סעהא אשתן ל_ית דין כי כן הדין כמוט · ונתיוכחו יחד על זה :

תשובה

אין הדין פשוט כל כך כי מה שכתב הטור חא פי'קבד נבן
כנשיב הוקרותלא ויתר לתב בדין וזה רב אלפס אלא לשור
להן סופרי הדיינים. ולטשון לפניהם חבל לא לחסיר טעבותיהן לאחריס והר'לום
ססכים ליה וכו' · אבצר לומר היוכנשיב דחין להם כתצלים או הבעל איונ פקח
לטשון ולרך נקט לאחרים דבכצל נכי איתתיה לא מיקרי אחר דבעל כאשתו והנע
פצמן הא דהוצא פרק השולח ומייגע לה כהא סי'קד'ב הבעל סכא לדין לם אחר
סמחניק בככסי אשתו א_שתי זריך הרשאה ואם יש פירות בקרקק אין נרוך הרשאה
וממשמע בכהא אף על פי שאין לו אלא הפירות יכול לדון כלא הרשאה אף על בקרקק
וכל סכן בבדדן דידן שהבעל משלו שובל לטשון ואין לו לכסבנדרו לומר כבעל דברים
דידי את וכל סכן שאמר שאם וולתה לא ינמר הדין סיביא אותה לבית דין כן·
 הוכה התע' רב שבועת העדות כתבו חבל לדין יכולה למסור טעבותיה ביד אחר
ואבצר לדחותה מפני שאמרו אותו דרך יסלומר נלא דרך פסק · מכל מקוס און
לשבע אותה לגמרי כי ניכול לומר דלא דק כאחר ונרין לומר ביד בעלה · כי היכא
דלא לההו פלוגתא כיני פוסקוס · ונס במרדכי פ החובל מצמא סכו וזה לשוכו
פסק ראבן כיין שהנכסים רגילות לישא וליתן כוזה הזה הרי כאלו מיכנס בעגיהם
להיות שלוחים ואם יש עדים חייב סבע: לשלם מפני תקנת השוק השאו ויתבנ
עמהכ ואם אין צרים נשבעת והל לדממרין אין חדס רונה סתתכוה אשתו בבית
דין_אבני מילי נכי כדר דנריכה פנמים לפרט סנדר כפני בית דין אבל בכא אבשר
על ידי אביסרומפוס וצור תתבוה ותתבוה ולא תעוול וכו'ויס לדקדק על זה אמלא
בקט ואם יש עדים חייב בבעל לשלב הוה ליס למיתר מייכת היה לשלם מלומ הבעל
אנא נלהי הוא טוען כשהוללא וכבודה כת חלק בביתה · ועוד לכחורס מצמא חזת
סכתב;ואם אין עדים כשבעתיהא והל דממרין וכו'פד אבל סכא אבצר שי אביסטרופו
וכו'· דאין הכדין דומה לראיה בו אין אביטרופוס לשבועה · אבל לרתתי
יתינשב יפה סמתחילה אחר חייב הבעל לשלם ורנס לומר פטוטן בשכילה · וצל
זה כתב דאבשר על ידי אביטרופוס דהייכו כל סכן על ידי בעלה · וכננד האחר
ואם אין ע_דיס כשבעת ועוד תתבוה ותתבוה וכו'ס_ריכה היא כעמס לבא
לבית דין וה_ח מחמ בתוכבדא דידן שרבא לטשון בשכילה קודם ואם תטריך לבא
כשכיל

שאלות ותשובות

נ̊ סוס כרוסיה לא שוו המורה משה דרוזה · משמן כשרו ירזה :

ס̊ עייל פילא בקופא דמחטא · להתיר אסור לבני דאטא :

ק̊ ידוע גיהנם יורתין באחריתם · ועליהם את־מוו מיום דעתי אתכם
ממרים הייתם :

ר̊ פות על רעות אוכון מוסיפין עם מוריהן · כללא דמלתא כל רע״ת לא
אכם להון :

א̊ יכון בויתין למשה דור עזי · עיזר ושור לנו אתין כורא למיזי :

ק̊ לקולי דארמאי גלגלו על גופא וממוכא · להכהו קדישין כבי בכורדלאכא ·

א̊ סר כלכהון אומתא דאלפא עילאה ודאלתא · סכא נפרכן דכורדלאכי
מכרוסן דבכי דאטא :

והפלא ופלא עליך משה דרוסי דאת רודף ודורם ומטיל אדם לעם קדישי עליונין לבלתי שמוע לגזירת כל גאוני עלמא · וכפלא ממך פסוק כי יפלא וגו׳ לא תסור מכל הדבר אשר יגידו לך וגו׳ · והאיש אשר יעשה בזדון לבלתי שמוע וכו׳ · ומת האיש ההוא אך אהכי לך שטותך וחסרון ידיעתך · דזקן ממרא שחייב מיתה האמור בתורה הוא תלמיד חכם שהגיע להוראה ולא בתעלם מיכלם אלא דבר מופלא כדאיתא פרק הכהנקין · ועבשיו מופלא וטמיר מינך אפילו מאי דלא טמיר מדרדקי דבי רב כי לא כגורכו גורם ואויביכו פלילים · ואי אית בך דעת אכת יתיר נריעא ופתיתא דאכת יודע רבונך ומכוין למרוד ביה ומכריס לאחר את מתקרי ועובדין דילך יוכיחו בן קמצניות קדישין לבית הפס״ול לדון בבתי קרקסאות ותרטייאות של עבדין אלילין אחרים · וכדי בזיון וקצף עלך דעל מארי שמיא התרוממת ולאלקא כספא ודהבא סגדתא · ולאלקא די נשמתך בידיה וכל אורחתך ליה לא הדרת · להן מלכי יספר עלך וחשלך במשפט ונדק פרק · ותחזור הדין לסיכי והמשפט ליושבו · ואז תתחייב מגזירת כמ״ש · ותהא ארכא לשלוותך · הדובר באמת ובנדקה ·
דוד דרשן יוקראקא :

ואת השאלה חברתי שנת שכ״ז כשבא אלי כ״מר אליה גלאן שכתובים עם דיון אחד מאודות אשתו ·

שאלה ראובן תבע לאשת שמעון לדין · וכא שמעון במקום אשגו בפני הדיינים ואמר רבותי ידוע לכם שאין אדם רשאי שתתבוע

אלקים וכל סתריה כן מלבד ניכופיהן וגמטריאותיהן של שמות עד כאן לשונו ·
והפלא שכתב זה אף על פי שעדיין בומכו לא כתבנה הספר המופלא שאלוקי ספר
הוודר כאשר כתב כעל מנהקת יהודה כפתיחתו לפירוש מערכת אשר הגא מוונקן
שבעתים כנרופין וכגלגולין כאשר כודע למי סקריא כתיכו וכמסמו כן הוא ערך
לתהלתו ·   ומה מחד כודע יותר ויותר פעולת השמות והקמיטין מי סוכב
לראות כספר סיעור קומה ·   וכתפלת רבי כחוכיא בן הקנה ·   וכתפלת רב
המכוכא סכך ·   וכספר עב שמות של מטטרון כתוספות פרק קמא דיכמות נכי פסוק זה אף
סעולם איורו ·   ולפי מה שראיתי כספר אנרת חמודות כראה שהרלמכה לא
ידע כחכמת הקכלה עד סוף ימיו שכתכ מס כמס הרלמכה כשכאתי לארץ הנכי
מנאכי זקן אחד ומסר לי חכמת הקכלה ·   ואלו זכיתי חלוק כימי חורתי
הרכה דכרים לא כתכתי החלו שכתכתם ·   וכן כתב הרכמכאל סלהי פרק ג
ואכחלת חכות כמס הרוכס ·   ואפטר מס שהזכיר סמגדל עוז כספר סומס
סיה גס כן כסוף ימיו :

וכן מה שפראס לי כתכתי כפחיכס כאס הזקן דוד דרסן מקרוסקו ·   שמואל לכאת
פתכ ככית ספסוכים כני כורונצ'ו :

כטמת סכ'ח תכר פה זקן קרילאקל סרכטא כמל מסה כורדלאן וכידו מעולות מעולות
שהכמי אטולא וחכמי דו סאלס מסתרי001 וכולו נרני מסה כלדוו על ססכר לכב
החלו ללך כפרכאות סל נויט על כמו כורדלאני ·   וכטכור מכיכרים לי כמס
כנויס ·   כאתי נס אכי כטקכי הנאוכים ·

א | החרין ככל ארטא סלוחכן יסנא ·   אלכטו סמיא קהרות ולחטיכו
     כוככי מונה :
כ | וו לאוחכין רכך סוחין ·   וכל פחיכין חלון רמחין :
ג | גרו מטויס וחמורתה סויטא ·   על דקס כנו יסראל ססוכ סכיט'א :
ד | לא כפח ליכוית למולי אוריחא ·   וכקיסוכסו מכרי כריתא :
     סיט סיחן רטומין ·   לפחוין כלמי מסערמוסין :
ש | סוכך מטווג דיככ דכר יסראל כפכניקטיכון ·   ואחיוקר סמל דאלסטין :
     כסוס

שמכין פגמו לה לפשר שלא יתפכח כידוע מעכין כרוך בן כרים שהלך לחר ירמיהו
וסכיכו ולמדנו והיה מקום להתפכח ונמכע כמו שנאמר לו על ידי ירמיהו כה אמר ה'
כה תאמר אליו ואתה תבקש לך גדולות אל תבקש וכו' ׳ אמכס היות יסודכב
מסכנה וסהלמות כחרות וכדכריות על כל פנים הוא ולערם אין הנכוחם סורם
אלא על חכם נכור ועטיר ׳ וכדומה לוה כתב הרשב"א סימן תל"ב וזה לסוכ]
וכעגי הקמיעין שאמרו דאיתמחי נכרא דאיתמחי הייכו שהוא בן מזל מקמיעיו וכולך
מפניחין לכוין מלאכתם כמזל ידוע כחדם וכיום וכן כותכין בקלף ילדות וסמוכם
תהילים סמוסכם כיד גדול ישראל כולם מסכימין סנריכין עוכב ידוד עבל הכס
הכתכאר דלאו כסכל עמיקין מדכקט וכולן מסניחין לכוין מלאכתם כמזל ידוע וכו'
דסכל ודיעת המזל מכל ליה ׳ ׳ ואם תאמר וככר רחיכו כמה קמיעין כאו מיד סכל
והבליחו על מנע אתמחי קמיעא וכמו סכתכ הרשב"א סם וזה לסוכו וכמו סאכו
פונמכין על חכמי סרפואות כאותן הרפואות סאין הסיקם הטבעי נגזר אותן ׳
(עיין כתריך ערך קפ׳) ולא על חכמי התורה וחכמי הרפואות כלבד אלא על כל
הלכסים סאומרים סכתנמסא העכין סהוא סתירו לנו לסמוך עליסן ככעל׳ הקמיעין
מהס סתירו הקמיעין כין סל עיקרין כין סל כתב ולא פירפו לכו חכמיס חיזס קמיע
סל כתב ואיזס עיקר מן העיקרין עבל וכהלי גוכא איתא כהגסת אסירי ׳ ׳ וואסי
לסוכו רופא אומחה סעסה קמיע חדס לסוס חולי אותן קמיע לכל מותר ואם יעסכא
אדס אחר איכנו מומחה חף על פי מריפא ג׳ פעמים מיד הסומחה חיכא למומר מזל׳
סרופא נרס אכל קמיע סעסאו מיד אדס סאיכו מומחה וריפא ג׳ פעמים כעסאם מומחה
מיד כל אדס דלאין כאן לתלות כמזל הרופא כגנן סלא היה מומחה כסעה סעסאם
פעכ"ל ׳ ולפי דעת זה יס לקיים קנת דכרי רסב"א דאתמחי קמיע סכומאס לסעמים
קמיעין מומחין מיד כל אדס ׳ וסס כמו סגנולס סאין הסיקס הטבעי נגזר אותן
ודעת נכון הוא ׳

ונגלאס כסנכה כעיכי על סכרכוכי כפירוס הסמורה חלק מ׳ פר׳ סב׳ איך חסב עעלת
(הקמיעין וסהסמות מכת הכ"מכע ׳ איך כילה כעגמו סהיה ערוס ומעולל מחכמת
התלמוד כפי מס סכאחרנו למעלה ׳ ואף על פי סאוא סכין כך מדכרי הסמורה
סגם לא הכין על ככון כי הרכ סמורה לא דכר אלא על הסנולאים מלכם ׳ אכל
נורה סיס מחם כיודעו לבדף וסראיס סלא חלק כחכורו התלמודיו על עגין הקמיעין
כבגור סס כסלכות סכת׳ ׳ וכדאמרינן כמדרס יודע סיס בכגלאל לבדף אותיות
סכהן נכרחו סמיס וחרן כדחיתא כספר יגירס ׳ וכנערם מלחר מספר פנ]וכ]
נור האלפי חכמת הקכלה אסר סיא מלאס כל טוב כתירוף סמות כחסר כתב
סד]מכן כפתיחתא לפירוס התורה וזה לסוכו עוד יס כידיכו קכלה על אמת כו כל
סתורה כולס סמותיו סל הקלס מסתיככת מתחלקות לסמות כעכין אחר כאלו
תחסוב על דרך מסל כי פסוק כראסית יתחלק לתיכות אחרות כגנן כראסית כרא
אלקים

סגולה הטפסר כמ״ר מאיר לוי שיהיה · ומעבין הקדמת חכמתי לאלפים · וכל
בקהלה המפוארה קק קראקא · כללא דמלתא אף על גב דכחונית מילתי טובא
זמנין סגיאין · כמה וזמנין כעביכא למעבד עובדא חדתא דלא עבידנא זקדמת
דכא ולא עלה כהוגן · ואשכחינכא דדכרי רש׳ לא נהירין · ומליישכא דירושלמי
שאתע כמי דלא כרש׳ דכתב דכאן כאמן אדס לומר בקמיע וזה רפאתני שלשה בני אדם ·
ולא כתב כאמן אדם לומר מומחה אני · וכפירום איתחימו קמיעא כמי דלרש׳
דוחק לחם זה אפילו כתבו אדם אחר · הא כמי ליתא דקוומן כמה כעמים העתיקתו
גדולי הסופרים הקמיעין שכבתבו מזה פעמים ולא עלה לידם :

ומה שכראה לי · בטעמא דהא מילתא מדרך הסבכא כפירום איתחימו נכראה דלא
איתחימו אלא לקמיעין שממין אותו לאם דוקא · דרך משל ראינו המלך הרמא
בעבור ישרותו לאחד מעבדיו לעשות שלשה עבייכים זה אחר זה על עבייכים שכבר
הכריז עליהס שלא לעשותם · וכי נאמר בעבור וה מיכול להרום נס כעבייכים
המפורסמים כגזילה ורניחא אם כן לא סביק חיי לכל בריא · וכן כהפך זה כעבין
הקמיעין אם היה מומחה לכל קמיעין סיכתוב כדברי רש׳ היה יכול להחיות המתים
ולהצמית כמה פלאים מה שלא ישוער · וכהאי גוונא כפירום איתחימו קמיעא
דלא הוחזק אלא אותם סניית עצמה לכד אבל לא אחרת סכתוב כה לאם זה
אפילו כתבם אדם זה אלא אם כן איתחימו נכראה · דרך משל המלך נתן רשות
לראובן כווחן מה סירטום על קלף שמו של מלך ככתיבת ידו · ויראה אותו למוכם
ויביח לו המכם · וכן תעשה עד שלשה פעמים אחר כך המוכם כבר מכיר זה הקלף
ומביא המוכם כל מי סירלהו לו · וכי נאמר בשביל זה אבל אחד ואחד ירסום שמו
של מלך על קלף ויראהו למוכם וכעבא המכם כתב של כולה ·

וכן כעבין הקמיעין לדברי רש׳ סכתב אם תוחים לחם זה
אפילו כתבו אדם אחר לפי דברינו קרוב סהיו כל הקמיעין מומחין סכתולם מיד כל
אדם מפכי שהיו כאפשרות סכל קמיע כמוכה פעמים ונכל מה סכלאפשר אי
אפשר שלא יסיה שאם לא כן היה אפשר אלא כמכ כידות לכעלי הסניין :
ומה שכראה לי על פי דרך הסאבל ומעבין הקמיעין מי סאכלו יותר רחב וסלם כטבעו
והמחכם סרבם כעולותיו ומלאמין יותר כעבין הקמיעין והוא מחם על דרך הנעת
הסלחת בכואה לכבי אדם כמו סוכר הרב סמארם חלק כ״פר לב רעת אדם ככנואה
סלאם רעות · הרעת הא׳ דעת המון הפתאים אהסם יתברך מי סירונה חכם
או סכל כתבאו סיחוורדו למוסך תחילה וישרם בו הככנואה · והדעת הב׳ דעת
הפילוסופים והוא סהככנואה לא ינוע לאים מכני אדם אלא אחר למוד וניניא מזת
מבכח למעל ואי אפשר סיהיה ראוי לככואה · מכין מבמו לם ולא נכבא נכבא ולפי זה
דעת אי אפשר סינבא סכל · והדעת הג׳ והוא דעת תורתנו הוא כמו זה
דעת הפיולטופי כתעמו אלא כדבר אחד ווה סאנחנו כאמין סהראוי לככואה
סיתכין

נרסינן בפרק כמה אשה כמשנה לא יצא האיש בסכדל מסומר ולא
ביחיד בזמן שאין ברגלו מכה ולא בתפילין ולא בקמיע

בזמן שאינו מן המומחה וכו' • ופירש רש"י ולא בקמיע שאינכו לרפואה •
אלונו מן המומחה אבל קמיע מומחה שרי דתכשיט הוי לחולה כאתר וחולבונשו •
ואיתא בגמרא אמר רב פפא לא תימא עד דמימחא גברא ומימחא קמיע אלא
כיון למימחא גבר' אף ע"ג דלא גב דלא מימחא קמיע • ופי' רש"י דאיתמחי גבר' ואיתמחב
קמיעא כגון מעשה אדם קמיע זה לשלשה כני אדם דכעשה אדם זה מומחה שריפא
שלשה בני אדם והקמיע מומחה שריפא שלשה זה שלשה זה בני אדם או במו שכתב
אדם זה שלשה קמישין של שלשה הויכי חולאים לשלשה אכסים הויכו איתמחי גברא
בכל קמישין שיעשה כיצולה ואיתמחי קמיע שנעשה קמיע זה לשלשה אכסים לחולה
זה כין שכתבו רופא זה כין שכתבו אחר כעשה הקמיע מומחה • אבל וספר
פרומא וסמו וסמק העלו כדברי רש" דאם ריפא ג' מיכי חלאים בג' מיכי קמיעות
איתמחי גברא לכל הקמיעות גם לחלאים אחריס • אבל התוספות והרא"ש
חולקים • וזה לשון הרא"ש פרש" אם ריפא ג' מיכי חלאים בג' מיכי קמיעות
דאיתמחי גברא לכל הקמיעות גם לחלאים אחריס ולא נהירא דלאטו אם בקי
בג' מיכי קמיעין וכי בשביל זה יתבע ג' מומחה גם לקמיעים אחרים שאינו בקי בהס
הלכך מראה לפרש איתמחי גברא היינו שאם כתב לחם אחד בג' אגרת ורפאה
שלשתן איתמחי גברא לאותו לחם בכל פעם שיכתוב אותו אבל לשאר לחם אינו לא
גם אין הקמיע מומחה ויכתבנו אחר • ואיגרת ש" יפתח גם מומחה לכל אדם
ותכ'ית קמיע לתלת גברי תלתוזמני הם אם כתב לחם אחד בג' אגרת וכל אחת
הועילה לשלשה אדם ס או לחם אחד ג' פעמים איתמחי גברא ללחם זה בכל אגרת
שיכתוב ואיתמחו אגרות הללו לכל אדם וכן כתבו התוספות והטור בהלכ' שהן
חולקין על רש" בפירוש איתמחי גברא וכפירוט איתמחי קמועא • ולפי' איתמחי
גברא דלרש" איתמחי לכל מיכי קמיעים שיכתוב ולדבריהם לא איתמחי אלא
לקמיעין סממין אותו לחם לבד לא לקמיע לחם אחר • ולפי' אתמחי קמיעא
דלרש" הוחזק לחם זה לפי' כתבו באגרת אחרת ולפי' כתבו אדם אחר ולדבריהם
לא הוחזק אלא אותו לחם באגרת שכתב לבד אבל לא אגרת אחרת שכתוב כס לחם
זה לפי' כתבה אדס זה אלא אס כן איתמחי גברא • ואף ע"ג דברי התוספת
והרא"ש נהירין וברירין ואיכן צריכין סעד למאומה מכל מקום חזוכא לאסהורי
ולאיהו דכרבדי הוה עובדא בתרוויהון כדברימן כפי' איתמחי גברא דלרש" איתמחי
לכל מיכי קמיעין שיכתוב • כבר כודע ומפורסם בכל הגלילות שעברתי שנגלו
לידי כמה מיכי מיכי קמישין דהייכו לפני הכשוף והסנטוג והקדחת ופחד התכוקות
ועביינכט אחריס הבו מספר • והחזקנו היותר מפורסם מה שבחנתי פה פיררס :
וכדומה לעביניט הללו בכתכת בקק פ'וזכא למאה בזמן במרותי כשמוכת אבל הסר
סכעלא

שאלות ותשובות

אסי משום כבות ולית ליה בכתא דסהנא דרא אנטרויי אנטרוי וכו' • ולפי זה נרך
אמר דשמואל לא הכין דברי רב אסי שהטיב כנך קרוי כנך ואין כנך טבא מן הנגיס
קרוי כנך אלא כנה • וזה דוחק • ומשום סכי זעלו התעלו התוספות כתימא אף גב
דתרנו' • ודברי שמואל דקנן לרטי לפרט מה ספירם • משום הכו
סונרך להבוא איכא דאמרי לא זו ומס ער מטאחוס גוים נמוריס וכו' • אפינו
מהככות והסיב שמואל כהנן ותלמוד'א נמי לא הונרך להקטות והאיבא כנות •
נמא דאמרינן ער מטאחוס גוים נמוריס וכו' אפינו מהכבות וזו דוקא לכני עטרת
הטכטיס דקרא רכה'כבנו עליינו כתיב • ולאיכא לאמימר ושא נכי יהודס כמי
כתיב כגדה יסוד' • שאני התם דלא כתיב כס כגנים וכו' • ודומיא להא אטכחיינן
כפרק האומר וכפרק אין מטמידין לפריך תל'יו'דא נכי כי יסיר הסוא כטבטה נוים
הוא דכתיב • וטעמ'א התם משום דטבעה גוים מטירין
טפי מלאומות אחריני • הכי כמי נכי עטרת הטבטיס משום דכגידמא הוו טפי
אחריני • גזר הכתוב על כניהם אפילו מהכבות • מס טאין כן כדורות הללו
דהא אמרינן אפילו גוים כזמן הזה לאו טובלי עבודה ורס כס אלא מנהג אבותיהס
בידיהס • והכי מטמע כמי במדרכי כהנהות וזה לטוגו עד נרטינן מס אמר רב
אסי נוי סקדם כזמן הזה חופטין לקידוטיו דלמא מטערת הטבטיס הוא ומקי לס
כדוכתא דקביטי כנן בלחלם וחבור וכו' • כו לאמרית' קמיה דשמואל אמר לא
זו ומס ער מטאחוס גוים נמוריס • פסק רבי אכנאל דליתא לדרב אסי ואטיגא
כדוכתא דקביטי דכל אמר סקידם סוו קידוטין דאורייתא כדתניא פרק כחולן וכו'
אבל • מטמע כמי קנת מתוך פסק רא' דכתב דליתא לדרב אסי ואטינו כדוכתא
דקביטי • דלא זוז ומס ער מטאחוס גוים נמוריס דוקא לטערת הטבטיס •
ודכוותה אטכחיינ כפרק חלק עטרת הטבטיס איכן עתידין לחזור דברי ר' עקיבא
רבי אלעזר אומר מס היום מחטיל ומאיר אף אפילה טלהם עתידה לסאיר לסס וכו' •

וכדין קרין תירונא דתריונב'כדטתין דחטירא סלקי אליכא דכולהו ואין פוסקין ואין דכ
לדקדק כהנן דטריך מכני דוד דרטן מקראקא' • דקחו נטעירכא דנא כבתא
קדטא דכורדכאטכי פס פיורדה :

אנ סאנרת טעם סקעיוטן טכרטי כפורדם טבת סלא טטלם אלי טגאון טסליר יומן לחרם
פינס ד כר על סק קעוטן כדרך סוכטן :

מככי טאין מטרכין לגדול אחוט דעתס בקברט•

ג   ב   3   נרטין

אבינו מתיימם אלא אחריו • אלא ודאי רב אסי לא דקדק בייחום דאף על גב
דאבינו מתייחם אלא אחריו לענין קדושי ישראל מקרי • והכי משמע מדברי
הר'אליעזר ממיץ דמייתי לה בסמ'ע עשיין סי קס'ב וזה לשונו אומר הרב אליעזר
ממיץ שאב הוה מברוגן בחוד מכל המצות סלחמורות כנערין ולא עשה
תשובה איבו מחייב לסחיותן ולא לסלוותו דכתיב וחי אחיך עמך וכתיב מאחד אחיך
וכיון מעבר כמיד יצא מכלל סאחווה עד פילקה דתב'וא כפרק אלו הן הלוקין ונקלה
אחיך לעיניך כיון סלקה הרי אחיך הכל קידם לכן איכו אחיך ואף על גב דתב'וא
כפרק ב'דעל לכל אבידת אחיך לרבות את המומר דנקח לענין אבידה כתרבת
לסחזיר לו את אשר לו ואין לכלל ליתן לו מסל אחרים וחה סמסמע כפרק סולח
סרכי סמי היה רוגה לפדות מומר אובל כבילות לתיאוכן לפנים מסורת סדין כיה
ועוסק • וגם כרכית כמי הנם אסור לסלוותו אבל המומר לסכעים מותר לסלוותו
כרכית סהרי נכי רבית כתיב לאחוס כי ימוך אחיך ונג'אל תקח מאתו כסך וזתרבית
וזה דאמרינן כסנהדרין אף על פי סחטא ישראל הוא דנקח לענין דברים דלא כת'י'
לזו אהוס כגון לענין קדושין וגיטין כדאיתא כיבמות פרק קמ'א בני סקדם כוותן
כזו קנוסין לקדוסין סמא מעברת הסבטים הוא כא' • אבל • ומאום דתלמודת
מסתפי דלמא רב אסי כדרקאי קאי אף על גב דהוה סמיע ליה לסא דסמואל לא הוה
סבירא ליה מסום דקר'א לא אסכקיס כסדיא ורלוי לסחמיר לענין קדוסין • מסום
אכי ומכ'י לסו לסוויית אוכא דאמר כי אמרית קמיה דסמואל אמר לי לא זוו מסם
על מסאאוס גניזם נמרים סכאמר כת כנד'יה כי ככוס ורים ילדו • וכנראו או סוב
סמיע ליה רב אסי לסא אלות לא הוה פליג עליה • מדא דגזירת הכתוב הוא כסדיא
ועוד לעמאא דלא זוו מסם סלכתא פסיקתא הוא כדתרסינן כפר'יס כוחלין הבן
רבכן אין כולדין הלכה מפי תלמוד ולא מכי מעסה עד סיומרו לו סלכה למעסה
וכו וכתב סם הר'ב ופיה כאומר כמתכיתן לא זוו מסם עד דקב'ע סלכה כמותן
אין לך פסק גדול מזכו כדלאיתא פרק קמא דפסמים סבל • ומאי דלא סייוחס
כמו כאלכא דאמרי וסאיכא כבנות אפסר לומר מסום דלא כתמרתם בית דכר לא חמ
תלמודו לסכיאו • ואית לדקדק למאי לא סמיחסו נדולי הפוסקים דין
כימקרים את המומרת וכראה דהוא מלתא דפסמיטותא נכי מומר סקדם סקדוסיו
קדוסין אף על גב לנגרע כמוקים אחר דלא סדינן זרעיה אכתריה • מכל סכן
סיא דקדוסין תפסי כה דיפא כחת אפילו לגכי דסדינן גו דפ'ם זרעה אכתריה •
ואו לאו ליוסת פיבא מחס מסערם סד'ב כי ככוס ורים ילדו אלא סן ישראל סבא על
הבויים ור סני • סוו מוקמינן סמניא דתלמוד כאחיכא דאמרי כלא קוסיא כלל •
וקכת נראה כן דעת התוס פות דהקסו לפי פי'רסי דב'נני סקדם כוזן הוה מנסטין
לקדוסין כו'קסכר בויה סילדיב'מיסראל הוזלד מומר ומוחסין לקדוסי מומר • ותית'
דהכחה מצכיות מוכח דאיבו מתיינמם אלא אחריס וכו'ותר'נו וכראה' לטעמיה דרב
אסי

בחסמי הנמרא בנך הכא מישראלית נמורה קרוי בנך פכך רעת המפרשים סם
בזלן בנך הכא מכתן קרוי בנך ואפילו בכא עליה כותי · וכבר איפסקא הלכתא
כותי ועבד הכא על בת ישראל הולד כשר כדאיתא פרק החולן ולפי דעת הריף
כשר אפילו לכהונה · זמליסכא דמגיד מסכה פרק ד' דהלכות אישות מוזכן כמי
דסמך על וזהיוכא כבות דכתב נכי ישראל מומר סקדם וכו' · וזה לשונו ומן המזנג
מבפך ריבמות תבל שאפנ' זרעו שהונניד מסשמיר אה קדם אותו זרע ישראלית קדושין
קדושין · ודוקא סהונידו מישראלית ואפילו מומרת אכל הולידו מן הנניה אין
חוססין לה שארי אפילו ישראל נמור הכא על הנוייה והולד מחכה כן איכו קרוי בנו
אלא כנה וזה כרור' · עבל' · ומה סכתב · ודוקא שהונידה מישראלית והנא אפ'
נלי הכא על בת ישראל הולד כשר לא הונרך לאשמועינן אלא כשביל אבל הולידו מן
הנניה וכו'· והכי איתא כמי במרדכי סוף פרק החולן וזה לשונו ונ"ל כיון דבפסקינן
פרק החולן הלכתא גוי ועבד הכא הכא על בת ישראל הולד כשר אפילו נא מל ולא עכל
אך קדם קדושין קדושין אבל ישראל הכא הכא על הנכרית הולד כמוה · וכל שכן מומר
דהולד מן הנכרית כיון דפסקינן כותי ועבד הכא על בת ישראל הולד כשר לא
כבניה ולא אשת איש כי השמירה והולידה מכותי הולד כשר וקדושין קדושין ואמר
להלוותלו כרבות · אפיאסך · עבל ·

והכי כמי איתא בתרוזבת המיוחסים להרמבן סי' קם שאלה מומר לשם שקדם בת
ישראל שקדושין קדושין ואפילו נא שבתי זיר וחזר לסורו כדאיתא ביבמות מה ראו
חכמים שלא אסו לעגון וכו' · והשיב כאוף דבריו ומיהו כשקדם קדושין קידושין ·
ומשראל כמי שקדם מוחרת תפמי כך קדושין ואם חזרה בתשובה אסורה בקרובת
זכה אסר בקרובתיה וברינכה ממנו נט ואם הולידה בן אפילו בן מנוי ישראל כשר
ברא ומיוחם היה כדאומרכן סלה פרק קמא דיבמות והא איכא בנות בנות כלומר בכות
שהמירו תלד לנוייס ואמר רביוא בן בתך הנוי קרוי בנך וכא אם כלקם
ישראל עבל · וכל הדא כמי משמע דליכא למימר דאיכא פלונ על
והאיכא בכות כיון דמוין דנגלולי השומרים נסכי לה עקר לואהיכא בכות ·
ולפי זה קשה לחלק בין לישכא קמא לאיכא דאמרי · ומאי דמזי לך לחלק דלגלגלסכא
קמא אף על נב דקאמר בנך קרוי בנך ואין בנך סבא מן הנויה אין הכא כנה אלא כנה
מכל מקום יב ילפכא למימר דרב אסי כי נא חם נא מלא משום מומרת דקידושי כדתנכסיקן
בפרק החולן נכי גר טבל ופלה סר היה כישראל לכל דבריו למאי הלכתא אמר ר'
יוכס בר חכינא דזי זא הדר בים כישראל מומר הזא ואי קדים בת ישראל קדושין
קדושין · ועל כרחין אית לן למימר סכי רכא מם רב אסי דזו ואי תימא סכי
דווקא לומר דרב אסי לא הוה ולא ידע במה מתנייתא דתנן בפרק ב' דיבמות כי שים נא
כן מכל מקום פוטר את אשתאכיו מן היבום וכו הוא לכל דבר חון מהם שים נא
מן הסטפחה ומן הנכרית וכהני גוכא אותא כפרק האומר בקידושין דוולד בנכרית
נ   א ן   3   איט

שאלות ותשובות

קמיה דשמואל אמר לי בנך קרוי בנך ואין בנך הבא מן הנכרייה קרוי בנך אלא בנך כבת
ופי' רש"י תיישינן שמא מצבארת השבטים הוא כו' שנשאו גויות ונסתבר גווים פילדים
מישראל הולך ממזר ונחושין לקידושי ממזר. ודוקא בדוכתא דקביעי בני
עשרת השבטים דכל קבוע כמחצה על מחצה דמי. בנך הבא מישראל וישראלית
קרוי בנך ואין בנך הבא מן הנכרייה קרוי בנך אלא בנך כבת כדנפקא לן מכי יסיר את
בנך ולא כתיב כי תסיר כי תסיר את בנך אלא לאו אבתך לא תקח לבנך קאי ראם כן
עובד כוכבים לאו כנך מיקרי ולא קרינן ביה כי תסיר את בנך מאחריו דכוותיה נמירא
הם דאין קרוי בנך אלא בנך. אבל מהכא משמ' דלא משגחינן כמאחרם
לא כתנייר אם לאו דהא גוי סתמא כמ ולא אית לספוקי אלא אם הוה מעברת
אשבטים דהיינו מורבצ' דישראל. והדין כן עברן המאחרם ידעינן בודאי לבודאי דמורבצא
ישראל הוא. ומאי דאמרינן בנך קרוי בנך ואין בנך הבא מן הכותיייה קרוי בנך
אלא בנך כבת. והדין כן עברןהמאחרם כמו ידעינן בודאי דמאני מורבצא דישראל קלא
אתיא. ותו גרסינן התם והא איכא בנות ואמר רבינא בן כתף הבא מן
בנוי קרוי בנך. נמירי דבבתיה דההוא דרא אטטרויי אטטרויי. פירס רש
והא איכא בבנות ישראל שנשבו ונשאו כותיים והולידו מהם. ואמר רבינא כן
בתף הבא מן הכותייה קרוי בנך. נמלא כתיב כו
תסיר מכלל דא כתף לא תתן לבנו כ"י. והכי קאמ' שמא תוליד לו בן ויסירנו
האב מאחרי וקח קרוי בנך זלחוש לקידושין. דההוא דרא לעשרת השבטים
אטטרויי. כתבקץ רחמן מנקלוט את הזרע ונצבאו עקרות עד כאן לשונו
אשמעינן כהדיא דאי לאו דמיעקרן היינו מוטשין לקידושין אף על נכ דאכיו
בודאי כותיי הוה. וכל סכן כן עברן דבודאי אביו נאמן מישראל קאתו. ואף
כל נכ דאמרינן התם איכא דאמרי כי אמריתה קמיה דשמואל אמר לא זו מסב על
אטשאלות כותיה גמורים סנא"ח כ"ס כבנו כי בנים ורים ולד. קא כמ' לא אמרינן
אלא לבר ישראל הבא על הכברית דולד זר הוי ולא קרוי בנך כדפירס סלן כפרק
כאשר בקידושין. אבל כותו הבא על בת ישראל ליכא מאן דפלינ דקרני בנך
מכל הדא משמע דכן עברן המאחרם קידושין קידושין. ומדילה כשמע לדידה
המאורסת בת מומר גמורת דקדושין תיפסי כ"ס. והנחיל ונמירי לן דהלכתא
בליסכך בתרא כיחא כיה מולתא. אית לדקלק מחו כיכיהו ולנשון כלנשון דאחבוכ
לאמרי לפי פירוס הדן. נחויכן לברורי כריסא דליכא מאן דפלינ על והאיכא
בנות דסלכה פסיקה היא רבן כ"ד דתב תפ מן הבוותי קרוי בנך דלא סבחינא כבמא
דוכתי דתלמודא מייתי לה כפשיטות' כדגרסינן כפרק כיבד אחיו וכפרק
האומר בקידושין נכי כבריית הולדה כ"יונ חכלן אמר רבי יוחנן משום רבכ' אמר
קרא כי יסיר את בנך מאחרי בןן הבא מבתך קרוי בנך וכו'. ואף על נכ דהאית
בנוסחי

על פי שלום כשחטו צוכרי עברות ככר אין מרסים את דמם ונופם כדי סיביז
דירחון לכל כשר כדכתיב סוף ישעיה והיה מדי חדש ומדי שבת בשבתו
ובאו כל בשר · וראו כפגרי האנשים הפושעים כי וכו' · ורחמכא לשבן מתגן אשר
הצונשין עניים באים · ונזכה להיותמן הרואים · אמן :

מאת הסאלה בכן אוני אצטן מ"לר יעקב רייכר ריש מתיבתא שבת שלז לפק בקק פורדשי
והוא ריש מתיבת לעת עתה בארץ אשכנו ·

שאלה רב סקם שהמיר ולקח לו לאשה תארורית שאמירק גם היא ולקחה
בניותן וקדשה כדיניכיס וילדה בת ממכו והולידה והסמיחה בניותן
עד סגילה כומכיס · וסאישאו אותה לעברן מומר גם הנא · ויקלידו בן שאל
מ... עברן על רלשו וכתגדל כיכיס מפתה אכל ומכוסס סתן ואת אלהים
סמה עובדיס ככן כאב כעושו ביכיהס לגמרי · ויהי כאשר הגדיל הבן כמראם
מלוי כתעדע כי מורע ישראל הנא וסמא כסכו ויטת אל לבו לסוב אל אמות אבותיו
ככה אשר למכולין אך לא כימול ולא הכוim עדין דרכיו אשר סנסיג מקדם
להשתמות אל כית נכרפו אלקיהם · רק לכו אמר סוב · ויהי היום נתן
צוכיו ככת ניגו כת מומר ומומרת אשר גם המה פוסחים על שתי הסעיפים ויאמרו
לסוב ליראת אתה' חלקו אבוקם ויהי המה מתלחשיס ויום יום ידכרו יקדנו מפסק
גם קול דכרי סהמ' שותצוס ולא יכא שום פועל מהם כשתנו יקדנו להשאיל כת המומר
סלוs לבן עברן סנל אשר נדכה רוחו לסוב ליראה את ה' · וסהכו ביניהס כדרכו
כתבאים וכמדו מתוך הדברים האלה וסלחו לקרית שני יהודים יסנו עבדים לקדוסין
ומ*ר כן עברן וקדם את הכתולה הכל כפני הצבדים כטבכת כלת מסה ופשראל ·
וסעינ יוריכו רבינו אם קדוסין אלו תופסין אם לא מאחר פלח כתעמר עדין אשר
מהם רק זמר וזמן כתגניריס הכת המאורסת כהלכתה · והמארם עדין לא כתעניר
ונהן למרחקים כמקוס סאין דריס סמה יסנדיס :

תשובה הדיק לן מר כמלתך צמיוקתך אבל לפי מולכת דעתין ירום
דבר כרור דמזיסין לקדוסין סולחי דילדתין כולחי דתרווייהו
במקום וסמקוi ילדת מרעבל דיסראל קאתי · לגריסכן סוף פרק קמא דיכמות
אמר רב יהוד אמר רב הכני ננ סקם כזמ היה זה מוכשन לקידוסי היוסינן סמא
מעסרת הסבכטיס הנא' · ויאi כל דפריs מרוכא פרוsכ כדרוכתא דקכיעי
וסיבן קטיעי כדרכתיb וינכס בלמלם ובקור כדר גון וטרי מדני · כי אחריתא
קמיs

לתמלקים שישחטו לישראל אותי הבכוי כעוס טוב שלהם שינושין כל ומיהר כתכויב
למה ׃ ואם שחטו אין מכסין את דמו כלומר היה לה לוכור אב ישחטו
לישראל שאין מכסין את דמו שהזקבה יקח נקמתו מהם כדכתיב ונקנ׳ע
דמם לא נקתי ספירו׳נו אף על פי שאנקה את הדומות מסאר עבירות אבל מה
שנשפכו דמן של ישראל לא הנקתה אותן חנה שקח נקמתן מהם ׃ ומוע יהיה זה
אומר סוף בפסוק וה׳שוכן כ׳ציון כ׳שיהרה שכינתי בציון דהיינו לותן הנחולה וצל
ידי מי ועצשה הקבה נקמת כ׳סיית הדם על ידי מ׳שיח בן דוד שכא מיהודה שאמר
עה צנע כי בסרנג את אחיכו וכיסינו את דמו׳ ׃ וכאותי הזכות יהיה מנהיג לכל
העולם כמו שנרמו נס כן כמשכה ׃

כיסוי הדם שהוא מ׳שיח שכא מיודא שאמר וכיסינו את דמו ׃ כוהן ׃ יהיס
מכהינ ׃ כארן אותי שצדיין קיים כארן ׃ וכמונה לארן ׃
פלו׳ שיהיה נב מכהינ לאותן שינאו חון לארן יהם המתים שכליהיתי הזמן יהיה תחייה
היתים כדראיתא כמדרש רבה פ׳רשת ויחי בשם רבי חלבו למה הלבות ומהוכבין
קבורת ארן ישראל שמת ארן ישראל קיים תחולה כ׳מות המשיח ואין כלין שנות
המשיח ׃ כפני הכית ו16לא כפני הכית כלומר כין אותן זמן שמתי זמן הכית ושלא
בזמן הכית כנון דור המדבר והנג׳ ׃ במולין אבל לא כמוקדשין ׃ כלומ׳ דוקא אותן
שהיו מולים כאהבת הקבה כדכתיב כי חולת אהבה אני ׃ ויהיה להם שארית
ותקניה ׃ אבל לא כמוקדשין ׃ הם הריטעים סלכתנ בהם המנקדסים
ונהמטסריס אל הנקנת ׃ ונקח לשון כוהן כמשנה נ׳ פעמים נגד נ׳פעמים שכמ׳שא
במקראל נשויכין על משיח כקהלת ולכי כוהב כמכות וכתיב כמשיח ונחה עליו רוח
ב׳רוח חכמה וכו׳ ׃ וכער חטן כוהב כ׳ב כישעיה לימות המשיח ׃ רועא ישראל
ה׳זויכה מוהב כאהן כ׳ כות שאחור על יוסף מה כנע וכסינו את דמו׳ ׃ ואמר כך כאר
אפקייס כו אדום ומואכ משלוח ידם וגנ׳ ׃ ויהו שאמר וכוהב כמיס פסוא כותעיס
כדכתיב יכרסמהה חזיר מיער ׃ וכעוף כודד קן משולא תהייכה כבות מואב וגנ׳ כמוון דסיוכו אותן מבוכרו שיהיו
מזוהכים תמיד כמסלהתידם ׃ וכ׳שחינו מזומן כדכתיב נכי דוד עם לא ידעתי
יעכדוני ׃ וכוהב ככני חיתא פלו׳נתא פרק אותו ואת בנו כינר׳ אלישתר ורכנן
מזכרו סוא תים הכח על הב׳כייה ׃ כלומר ויהיה מ׳שיח מכהינ כישראל סהיו
מלשיס ותמ׳שים סכאו על הב׳כייה מהוא ארן ישראל סהוא נכי לכל האומות ׃
מפכי שהוא ספק מפכי שהיא סכל די ספוקן כגלותורלאו לגאולה כמו סיסד ספירוא
בחמוכה כנתחנלא מפקו וסדי מכן וכו׳ ׃ ואין שוחטין אותן כ׳ט סכאותן הזמן יהיו
לישראל כעולם ישו ויקנו׳ כ׳נלא המות לכה ח׳ גנ׳ ׃ ואם שחטו א׳ן מכסין את דמו כלומ׳ ואף
על

ועל דרך המדרש

בא לבאר ולרמוז איך כזמן ביאת משיח ישחוט ויכלה הקב̇ה עמלק הרשע
סופכי דמים · וגם פושעי ישראל שהרבו מעשים הרומיים כדס ·
וזה שאמר כיסוי דדם מלשון לא אכלתי באשר כוס פרק הסוקט ופר̇ אלו טרפות
והוא תרגום ש̇ שחיטה · כלומר שישחוט הקב̇ה לשופכי דם · אותה המדה
כוהן כאו̇ן כאומות יושבי הארן · וכהונה לארץ היינו כשרי האומות מכב חוץ
לעולם התחתון שהוא על סולן · כדכתיב ויקוד ה̇ על נבא המרום כמרום ועל
מלכי האדומה כאדמה · וכתיב כי קנא לה̇ על כל הגוים וחומה על כל כבאם
האדומים נת̇ס לטבח ולהשני כי רוחה כשמים חרבי הנה על ונומר · וננקם
כוהן שמתינו אותו הלשון כפורענגות האומות וכהנהו ככבדות : כפני הבית ·
ככאן רמז איך יכלה הקב̇ה נם כן פושעי ישראל עד שלא ישאר מהם רק המעשר ונם ·
מדונתן המעזר ונכ̇ הפ̇ סעטים דכתיב ועוד בה עשרים ושבה והיתה לבער ·
אוה סכקט כפני הבית שמתינו אותו נכי מעצר כלל ת̇ל פרק הפועלים ופרק קמא
דניטין אומר רבי וכאו אין הטבל מתחייב כמעשר עד שיראה פני הבית שנ̇ בערתי
בקדש מן סבית ושמואל במשלו לתבואה כדכתיב כדם ישראל לו̇ ראשית וגו̇ תבואתו ·
ועלא כפני הבית · כדנג הפ̇ל דסייכו וולנ המעצר דהיינו דהיינו אותו סיבער קודם
שנית לעשיריב · ואין מוקדם ומאוחר · כמולין · דווקא אותו שלא היה
קדושה שמ̇ל תליי כמולין כמולין ויהיה כהם מדת הכליון ונהישוטר אכל לא כמוקדשין
אותם סהיו ק̇דות ע̇יהם יהיה להם מצב וקיום כדכתיב כס זרע קדם מצבתה · ואמר כך יחזר
לבאר מדת הכליון כיכסנג כאומות אפי̇ אותם שזומן הקב̇ה סיסטבדו פישראל כמוש
כפש̇ס כתבור סמצבדו יתר מדלי כדכתיב כזבריה נדול אני קוי̇ף על הגוים
סא אבנים אשר אני ק̇פתי מעט והב ע̇ירו לרעה כדכתיב וזה שאמר וכוהב כמיה וכפוץ רמה
לעוולי האומות כדכתיב כדניאל וארבע חיון רברבן סלקן מן ימא ונו̇י· סהם
פורפין כמיית ודורסין לישראל כשפות · כיחוזון כמו סהקדמכי · וכשאיכל
מחוזן מכל סבך · אמר כך כאר כסתם הפוסעים או יכהג הקב̇ה לישראל כדכבע̇
והוא יכסב̇נו פלמות · ולמי יכהו · אותן סבכו כנלות כדכתיב כזרחיב כזרחיב ככבד
וכוא̇ וכתחבוכים אוכלם · וזה וכוהב ככוי קרי ביה וכוהב ככוי כבוי ככקמן הבית לסא̇ן
בכו̇ · ואמר כך כאר כך כאר הטעם מפכי שהוא ספק · מפני סהיו מיו̇ ת̇ו̇ לים
נם ספק כנלות שלא ישחפו אותן כל מצב על מצב קדום הבא̇· כמו סצפו כתבונתיכ̇
ברכיס ככמה פורעכויות סעברה על ישראל סכסחטו וכסרפו כמס חביולי עולם
עמו סכאר אמר. כך · ואין סונהנין אותו כיום סוב כלום ואין מן הרלו̇
כתמלקים

בעבור תעבר · כי עפר אתה ואל עפר תשוב · ולאן אתה הולך וכו' · **ונב**

דרך זה כוונת המשנה :

על דרך השכל

עיקרי הדם רנה לומר מה שצריך לכסות מן הלחויות הבאים מתנבורתהדם
שלא ימך אחריהם ואלו הלחויות כמשכין אחר ארבע יסודות
הגוף שהם כמו מנהיגין ועל כן נקט כונב כאלין רנה לומר

ביסוד סלרץ שהוא התחתין · וכתונה לאלרץ · רנה לומר כיסודות הזכרים שהם
מין ליסוד האלרץ כי כנלם סובכים א'תי כידוע לחכמי הטבע · בפני הבית ·
רמו שיכםה גם תהרוח שכח מארבע יבודותכמה דלם אמר ויהכה רוח גדולה כאם
מעבר המדבר וינע כארבע פינות הבית יגנות סהרמו על ד' יסודות של הגוף סהיא
כמו בית · וקרי כאן כפני הבית · וסלא כפני הבית · דהיינו הנסית הרות
סכח ינד הסכל · וכאר אחר כך סאין ראוי לדתות לנתרי עניני אתגלות
במאמר רזל סלסה דברים תכל סמאל דוחה והימין מקרבת ינר תעונק ולסם ·
וזהו סאומר כעילין דהיינו כמותרות סאין בנ.מנה · אבל לא במוקדסין דהיינו
סים בו מצוה כגון קינם פריה ורכיה וכדומה ונד הזמרינן לתולב יקדם אדם כסעה
תגמים וכו' וכנגן קדום סל סבת · ואחר בך דבר מסלם ראסי מנהיני הגוף סמימנם
מין וזהו סאמר וכנהן כמיה רמו לנב סכו התויות · וכתוף רמו לסכל סהוא מנכיות
לחטבה ומתופף לדבק כסכל כסעל סן ויתף אלו אחד מן הסרכיב · כמוזם
אכו' · כלומר סיעזם הפרם כלכו וכסכלו בין אלו סיתוומכיב לחיי עולם כגון
מאמינו ן עיקרים · וכסאינו מוומן לחיי עגלב הכא כגון המלאכים והאפיקירהים
כמו ולא תתע־ן אחרי לכבכם וחמרו עיכיכב רנה לומר עיניכב סהוא מנד הסכל ·
אנו:נ בכו' · מנסון כויה סהוא רמו לתמוות הכבד סבו תעכורת הדם מסורה
באדם כדאמרינן בכברות־ים רבה סגין רבה וסקין נסון קמיוות בדחיתא כוורא
כתע־ינלת כהן גדול סהה סמונה ונסומה וכו' · כלומר מה סהוא תלוי כסכל וכלב
מדע ת כוזכית ומחסבות מסוכסות ירוך להסיר לנתרי ; אבל מה סתלוי כפו
סהוא הככד דהיינו אכילב וסתיב חם להסירו לנתרי · מפני סהוא ספק סברך
סיהא לו כה ספוקין סיב: ל לחיות ולא יותר · הייכו דוקח כסאר ימותהסכם סלא
ים מצוה כתעב:נ אכילה · אבל כסבתות וומים סוכים סכתיב כהם סינב
סתמיה יכול לאכול יותר והם כאחר וזה כאחר ואין פוחטין א'תי כיום טוב כלום 'מונעין ·
וכאב סחטמו אין מכסין את דמו סצ:רין ליתן הדין :

ונב

ואריך להקדים עניני הפרשה

אוסרי לגפן עירה · בכאן ביאר מי הם הצדיקים שיזכו לעולם שהוא משיח
אלו הצדיקים שנמשלו לגפן כמו שתרגם אנקלוס · והם שמשלו
בעולם על גופם שנקרא עיר כדאיתא בנדרים עיר קטנה וכו' ואסרו
יצר הרע שבת ∶ וזהו שאמר אוסרי לגפן עירה · ולשורקה בני אתונו · רמז
בלשון הזה כשיקויים לעולם שיקריבו להם ואקבצם · יהיה הכנין מהגוף שהוא היכל
הנשמה והיכל נקרא איתון כמ שפירש רש׳ ויהיה דעת התרגום
ובנין היכליה · ומטעם שברמז על תחיית המתים הוזכירו כנגדו בלשון שהוא אמר
ואמר כך מבאר שיזכה גם כן לעולם הבא למות הנכון שאמרו עליו שכל הכבשים
לא כתיבנאו אלא לימות המשיח שכל לעולם הבא עין לא ראתה אלקים זולתך יעשה
למחכה לו מאי עין לא ראתה אמר רבי יהושע בן לוי זה יין המשומר בענבכו וכל
כפריק חלק · ויש להקשות היכן רמז שברמז על היין · ויש לומר מאחר שאמר
עין לא ראתה ∺ הוא בגימטריא יין אלא נראה שעתידו בענבכיו · והטעם מאחר
שאמר האדם הצדיק את עצמו ולא כמשך אחר הד׳ לחויות אומנין ומסיתין את
האדם לתאוות המתוכות כידוע להכמי הטבע והם מתרבכים מתנבורת הדם כדומה
ליין · ראוי שיזכה ליין הנבול מדם כנגד מדה ומאחר שכבה את דמו בלומר כאלו
לא היה כעל חומר ודם כך תקף יצרו ולא היה כראה · ראוי שיזכה גם כן לנכל
אלא כראה שהוא יין המשומר בענבכיו · וזהו שאמר ככם בזין לבושו כלומ' בזכות
שככם לבושו שהוא החומר שלבוש הנשמה כמ ככבי מרפה לבך ולא נטה אחר
הלחויות יזכה לכך ככן · פירש רש׳ כותיו מיין לבוש · שהוא
כמו כסותה · ודם ענבכים כותה · כלומר מאחר שכבה דם כאלו לא כראה בעל חומר ודם יזכה
להמשומר בענבכיו אלא כראה · ויסיס הפסוק מסורם · ככם לבושו ביין
ודם כותה ע∶בכים · ומה שכחמר הד׳ מן כותה רמז שהוא לשון השתה שאדם הוא
מסית את האדם לתאוות · ומטעם זה כראה לי כאה בתורה מנות ביסוד הדם ·
הוא מהכתוב אומר איש איש מבכי ישראל ומן הגר כגר בתוככם אשר יכוד כיד חיה
או עוף אשר יאכל ושפך את דמו וכבתו בעפר · וכראה לי שרמז גם על זה העכין
כאים איש מבכי ישראל · כלומר כל אחד מישראל ויעבר על יכרו הזמנרים כאים
וזהו שאמר ומן הגר הגר בתוככם מן המגרה אשר בתוככם שהוא היצר הרע · אשר
יכוד כיד חיה או עוף אשר כא במצודת היצר הרע כדכתיב וכם עליו מצודים
ויכוד כיד חיה או עוף רכה רכה לומר מדת הכווית והנגלוה · אשר יאכל · שמכלם
את האדם · ושפך את דמו כלומר שהיצר מגרה אותו עד כן נס כן שיספוך וימשוך אחר
הלחויות הד׳ הבאים מתנבורת הדם למלאות תאות הגונבניות · ומה תקנתו וכ סהא
שיתגבר עליו וכאנו לא כראה שהוא בעל דב וחומר · בעפר · שיכסה זה
כ ב ד   ב ב   בעבור

ט

דהיינו ברכה אחת לעולם הבא הצפון לצדיקים • ואחד מפני'רו לדרום דהוונג
ברכה אחת ליה העולם שהוא דר כו ונצק דירת זה העולם הוא כשצהיה מתוקן
דירת רום שהוא בית המקדש ועל כן הנביאו בלשון דרום • והוא שאמר אלכו להכנ
לו סגולת וכין טובים ואבנים טובות ומרגליות כדאית'בפ הספינה דיתיב ר'יוחנן
וקא דריש עתיד הקבה לעתיד אבנים טובות ומרגליות שהם עלשים על שלשים
ומצמידן בשערי ירושלים וכו'י • ולא עוד אלוה בלבד זוכו ישראל אלא שוכני גם
כן לראות נקמת עמלק ונותיים להלקותם במקל ורצועה עד שיחאו מן העולם וזה
שאמר שהתפילין לו רצועה של מכות תחת וכני תחת שכתיב כו ניזכב כך כל
הכתלים אחרין • ונם כתיב תזחה אתזכר עמלק ונות'ונדע כי'אין
בשם שלם ובכסא שלם עד שימחה והכוונה בשם רמו לישראל שהמו של הקבה חסותר
כשמינו • והכסא הוא המקדש הדום רגלו • ונם שאמר אחר כך ומניאו כא
כעמלק קרשעה • ישראל שהיו שפלים כעפר כדכתיב התכמרי מעפר • ולהיכן
תכואם לנבטו שהוא המקדם ולמורכתנו שהיה חרב ואו יהיה השם שלם ישראל וסכם
שהוא המקדש • ונמו הענבין מדרשנו מעושה והכנאם כי לא ימרק חטאו של נאם עד
ביאת משיח ועל כן מכייכם סנם ואו כיכה נלמושן סכו האחרים והתנומים • ויסזה
בעורינו רם על רסים • ויוללט מאויכים ומקמים • וניכאנו עם כל ישראל
אל כית עולמים • אמן :

דרשה אחרת

בימוי הרם כוזב בארץ ונמהנב לארת כפני הכית ושלא כפני הבית כחולין
אכל לא כמוקדשין וכוהג כמים וכתוף. כמוזמן וכבטלינו מוומן
אוסג ככמו מפני שהוא מפק נלין סוחטין אותו כיום טוב ואם סחטו אין מכסין חת
דמו ג פיין כרסי וכתספוות•

אעפא גם כן מה צריך לכקוט כוהנ יאמר עבסין אף סדם בארן וכמונה לארן • ועוד לאס נקם
בתני הכית ולא כוין כבית• נלעס וכר ג סעעים כנהנ:

הרין

ותגזר אלא שגם ענו היו כפופים תחת רגועתם של ישראל לעשות מלאכת כחורב'
וכנינה כדכתיב וכני נכר אכרכם וגו' :

על דרך השכל

ר' שמעון בן מנס א' אומר חכל על שם גדול שאכד מן
בעולם רמז ליגר הרע שנקרא מלך גדול כדאיתא
בנדרים שנאכד מן הלאם שנקרא עולם קטן   שאלמלא לא כתקלל כחם דהיינו
פקר היגר הרע והכחם הוא הגוף ואלמלא לא כתקלל הגוף למשוך אחר התאוות כל
אחד ואחד מישראל אל היו מזלמנין 'ן שכי נחמים טובים דהיינו הגוף והכשמה יהל
מנחשים ומסיתים כו לטוכה • שהכשמה היתה לה מחשכות ודעות טיבות •
והנוף מדות טובות וזה שאח' אחד מסגרו לבשון דהיינו הלב כדכתיב בלבי נפנת
וסוא מלך כגוף כדאיתא כסי' לב כנכם כמלך כמלחמה • ואחד מסגרו לדרום
שהוא השכל כמח שהוא דר כרום הראש לשכיל לו מכלכפומין ואבכים טובת
רמז למדות טובות ולמחשבות טובות' • ולא עוד שאם לא היה היגר הרע מהגף
אלא שמפסולין לו רגועה תחת וככו כלומר לא היו נלו תרוה מונכה והיה כאלו
תעלה רגועה אחת כמקום וככו שהוא עריותי' • ומניח כה ע'פר לבינתי רמ
שהיא מעושא כפריתו כדכתיב יהיה ועד כעפר כעפר • דוקא לנגתב מתגו
מתגי ופא כדכתיב כאתי לנני אמותי כלה ' נג כטל מועין חתגים ואחין ולד ופא
א שגו לא היה מזוון אלא כדן לקיים פרים וגרכו להעמיד העולם שלא יהיה חרב
כדכג כ לא לתוהו כראה לשבת יגרה' • וזה כוונת ולקורכתו להעמיד עורגן
סעולב :

ועל דרך המדרש

רבי שמעון בן מבמיא אומר חכל על שם גדול רמז על משיח שכתוב כו לפחם
שמם יגון שמו '   ונקרא גדול כדכתיב מי אתה הר הנדול ודרש כו זה
משיח שיהיה גדול מהאכרים ומחשא כדכתיב סגל ישכיל עכדי ירום וכו' • והאזור
הנדול שהכדיל הקכה לכ דיקים הוא אזרו של משיח מאזמן שנאמר כיאזתו יהיה השמש גלא
שמן חלקים • כדכתיב יהיה אור הלכנה וכו' • שאכד מן העולם • כומן
שכראה שהכדילו הקכה לכ דיקים כעכור שהיה נלוי לפני מי שאמר והיה סעולם
עכין ספתי מהנחם שאלמלא לא כתקלל הנמא כלומר שלא היה עכין הכתי מקללת
הנחם ואחרו של משיח היה זורח תכף וידוע כי לא כברא הע' שלא לם אלא כשכיל ישראל
שנקראו ראשית וכו' • אך כל אחד ואחד מישראל היו מזלמנין לו ' כ' נחמים טובים
דונה לומר כ' מיני ברכות טובות כדא נחמא ויכרכו•   אחד מסגרו לבפין

א   ה   ג   ב   דהיינו

וסחכמה שכתוב בם כי היו קיוך ונגמ׳ ‏ ‏ בלע נכל אחד שהם היו כלים וסחכמם
והעושר לא היו כלים ‏ ‏ אבל הם לא היו בולעים את־החכמה והעושר:

ואחר זאת הקדמה נבא לבאר סיאמר

על דרך הפשט

תניא ‏ ‏ רבי שמעון בן מנסיא אומר חבל על בת גדול ‏ ‏ ר״ל הכהן הגדול
שהיה בבית המקדם שאבד מן העולם מלהתגלגל עליהם על ידי חטא
שהיו קבועים בו חורים ותומים ‏ ‏ אבל הוא איכו אבוד כי הוא כהן גדול למעלם
וסיבכו שנקט לשון חבל מכל שמורה על חורבן המקדם כדאיתא בולעולמנו פרשת פקודי
למה משכן משכן שני פעמים שכתמשכן על ידיהם הוא שאכבי ככסת הגדולה אמרו
חבל חבלנו לך הרי שנתמשכן כ׳ פעמים ‏ ‏ שאלומלא לא נתקלקל בחא ‏ ‏ רנב
נומר אלואלא לא נתקלקל חסן לעתות ממכו בחא וסיו חורים ותומים בשלמותם
שהיוכו יודעים להגמיד ולהבר האומיות כמו שהקדמנו ‏

כל אחד ואחד מישראל היו מוזמכים לו סכי בחמים מובבם וסיבכו מביחנו קורבים
בכם חטן שהוא טוב לסבי דברים להתחלל על חכמה ועל עושר ‏ ‏ וזם סאמר כל
אחד מישראל וכו׳ מטום שהיו מפותחים על אבכים טובות סל החוסן שמות בני
ישראל כדכתיב ופתחת עליהם שמות בני ישראל ‏ ‏ ואם כן כל ה׳ ואחד מיאראל
סיה לו חלק כו לוכית כשביכו לחכמה ולעושר והוא סביום אחר כך אחד מסגרת
לבפין סרוכה להמעמיר יבפין ואחד מסגרו לדרום סרוכה להחכים ודרים ‏ ‏ להכית
לו סכלפוניכין סו כים ‏ ‏ רמז סהיתה תפלתו מקובלת מסכי דברים סל עורה ועוסר
וסכלדפיון היה קנסר כתר לקנוס מאלו הכ׳ דברים ועל כן לאחד בלסון רבים ‏ ‏ כמו
סביירם אחר כך וחבכים מובבת רמו לחכמת התורה ליחות אבכים סבהם כתקקס
סטרה שכקראת טוב וחרגליות רמו לעוסר ‏ ‏ וידוע סהאחפוד היה. מחיבר תחת
האוסן כדכתיב ולא יזח החוסן מעל האפוד וירכסו את החוסן וג׳׳ ‏ ‏ ואמרו רז״ל
בזוכחים פרק האיס מקדם מקדם אפוד מכפר על עז אין אפוד ותרפים וכתב בעל
העקידה אפוד תכסים מורגל לעובדי פסילים ופסל מיכה יוכיח וכו׳ולזם זה האל
סיעטו זם האפוד בכבדי הכהן אך סיהא תלוי ומוסלך אחרי גיוו סל כהן מהחגורה
ולמטה במקום הטפל מכלכם וסיא ולאי דרך כוון על דרך סאר״זל פ׳ ארבע מיתות
כל ליבכותא אסירא כר מליבבותא דעז דסרי ליה למימר לגני ען שן סלך סני
כטין תיו סלך ‏ ‏ וסיוכו שנקט בעל המאמר ולא עוד אלא סמפסילין רגועה תחת
וכבו סל חוסן סהוא סהוא האפוד סהוא רמו לעובדי עז וסל כן סוניאו בלסון מגוכ׳ ומוכיח
כם עתר לנבתי ולחורבתי וסכונכס אלנו זבו ישראל לחוסן לה די סהיה להם חכמה
ועוסר

שנקדיס ק״ת מפרק עקבי״א וזלתמיה שהקדמנו עליו תוך הפרשה ועם זה יתפרש
הקושיות :

רבי חנניא סגן הכהנים אומר הוי מתפלל בשלומה של מלכות שאלמלא מוראה איש
את רעהו חיים בלענו :

רבי חנינא כא לרמוז רב חינוכיס שאלים מתחכן ומתפלל הוא מה סגן הכהכיס
אומר דסייכו כהן גדול זקרחו סגן הכהכיס משוס דאיתא בירושלמי
חמשה דברים כאמרו בסגן ואחד מהם לא היה מתמכה ככהוכה גדולה עד שהוא
בעשה סגן • הוי מתפלל בשלומה של מלכות • רנה לומר תצבס תפלתך
בכוונה רכוייה שיהיה שלוס לך ושלום למלכות שמיס ויהיה פירוש בשלומה עם
שלומה של מלכות שמיס כדכתיב או גחוק כמעוזו ועשה שלוס לי ונומ׳ • וידוע כי
אהרן הכהן הגדול היה אוהב שלום ורודף שלום וקיה יודע לכוין כתפלתו יותר
מכל אדם לעשות שלום למעלה ולמטה על כן סיים ברכת כהנים בשלוס • וזה
בסיבת אורים ותומים שהיו כפל כאמן שהיו על לבו כדכתי ונתת אל חשן המשפט
את האורים ואת התומים ופיו על לב אהרן ונומ׳ • וידוע כי נקר התפילה כלב
כדאמרינן כספרי ולעבדו בכל לבבכם איכו היא עבודה פאוה בלב הוי אומר זו
תפילה • ונתב הרמבן וכל הדבר כאורים ותומים שהיו פומינן קדושיס מכחם
ידע הכהן העתיד וישמיע לכל שואל בכאות • והשמות האלה ב׳ חלקיס האחד
מכחם יאירו אותיות השבטים הקכועיס כאכני החשן וסם הנקרא אורים כהיונה
אורים לעיני הכהן • והשני מכחם יכא בלב הכהן סידע להנמיד ולחכר
האותיות ולהנמיד מהם כדי שיהא מכוין כתשוכה וכו׳ ושמאל כזה אם היו
מאירים אותיות חכם לא היה יודע מה הוא אם הוא מורה כחא או חומן ועל כן
היו התומים שידע לחכר • ועקר השלום שעשה הכהן גדול להמה כתפלתו היה
שהתפלל על החכמה ועל העושר שכנגד אלו השכים היו שני כלים בבית המקדם
מנורה ושלחן • מכורה רמז לתורה כי כר מנוה ונומ׳ • ושלחן רמו על העושר
וכדאמרינן הרונה להחכים ידרים והרונה להעתשר יצפין וסימניך יבכין מכורה בדרוס
ושלחן בנפון כמו שכתב רבי יונה פרק קמא דברכות • והשלום של מלכות
שמיס למעלה הוא שקיבל תפילתו דהייכו שהמלאך סנדלפון ממתין עד שישלמו
ישראל תפלתם ועונשה מהס כתר להקכה כדאיתא כמדרם שמות רכה פרשת בשלח
וכאשר יסד הפייט כאראלים ומלאכים • וזה פירוש בשלומה של מלכות עם
שלומה ויעשה שלוס למטה ולמעלה • שאלמלא מוראה של מלכות שמים
ולא יתע׳ל׳ אלו כשכיל החכמה והעושר • איש את רעהו כמו עם רעהו •
חיים בלעו לכל אחד ואחד • דהייכו איש העשיר וכמו וילך איש • ורעהו
תלמיד חכם שנקרא אחיס ורעיס • חיית הגוף שהוא העושר וחיי התורה
וקחכמה

נסמכה אתחיל בעזור הנור שכל הברואים נמסרו בידו לגמיתית · לכאר הנגבא
על פרק ארבע מיתות :

תניא

בפרק ארבע מיתות רבי שמעון בן מנסיא אומר
הבל על שהם גדול שאבד מן העולם שאלמלא לא
נתקלקל (כח כנתקלל ועתר) כחט כל ח' וח' מישראל
היו מודמכין לו שכי נחשים טובים אחד משנגרו
לבפון ואחד משנגרו לדרום להביא לו סכדלפונים
ם:בוס ואכנים טובות ומרגליות ולא עוד אלא
אמפטילין רנועס תחת זכנו ומוציא כה עפר לגינתו ולתורכתו :

נקסה לי עס שאמר חבל על שהם גדול משטע שהסהם היה גדול ונדיק עגד עבטו כי זה הלשון
עכיכו נבי אברהם שאמרו רזל פרק קא פרק דקידוסין עניבו נדול שהם · ולא שכיכו שום נדקות
נבי כהם קודם שנתקלקל אלא ערמה וכהכמ שהיה ערום · ויותר היה ראוי לועד חבל על שהם
טוב שהיה טוב לעי שעשאט לו ·

ועוד קשה מה שאמר שאלמלא לא נתקלקל כחט כל אחד מישראל היו עורעכין לו ב' כחסים וכו'
אם עבין קללת כחט כבי ישראל אם זכו ישראל יודען לבם כל טוב הלי כהם · ואם לא יוכו מ'ן
אפילו לא נתקלקל הכחט לא יוכו בעבורו לאכנים טובית ומרגליות וכו' · וכי אם במקלל
הכחט לא היה לישראל שכר וענוט ואם כן מ'ו היו בטלון כל מנוט סעורט :

ועוד קשה מה שאמר היו עורעכין לו ב' כחסים טובים משט: שאפילו קודם שנתקלל הכחט היו
בט כן כחסים רעים · ואם תרנה לפרט טובים לעי שעולמם אם כן פרסה פרטני לועד
מתחילה חבל על שהם טוב :

ועוד קשה מאי שבא נפין נדרוס דבקט ולא בקט עורק ונעב-כ · כי ידוע לחכמי הטבע שרוב
אבנים טיבות במזרח ומערב בשערי שמים שער שלישי במאמר סכי ·

ועוד קשה מה שפירט רש' סכדלפון שם אבן טובה · מאי שבא דפרט ליה יותר משאר אבנים
טונות, ועבל שכן שאמר סחר כך ואכנים טובות ומרגליות אם כן בכלל הכלל :

ונקדיס

ואחר ואת הסקלדמה · אולי יאמר סאיתעקם עלי אין בידי מאומה · לעשות
מטומאות טהרות · הפך מה לכהן כבית הקברות · ויני יעמידני כבית מדרם
סקדם · הנאיל ואוכי יודע דבר לאדם · ואיך אם כן אוכל להאיר להם להולכים
כעיון באפילה · להדריכם ליושר המסילה · על כן הוכרחתי להביא למקדם
עולות · ולהדפים קטת·

שיר המעלות   להראות הטעמי והשרי' דבר שיהיה לפתחות תועלת הבחורים ·
אותן שמתחילין כעיון התורה · בכמה מעלות סובכי יהיה
להם אורה · המעלה הראשונה · יוסיפו לקח להכין אמרי כינה · לאשמיע
להם קדמות · כעביין הדרסות · על דרך הפשט והשכל והמדרם וכמה עביינים
מה שלא שיערו הראשוניכ ·

והמעלה השנייה   הוא להנדיל תושיה · בקסת תשובות ושאלות
לפקח כעולות · והחלם יתגבר · כאנרת טעם
הקמיעון אשר עליהם מוכר :

והמעלה השלישית   להחזיק כפם חלושית · כעבין אנרות יקרות·
כמלציתתי מפעלות · וכלשון האדרת הזהב
מכוונים ·   לכבד כהם אלותים וסנגים :

והמעלה הרביעית   היא כחכמת הנערים מודעית · כאנרת קלני
וקיכונים כמרוזה וקכת שירים · ערוכים בכל
ונמורים :

והנה   כמעלה הראשונה מהדרסות יתחלקו לכמה חלקים · א   מלתא
כריחותא לשמח כפם חלושה כתיזונקים ·   ב   לפעמים לא כיוון
סתכם אל הדעת והמוזמם ·   מפכי עיון הזמון הנם ואיכם מכיכים מאומה·
ג   לפעמים דבר עמוק הסעתרו מפכי הזמון ·   על כן כתבוהו כדבר טמון ·
ד   לפעמים סברות ימודים ·   סאין כולם מודים ·   ה   דרם מקוכל כסמך
על הפסוקים ·   ויש ללמוד מהם חכמות ומוסרים והכהנות ונחקים ·   כאשר כתב
רב סריא נאון כמוכא כהקדמת מכורת המאור ·   נס כתב התעכלות לכמה
דרסות יהל אור ·   וכן אחרון הנאוכים הרמוכם כהקדמת סדר זרעים· יכאר
עבין הדרסות כאומט סעטועים ·   וכן דברו מהדרסות כמה חמודים עליכים
ואת הטם יהיו כרוכים ·   אכן הדכרים מרוכני ואריכים ·   לכן הנחתים כואת
ספקע ·   וכראש סער משכיל לדוד אם ינוור הטם כתיים אכאלם ככיאור
רחק ונעטם :

ונתכנה

גדולים · וכל זה בתנאי נעור שלא יהיה לי שום עסק כמוס נד שרדה וכבוד בעולם כן בעסקי
הקהל כן בנד הרבנות · וגם לא אכנס לשום מעונה בעולם וזלת למעשת מנוה כטע סדרם
כעינטריך · וגם להיות אוכן בכל יום בקזיעות שעה לסמחות אן יותר לומר להשון עם איוה דבר
מספרם אשר אי בעוסק אחד או בעשרים ונרבע כפי שיסכיאן ונאויה שעם שיסמיאן ויסיס נק
גם כן לתועלת בכי עביים · או דקדוק ספר לסלעדי תיכונין · ויהיה זה תועלת כפלא לכל קדמון
של בית רבן סלועדים מכס · ונכבל כל עם שפפשר בחוקי לעשות לא אתרסל ממכן · ויעשך ענם
תועליות רבות ליודעם ולשלא יודעים ·   סתועלת לסאינם יודעים כלל כנר מכואר ·
ומתועלת ליודעים קנת ∙ והם נאוס בעבר עיאוס וינעים מן דרך העכיס יכול · כל אחד ליקח
ספר בידו בתוך ביתו ויקרא ב · ↄ∙כן · גם יקראם לו שעם פשט או מלס מעורס יכול לענין אוכו על
כיר אמילו כלשון אסככו ויסלח לבית העדרם וגם הסלוח לא ינברך לומר אי הוא סטואל ·
ואכי אפרסה· אם אדעתו־מאם לא אדעה אסאליהן ·   והתועלת ליודעים ולתריפים הוא
בלי סיעור ·   וזה כי כאשר יקטס איוס קוסיא שמקא וישלח אותם לבית העדרם אכי אעתיקס ו
ואסלחהו לתכרים הנכעידם והסריפים וכל אחד יחמ עלין איוה דבר · ואסר כך אברך אותם יחד
ונקריבינו לפני ראס הישיבה · נעס ונכתנו כדברים איוה עסס יותר חריף · ויותר נקי ויתעוררו
ויתריהכן הלבכות לאין תכלית מס סאינ כן לעת עתה שלא מיכר שוע לפני רל · וירהב סכער
בוקן ומי סים לו לשון גדולות ובנקי בקכטורין הוא סיותר חריף · ועוד למעמים אסׄ סלוי
ומכין וכמן לעבל איוב עספר סד ן · או שבמן או לדרוס עסמרי חכמות אן קהלא ונדעס וסין
לו אוכע הספרים יכול · לכתבו על כמר ולסלוח לבית עסלום לבית העדרם ואכי אפרים אסרד לעבל אותן ·
וסתועלת סגדול סוא לראש ישיבה · בלתי ערך בלתי קנה · כי לא יצטרך לסטסיד ומכיס ·
בעביניס סקטנים · כי לא יכעו לפכיו רק דברים קשים · ואכי אפטונ במזות שכלי דעריס
קלים וחלוסים · וגם למעמים אוכע ספל כמוני לאקור ונלדרוס · סיתכריים ילך לפכי כסיא
אן כרפס · ונעגור זה רפס הסל סגדול וסכנרא · לסעמיד ספל כערכי חלא יצטרך לפסד
מפכין ולא לירד :

ותכלית הסכל ועקר הוא דבר שאין לו תקר · כי כל העמזוין וזה העבין · בסכי
סעולמות יתומק לנ סכנין · ויוכס לחיים ארוכים ולטובס · כדכתיב עך
תיים היא למעמזיקים בס · ללועדיכס לא כאפר · כי העמזיק הוא הגוער · על בן בכל מקום
פילך ילך עבין נדקו · להסיר מכסולו' ולהסמוין נדקו · כי בעוד שהוא הולך לעסקיו
ולסמחורס · יעסקן במדרס בקדוסת סתורס · ננללה כי כל מעשה ידיו ינלחו · ויוכס לבכות
עסים · מרווח בקכייכו וכחמורתו · ויהא כינול מרעב ודבר וחרב הוא ונכי ביתו · ואלו
סאכסים אשר רונים לבעל דבר וה שלא לשם שעים · יכרגו לבכם ויעשו מספר סאייס · ותעעלידׄ
דבֿסעּלסֿ יהיה מוג סחרידם · ברוכים יקיע סלא להסקכס בתو סס ונכסתס · ויהיה ינואתם און
סעולם כביאתם · סם ורחבסם ונקבלף · ויאמן · אמן סדנ נער כאמת ונכדקא :

בית המידרש בקטנ...   ...דרשן קראקא   חסר חר*
                                         ואחר

ח

אגרת הקדש

אגרת הקדש

הקדמה

אמר הקטן דוד דרשן מקראקא

ברוך יי אלקי ישראל אשר בידו הממשלה מהמלוכים ותהמונים ונבחר בעמ...
ישראל להיות לו לעם סגולה ולבני קדוש ולמעלבת ככבים אך בתרצי אם
שמוע ישמעו לקולו וישמרו את בריתו שהוא ברית כתורה הקדוסה

סכבתי ובו בם מאשר האותו' כדי לזכותינו בעולם הזה ובעולם הבא' · וידוע ספיבת הנגלות
והנגרות והכבהלות הכל בעבור שאבו בעבו' מתיהוצ'ם בתורה ובמצות · והכיאו במדרם תבהומא
משל כאדק על זה הקרב בם כתן תורה ליס'ראל להבהילם הוי תולם חיי עולם הבא ולא הביש דבר שלא כתן
בן מנוס ינבל לחרים בו' לא תמרוים וכו' לורות לא תורע כרמך כו' מבל לאדם שבטבע בתים מם
עשם הקברקרבים קוטים לו את הקבל אמר לו תבום את התבל בידך ואל תביהכו שאם תביקנה
א'ז לך חיים אף כאן אמר בה'' ליס'ראל כל זמן שיס'ראל מדוכקים בי · את יש להם חיים שכאמר
ואתם הדבקים בה' אלקיכם חיים וכו' · והכה כעובהתיכו נעשו כרות עליכו מכובד הנגלו והסכמים
והרבה אבות ואין לבו כבאי לתבום בהכל התים רק אחד מעיר וסבים מסבחה · ויכל כבהל' וי'סיבו
ובהתיכו בנבהלה · לולי חסדי הסם סבברו עלינו כבר כיינו כלום ח'ו כלים קו'בעוכיינו · ובוא סמונינ
אתכבן מכמה תלאות · כדי סכמסר ממכו כסים וכפלאות · כל אחב בכסמו · וכשאלוני · כדכתוב'
ינרו לה 'חסדו ' ואם כן עלי לסבח ולהודות לאדון הכל · אשר אנבי ערמסית אחרית כל ' אסר
בטרם כבטן ינברו ידעבר · ובטרס ברמם הקדיסכי · כוכב לנגלים כתככי · ויתן לו לשון
בלמודים · להסמיע לרבים דברי המודים · ולברורות כדרך ה'שרם' · כהלכה וכתורה' · ותכליע

והכל יתברך בורא עולם אשר כתן כנבי נבי' להסמיד עדרם לכבוד ישראל אלקי ישראל בא'יזה מקום סימין
לו הקבה · ואכי אבכים בתובו ליקר הוד תפארת אלקי כסמיה והארן ארבע מאות כפרים
בכפרים ויותר ונתן כן כולן בתלי יפת תואר תואר מעבל אנרופין סל בית דוד אסר טרדתי בעבורן
עזן בחרימי כסהייתי כן י'ט סכך בידוע להנאן מוהר מתתיה מבריסק עד עמק נב סנם
וקבנבתי אותן מד' מובית המולם והכנאתי והבנאתם עליהם כ'דמם מאות והזגים וכראסם הכבכתי ספר תורה
הדסה כתיבה נסה כדי להבסול בייב עמודי הזכי לנרבי · ואלו כספרים יהיו מוכבים ומוזבים
לכל מי סירצה לידע ולרעת את ה' מתכו ס' · ומם כלה יתנבלו מה וכמה חידוסי ספרים אסר
בכנון כמם סבים · ועב אכי בינמי בצירכי הקטן לא אפרד מסם רק מעיב סבת לערב סבת
לכבין נרכי סבת · להיותי מוין תמיד לכל סואל ונדע ולהבין ה'כ'קור בתוכם ה'כ'פי מעוכו סבלי וקוכר
סכבתי' · והכ'סה זה ' אתה הקבסנה החלקיתיה להומין על ידי או ספרי' · ולהוסיבכי הוך המדרם
אפ' סאכי יס' כל הבעב · כדי סיתחזק כד נקהתרביב' והקבל סל החיים לא ינבק לנמיר מ'ו תרוב
כובד הטרוד ות הכפהיא' וה'הבים · וה'רונ'ות וה'כרנות והכלות והתלאות כים לכו בגלות הב'יס
ואין סכאי לטפ'ם ותסוק בתורה המנוה על בוריין · ולמעמים יס לו פכ'וי ואין לו ספר
ולפעמים יס לו דבר ולין ל' רבבה · ואם כן בסיכבם לבית המדרם יתבלא סטרוכו · ואם
יבין יותר עוכו לא בהכבים ללמוד המנו · וסא סיקסה מיסמואל וייבי אכי סטריb לסאול בן

הנגלים   1 2 ..6

זה
ספר שיר המעלות לדוד

הוא מהר"ר דוד דרשן אשר חבר לרשו' ה' חומשי תורה ועל כל כרשה
ופרשה ד' מאמרים או אגדות ובכל אגדה ב' או ג' כוונות לפחות·
ויקרא שמו בישראל
משכיל לדוד

ואחר כך חיבר קבת שאלות ותשובות ובקבתם כתבונהו חכמי הדור
ועמהם חובר אגרת טעב הקמיעין :
ואחר בך חיבר אגרות חמורות בלשון תרגום שכתבו לגאוני עולם
ולשרי מדינות ובקבתם תלו וזיניהם וחתימתם גאוני עולם מהר"ר
יוסף ומהר"ר משה איסרלש שיחיו :
ואחר כך חיבר אגרו' קלות בלשון נח בלשון הקדש בחרוזו להוסיף
בינה לנערים· והם קרוב לשני מאות עם קב"ת קיבוניס· בחרוזה
ונרכה שירים· ויקרא שמו בישראל·
מגדל דוד

ואחר כך התחיל לחבר וכירת תרי"ג מנות עם רמוזים וסימנים
כענין שנקל יוכל אדם ללמדם על פה עם הסרינגים המסתעפים
מהס· וטרם הוולדו יקרא שמו בישראל
תהלה לדוד

וכדי לזכות הרבים הניח להדפים מכל אחד שנים שלשה להטעים
התלמידים נופת צוף. אמריס ועל איזה מאלו המכוריס שיהיה
סמוסבס יותר בעיני חכמי הדור כדפיסהו אלה אחר זה · הסיבור
הקב"ר הלו יהיה לחן לעם כינות :   מאוס עגווה התלאונת מטונפל
בכנות :   יאר פ'עליכס פניכ :   ג בסנת
יקרה היא
עתניכיס :

כאדר שני יעיס עשרס·   ליסודים כותבֹ טורכֹ:

פה קֹקֹ קראקא

COPYRIGHT © 1984
HEBREW UNION COLLEGE PRESS

Library of Congress Cataloging in Publication Data

David ben Manasseh, Darshan, b. ca. 1527
  Shir hama'alot l'David = (Song of the steps) ; and,
Ktav hitnazzelut l'darshanim = (In defense of preachers)

  (Alumni series of the Hebrew Union College Press,
ISSN 0192-2904)
  Hebrew text and translation of: Shir ha-ma'alot
le-David, and Ketav hitnatslut le-darshanim.
  Title on added t.p.: Shir ha-ma'alot le-David ; 'im,
Ketav hitnatslut le-darshanim.
  Bibliography: p.
  Includes index.
  1. Jewish sermons—Poland. 2. Sermons, Hebrew—Poland.
3. Preaching, Jewish—Early works to 1800. I. Perelmuter,
Hayim Goren. II. David ben Manasseh, Darshan, b. ca. 1527.
Ketav hitnatslut le-darshanim. English and Hebrew.
1984. III. Title. IV. Title: Song of the steps.
V. Title: Ktav hitnazzelut l'darshanim. VI. Title: In
defense of preachers. VII. Title: Shir ha-ma'alot
le-David. VIII. Title: Ketav hitnatslut le-darshanim.
IX. Series.
BM740.D2913 1984   296.4'2   84-6696
ISBN 0-87820-116-5

MANUFACTURED IN THE UNITED STATES OF AMERCIA

שיר המעלות לדוד

עם

כתב התנצלות לדרשנים

מאת

דוד דרשן

שיר המעלות לדוד

עם

כתב התנצלות לדרשנים